ONE-WAY TICKET FROM WESTERBORK

JONATHAN GARDINER

ISBN: 9789493056763 (ebook)
ISBN: 9789493056756 (paperback)

Cover: Prams left at Westerbork 1942-44 (Beeldbank WO2, NIOD, R. Breslauer?)

Copyright © Jonathan Gardiner, 2021

Publisher: Amsterdam Publishers

info@amsterdampublishers.com

CONTENTS

FOREWORD

This book is about the trains crossing between Westerbork in the Netherlands and other Nazi camps in German-occupied Europe, especially between October 1942 and September 1944. It was written for all those who took that journey not knowing whether it would be their last.

On a moor in the north of the Netherlands stood a camp that came to imprison many tens of thousands of Jews. Yet it was not the Nazis but the Dutch who built it. They did so to confine the many Germans and others seeking asylum in the Netherlands from a world in turmoil: Germany was systematically depriving Jews and others of their rights. Homosexuals, communists, Freemasons, Mormons and other minorities were being imprisoned or faced harsh penalties. The Netherlands, as a neighbour of Germany, began to receive more refugees than it could assimilate into Dutch society, so the government decided to build a refugee camp so people could be held until they could enter Dutch life.

Many German Jews also found themselves waiting in Westerbork. Today, it is a camp that few non-Dutch people will have heard of.

This is a story of the trains that left Westerbork and Amsterdam, heading east to the extermination camps in Poland and to Nazi concentration camps across Europe. It features material from diaries and Jewish sources that have recorded the histories of individuals and families. This story is chronological and does not contain footnotes. It brings together source material from Yad Vashem, the Joods Monument and first-hand diaries along with many reports and obscure papers not commonly used previously. It is not meant as a scholarly reference. All events are honestly recorded.

It is an indictment against those involved in perpetrating the Holocaust and against the "Gentleman Kommandant" of Westerbork who denied until his dying day that he had known the trains were transporting people to extermination camps – this man who entertained Eichmann and associated with top Nazis when attending briefings about the Jewish Question.

I would like to extend my thanks to Dr Casey Hayes of Franklin College, Indiana (USA) for sparking my interest in Westerbork while I was researching the life of Willy Rosen.

OVERVIEW

I have come to know the last Kommandant of the Westerbork Transit Camp during the last few years. Some regarded him as a gentleman, whereas others took him for what he was – a malicious, stone-faced smiling puppet master. Etty (Esther) Hillesum, a well-known Dutch diarist, saw through the façade of a "gentleman." He might have played the gentleman, but as Etty wrote, it was "a peculiar job for a gentleman to have." I have found him to be charming and well regarded by some, but those who saw beneath his veneer saw a man who was a deceitful and manipulative liar, although he liked to think of himself as cultured. You might ask why I would want to know such a man? Well the answer to that is simple: I do not. Would I profess to liking such a man? No, definitely not. Then how do I know him? I came to learn of him through someone whom, if I had known, I would gladly have called a friend. You must read further to see how this came about.

Obersturmführer Albert Konrad Gemmeker, SS number 382609, party member 5620430, was proud of the camp he ran. He went so far as to have it filmed and photographed in detail. Gemmeker knew he ran a model camp; his visitors came to watch the shows presented at the theatre he had built and to see his star-studded cast singing, dancing and telling jokes. There Gemmeker sat, in the front row, tapping his foot in time to the music, slapping the tops of his legs when a joke made him laugh. He would turn to his guests to see their enjoyment of the shows he staged for them. His guests, notes Philip Mechanicus, could be local Dutch farmers, ones who profited from the cheap camp labour and who sat alongside high-ranking SS officers.

Even Obersturmbannführer Adolf Eichmann laughed and took an interest in a dancing girl at Westerbork. Eichmann and Gemmeker discussed her at length after the show and again after Eichmann had met her. She was just another Jew to Gemmeker, so what did Gemmeker care that Eichmann took a liking to her? He would not question why. This just enhanced Gemmeker's position. Others came from Amsterdam, guests of high-ranking Nazis, from all over, to be fêted by Gemmeker who would show off his tame Jewish performers of film and the Berlin cabaret. This was how Gemmeker got through his day, seeking distractions from what he knew was his real task, transporting the Jews out of the Netherlands. What number had he been told? Some enormous number, enough to fill a city. One hundred and forty thousand Dutch, German and other nationalities currently residing in the Netherlands.

Albert Konrad Gemmeker from Düsseldorf had taken up his post on 12 October 1942 with the rank of Obersturmführer - Kommandant of the Polizeiliches Durchgangslager Westerbork. Those three squares set diagonally on his uniform's collar meant a great deal to him. His time in the police force at Duisburg – and tedious Gestapo administrative work – where he was diligent and regarded by superiors as reliable, had paid off. But a three-year wait to join the SS had seemed interminable. By November 1940, he was told that restrictions had been relaxed and was then admitted with the lowly rank of Hauptscharführer, the highest enlisted rank. He was already in The Hague working in the personnel department of the Sicherheitspolizei and the Sicherheitsdienst, the Security Police and Security Service. Not terribly exciting, he thought, but an opportunity arose to demonstrate his administrative skills. He was put in charge of the Sint-Michielsgestel internment camp in the south of the Netherlands in June 1942. While there, orders arrived to execute four hostages taken in retaliation for a Dutch Resistance attack on a German train full of soldiers headed home on leave. The bomb had exploded prematurely, injuring a Dutch railway worker. General Friedrich Christiansen personally issued the execution order.

Christiansen had ordered the arrest of 25 civilians who were also well-known in their communities. He demanded that the guilty persons give themselves up; otherwise, he would have the hostages shot. When the perpetrators did not turn themselves in, the general was forced to keep his word. Orders went out naming four, but then troops turned up with a fifth man. The action would serve two purposes. The men had double-barrelled surnames and, in German eyes, were therefore friends of Queen Wilhelmina who was safely in England. Executing them would send a message not only to insurgents but also to their Queen. Christiansen had not been in the Netherlands long, or he would have known that many Dutch had double family names. Two facts Gemmeker and other Nazis failed to grasp was that Queen Wilhelmina did not know any of these people and that the executions would make heroes of those executed. Others then vowed to avenge their murders, creating a circle of hate which would take years to break.

Gemmeker carefully noted in his diary that General Christiansen had authorised the execution. He firmly adhered to the new ideology of Nazism. It had become his life, and he intended to play his part along with many others of the new faith, one that would ultimately dominate Europe. Yes, it was a faith, as strong for some as any religious faith in any superior being. For Gemmeker, that being was Hitler. The belief also encouraged a culture of blame and allowed someone who was insignificant like Gemmeker to become *someone*. People of little renown were becoming people to be reckoned with – created by a uniform and a title.

Gemmeker had repeatedly learned to note an order's source. Orders from on high were to be obeyed to the letter and with a good deal of zeal, ensuring that not only the letter but also the hidden meaning within the order was enacted. There was extremely little for him to act on at Sint-Michielsgestel. He had heard about concentration camps and how they operated, and he had spoken with officers assigned duties there. They were more than holding camps and more than re-education camps – more like camps for correction or punishment. Yet the camp he now found himself in was almost like a university. It was full of well-educated Dutch hostages who were mainly left to their own devices. The inmates had decided that no one should suffer from boredom. They held lectures and ran writing groups, discussion seminars and, interestingly for Gemmeker, a theatre group. Gemmeker viewed theatre as his type of culture. Gemmeker was there less than four months. Further orders arrived with instructions to report to Westerbork Camp, which was facing some difficulties and needed a Kommandant with a different approach.

Prior to the Second World War, the Netherlands had experienced an influx of refugees and immigrants from various countries, some of which were Dutch protectorates. To process these people seeking Dutch residency, a camp was built near Assen and just outside Hooghalen. Its very first resident was Leo Blumensohn. He was registered on 9 October 1939 along with 22 other refugees when the camp was still under Dutch control. It was reasonably well-established when the Nazis invaded the Netherlands in May 1940, following a month spent in a state of emergency. High alerts had come and gone after tip-offs from Abwehr General Hans Oster. The Netherlands had been in a state of readiness for many months, yet it could not cope with the tide that swept across the country. A few Dutch breathed a sigh of relief when the fighting ceased, which allowed a type of normality to return to which they could lend their weight. Gemmeker had come across these people in his work at The Hague.

Away from his wife in Düsseldorf, he felt that he could look around for some distractions. One of these was the recently separated Frau Hassel. Elisabeth Hassel came to have an influence on Gemmeker's life. In some respects, Hassel was influential, and in some respects his alter ego as well as . They began a sexual affair that, after a time, refused to remain hidden, and everyone came to understand that when speaking to Hassel, you were also speaking to Gemmeker and that she could, would and did make decisions for him. Even her former husband knew this. In some ways, Gemmeker was showing his weakness but also his strength through her. He was described as a good-looking man in his 30s. Some might say he was in the prime of his life, and by anyone familiar with the SS, he was considered quite a catch. Between the two of them, Gemmeker and Frau Hassel were to sort the chaos that had become Westerbork and to form a model Nazi camp in the occupied Netherlands.

Chaos? Was it not all Nazi chaos? A hell on earth, leading to death in the East in places whose names are now synonymous with cruelty, barbarism and death. Gemmeker would become familiar with names he had not heard before that day in October 1942 when he drove into the camp. Before him, hell had already come to Westerbork. With him, the face of Nazism seemed to be more kind, but perhaps more deadly.

Thursday, 30 April 1942: Klara Borstel-Engelsman celebrated her birthday.

Wednesday, 10 June 1942: Lidice and Ležáky were raised to the ground and the inhabitants murdered following the assassination of Reinhard Heydrich by Czechoslovak soldiers.

* * *

Sunday, 21June 1942: The Axis captured Tobruk.

* * *

Wednesday, 1 July 1 1942: The Nazis took over Westerbork Camp two years after the invasion.

Would you be surprised to learn that the Germans did not know about Westerbork? When the Nazis invaded, many fled. The camp at Westerbork was evacuated except for about a dozen people, administration, and detainees. The rest were taken to board ships to England, some 600 or so. But they were unable to get to England, as the German advance was too rapid. Jan Coenrrad Tenkink, the general secretary of the Department of Justice, asked the German authorities what to do with those previously who had been detained. Instructions were to return them to Westerbork, and Tenkink did his best to ensure the order was carried out.

THE FIRST TWO MONTHS OF NAZI CAMP WESTERBORK

15 TRANSPORTS WITH 13,132 DEPORTEES

15 July 1942 – 28 August 1942

Let me backtrack a little to when Erich Deppner became the first Kommandant of Westerbork. He came with a background of murder and execution as the leader of the Einsatzgruppen (Deployment Groups) against insurgents in the Netherlands. His experience in disposing of Soviet prisoners of war was expected to put him in good stead for his time at Westerbork. It came as a surprise to Deppner that the Jewish civilians at Westerbork were not as compliant as he had thought they would be. They were unaware of the fierce hatred of Jews simmering in this 31-year-old man from Neuhaldensleben in Germany. He was personally responsible for the deaths of at least 450 members of the resistance and 101 Soviet POWs in the Netherlands. His shortness of temper would be something the Westerbork Jews would come to know well and to remember.

Deppner was a man's man. He had rugged looks, a square jaw and a long straight nose. His haircut was like that of many others, shaved sides and a blonde mop, swept back over his head, parted down the right side. Yes, good-looking. Or at least his secretary thought so.

1

A short time before the camp had come under German control, it had been run "efficiently" by Dutch civil servants. They knew that the Nazis would leave them alone to manage the Jewish immigrants and refugees if there were "no trouble." This proved to be the case until July 1942 when the Nazis took control of the camp following a decision concerning Jews taken in Berlin. Looking for a suitable Kommandant, Brigadeführer Erich Naumann, chief of Einsatzgruppe B, ran his finger down a list of candidates where it came to rest on Erich Deppner.

Deppner was responsible for the very first train to leave with Westerbork deportees. There had been a change of plan at the highest level in Germany. In discussions with Hitler and others, Heinrich Himmler had been tasked with sorting the "Jewish Question." Jews were sent east for "resettlement," but it was proving a slow process. A solution was needed to remedy this. Himmler looked around; a name came to mind. Not knowing that his choice was already referred to as "Himmler's Brain," he chose the very man who was expected to succeed him: Reinhard Tristan Eugen Heydrich. Heydrich was the Reich's protector of Bohemia and Moravia, party number 544,916 and SS number 10,120. A latecomer. He was recalled to Berlin to chair a conference, now known as Wannsee. Heydrich's finger searched for an organiser and alighted upon Adolf Eichmann. Representatives from all areas of the German society were called to Wannsee, a pleasant mansion, near the lake of the same name. A letter from Göring was included to add weight to the invitation. The meeting was postponed several times, as it had clashed with the declaration of war on the United States. Eventually, it was fixed for 20 January 1942.

The 15 invitees spent the day discussing the "Final Solution of the Jewish Problem." Heydrich remembered the note that Himmler had put in his diary that Jews were to be treated like partisans so had to be executed. Eichmann took the minutes and later regretted having done so, as his notes would play a part in his own downfall. The outcome of that meeting was the establishment of death camps, where Jews were to be gassed, in a manner that was less stressful for

2

the executioners – Himmler felt that some forms were unpleasant for those carrying out the execution duties.

Before taking up the post, Deppner was called to meet with Naumann. Naumann had been called to Berlin by Eichmann to a meeting at the Reich Main Security Office in June. There he found himself with other representatives from the various departments for Jewish affairs in France and Belgium. Eichmann briefed them about the goals of the Wannsee Conference. The Netherlands would be expected to deport 15,000 Jews, between the ages of 16 and 40. Of these, only one in ten could be assumed unfit for work. Workers were needed, first to aid the war effort and then to construct the camps and factories. Those unfit for work such as the children, old and infirm were to be sent at a later date, when the killing centres were more established. Naumann noted the briefing with orders were from Eichmann. In the Netherlands, the lists of Jews compiled in 1941 by town and city mayors throughout the country were to come into use.

You can see, can you not, that nothing in Nazi Europe was done by chance? A harmless list of people in the 1940s was just a harmless list, but you are thinking, *how could they not know to what use the list would be put*? At that time, however, there was not the widespread suspicion that we now have today when lists are made. Today, protection of personal information is more important. When the Jewish Council formed the previous year was given the task of selecting Jews for labour, its members compiled the list of those suitable for work. An enormous saving of time for the Nazis and a system used across Europe: Let the Jews choose!

Little by little, the humanity of the Jews was stolen from them. That yellow star? All Jews over the age of six were required to wear it from 29 April 1942, onwards. And in June, a curfew was introduced, and shopping hours were limited. Here's something to ponder: Jews could not own a car or even a bicycle, and all phones had to be disconnected from Jewish homes. This would stop Jews communicating with each other if a raid were taking place. A few non-Jewish Dutch students wore the star and were sent to a camp for a few weeks, which soon put an end to that demonstration, whereas Jews caught not wearing the badge were transported to Mauthausen and labelled as criminals.

Before 1942, there had been a time when it seemed that escaped German Jews were tolerated. There was theatre, especially at the *Hollandsche Schouwburg*, the Dutch Theatre, which became known as the Jewish Theatre. The tide of events elsewhere had a profound effect on the plight of Jews in the Netherlands. The need for transports out of the Netherlands was a direct result of the chain of events triggered by that conference at Wannsee.

Deppner came to Westerbork to oversee the departure of the first transport on 15 July 1942 in collaboration with the civil servants still running the camp. Kurt Schlesinger, from the Jewish camp service, obtained permission from Deppner to keep 2,000 German Jews as long-term residents since they were *alte Kampinsassen*. Schlesinger had done this to thwart the Jewish Council, which had ordered that German Jews be deported first. Schlesinger was the most important Jew in the camp. His title was Oberdienstleiter or "Head Supervisor," but other inmates referred to him as the "Mayor of Westerbork." This act by Schlesinger ensured that many German Jews were secure in the camp from deportation and would lead to much bitterness.

The train's departure was reported by Deppner as having passed off smoothly, so much that Otto Bene, who represented the Foreign Office in the Netherlands, reported to Berlin that it was his aim to now deport 4,000 Jews each week. He beamed with satisfaction as he imagined how well this would be received in Berlin.

A new young woman, Etty Hillesum, started at the *Joodse Raad* (Jewish Council) the same day the transport left. She was quite well-known and very much of the moment, mixing with celebrities. People spoke of the way she could light up a room with her smile. If you were looking for a single word to describe her, it would be *dedicated.* She chose to work for her fellow Jews—it was her decision to do what she did. I will write more of her later. For the time being, she worked for the Jewish Council and could be seen entering and leaving the camp, mostly working in the camp hospital. Many people knew Etty, and many people know of her today through the diary and letters she wrote. She knew Westerbork as it stood and grew. But I will leave her for a while, as she had not yet entered the camp proper as a prisoner. She did not have to be a prisoner; she entered willingly.

That day also notes the larger influx of Dutch Jews into the camp, finding themselves at the bottom of the camp structure, below that of the original German inmates.

And I should note that the destination of that first transport was Auschwitz. I know, a name that brings to you pictures of untold horrors, but at that time, no one knew of it. Perhaps Deppner knew. It was the destination plate on the side of the train. One other man knew: Alfred Käsewieter. He was a Zugführer of the 7th Company of Battalion II, SS Police Regiment number 3, later *SS-Polizei-Regiment 3*, based in The Hague, and accompanied trains to various destinations, witnessing what happened at the destination point just as did all the members of his platoon who chose to look at what was unfolding before them. Käsewieter did that job until 1944. I would call that dedication too.

From that point on, two trains left Westerbork nearly every week. The train would come in with empty, old passenger carriages perhaps on a Monday or Tuesday, but it could be also do so on a Friday. Later it could be any day of the week. Someone was earning a profit there. The Dutch Railways earned 3,850 Dutch guilders per train. Other ways existed to profit too. As the workforce departed, bankers usually from the Lippmann, Rosenthal & Co. Bank (Liro) were there to take monetary deposits from detainees. Prior to that, they had reported to the Centre for Jewish Affairs to leave keys to their property for safekeeping. Their houses were sold or used by others. They took nothing with them other than a suitcase with working shoes, a food bowl and food supplies for three days. This created a false sense of security. Did the Nazis know what they were doing? Of course they knew. When did they not? It became common practice to draw rations for the journey, but for the greater part, the rations were divided among the Nazis along the route and not the Jews.

Deppner took well to the role of Kommandant. Superiors told him, which he noted, to make up the total for transport with inmates from Westerbork and to ensure the quota required. He was to guarantee that enough names were put on the list. He was to send people east. Orders from all of Seyss-Inquart's departments took precedence. From previous work, Deppner knew the outcome, and it did not bother him. Orders were orders, and he was contributing to the formation of the Reich across Europe. A total of 1,131 people were to be sent east, and there was a shortage of 100. Among that 100 extra deportees from the camp were 50 orphans and their teacher, who did not like the idea of the children going alone and had decided to join them. Their parents were probably not too happy either, as it was doubtful that they were really orphans. A slight upset to the smooth operation was compounded when Deppner had the women waiting to enter the camp dragged onto the train to make up for the lack in the numbers. A near riot almost ensued, which was just barely controlled and of course was reported through unofficial routes.

I know, as do you, what happened at that train's destination, at that place called Auschwitz. The deportees were met and sorted like cattle. Those 1,131 men, women and children were sorted as to who would die immediately and who would die later. They did not know it, but Himmler was there that very day to witness their end. He was paying a visit to Auschwitz for a few days. Not one person from that transport survived to see the end of the war. Himmler was impressed with the smooth operation that Rudolf Höß, the Kommandant, oversaw. Höß noted the pleasure of Himmler, the most dangerous person in the Reich; for him it was a day of note in more ways than one. Himmler was so pleased that he immediately promoted Höß to Obersturmbannführer.

Between 15 July and 31 August 1942, Deppner oversaw the departure of 15 transports. That is not many in the scheme of things, is it? Not really when compared with the total number of trains that Eichmann controlled from his office in Berlin. But that number, 15, stands for 13,132 people. Only 41 of those men, women and children lived to see the end of the war. Just 41 survived; can you imagine that? What did Deppner care? He did not. Deppner did not care that those 41 lived in hell for the next three years. Deppner lived into our time and never paid with a single year, living for another 60 years after the end of the war, protected by the German state and laws meant to save the innocent, like those he had murdered.

* * *

Thursday, 16 July 1942: 13,000 Jews were imprisoned in Paris.

* * *

Varying numbers were going east: 1,000 here and 1,500 there. What if I give you a few names? What if I make it more memorable and make those the names of children?

Monday, 31 August 1942, the transport was 12 short, so 12 people were added. Just 12. No more, no less. A precise dozen. And among that 12 was a set of twins, Elsje and Leentje Ketellapper. How about guessing their ages? Deppner did not care, but you might. Perhaps 10 or 13 years old? They were born Christmas Day, 1941. They were eight months old, old enough to be counted and to help the quota be met. Job done. Figure reached. Precise. Exact. Bonus even, as children took up less room. Deppner could have sent more since children took up less space. But here is the idiocy: It could not be one more nor one less than that list dictated without the proper paperwork. This was a transport for work details going east to further the Reich's work. Eight-month-old twins and also Dagobert Berliner, aged 59, from Breslau, were on that transport. What contribution to the work detail was meant to be theirs? Deppner could send ten percent who were not fit for work to make up the total number. For that particular transport, ten percent meant 100 people who were of no value to the Reich. Of the men, 490 entered the camp and were tattooed; 317 women had their numbers burnt into their arms, just over 80 percent who entered the camp. What of the other 20 percent? They were murdered within hours of arrival, including the babies. No one survived the war from that train so you be their witness.

Transport number seven took four days to reach Auschwitz. A Belgian Jew carefully advised the new arrivals to walk to the electrified fence. The Nazis gained more than 2,000 blankets that day along with coats, shoes, dresses, underwear, trousers, suits and jackets – all various sizes to be sorted and reused. Watches and pens, if they had not been purloined along the way, glasses, dentures, secreted money and jewels and a thousand suitcases, even prosthetic limbs. A total of 316 people did not live to see the end of that day, Friday, 4 September 1942. This transport coincided with the time that the Dutch Railways was worried it would not be paid and sought immediate payment for the train bookings thus far.

Deppner was responsible for the actions of the soldiers under his command, such as when a deportee got down from the train and asked whether he could go get a nappy from the baggage car for his child. The request was refused. He was incensed and slapped the German, whereupon he was shot dead. When the same transport arrived in Auschwitz, a rather large woman could not get down from the train. She was kicked from behind and propelled onto the ground whereupon she died. Another 380 souls followed hers that day. One of the most inhumane was Sturmscharführer Franz Fischer. He was known as *Juden Fischer*, "Jew Fischer."

* * *

Monday, 17 August 1942: Alfred Drukker, aged ten, stood by the tracks near Winschoten waiting for a train from Westerbork to pass by. He saw a train approaching and shouted out for his Uncle Simon. Waving his arms frantically, he saw his uncle waving back through one of the windows. It was the last time he saw Uncle Simon, who was murdered upon arrival at Auschwitz-Birkenau.

* * *

Sunday, 19 July 1942: Himmler spoke of the eradication of all Jews in the General Government of Poland by the end of 1942.

* * *

Tuesday, 21 July 1942: A mass demonstration was held in Madison Square Garden against Nazi atrocities which demanded that Nazis be brought to trial.

* * *

Wednesday, 22 July 1942: The mass deportations from Warsaw commenced.

* * *

Thursday, 23 July 1942: Treblinka opened 10 gas chambers with the total capacity of 2,000. The Germans used carbon monoxide first and then Zyklon B.

* * *

Sunday, 23 August 1942: The Battle of Stalingrad began.

* * *

Wednesday, 26 August 1942: In Vichy France, the arrest of 7,000 Jews started.

* * *

Heinrich Himmler personally complimented Deppner for his good work at Westerbork, but Deppner was transferred; his skill set was needed elsewhere. If he had made a mess of the first transport, as some have said, a goodly amount of time passed before he was actually replaced. Some may have cheered that he was leaving.

Wednesday, 15 July 1942: 1,131 transportees. Survivors – eight.

Thursday, 16 July 1942: 895 transportees. Survivors – one.

Tuesday, 21 July 1942: 931 transportees. Survivors – four.

Friday, 24 July 1942: 1,000 transportees. Survivors – one.

Monday, 27 July 1942: 1,010 transportees. Survivors – none.

Friday, 31 July 1942: 1,007 transportees. Survivors – none.

Monday, 3 August 1942: 1,013 transportees. Survivors – none.

Friday, 7 August 1942: 987 transportees. Survivors – one.

Monday, 10 August 1942: 560 transportees. Survivors – two.

Friday, 14 August 1942: 505 transportees. Survivors – none.

Monday, 17 August 1942: 506 transportees. Survivors – one.

Friday, 21 August 1942: 1,008 transportees. Survivors – six.

Monday, 24 August 1942: 519 transportees. Survivors – none.

Friday, 28 August 1942: 1,500 transportees. Survivors – eleven.

Monday, 31 August 1942: 560 transportees. Survivors – six.

Deppner was responsible for sending 14,237 people to the East. Of those, only 41 survived: 5,468 were murdered at the end of their journey, and 8,726 endured a living hell, until they too died. Your chances of survival were 330:1.

* * *

Leaving the topic of Westerbork for a moment, we saw that Marga Himmler, Heinrich Himmler's wife, was in Mitau. She had been there for four weeks, and half of that time she had been ill. She had been looked after by a "proper doctor," as she calls SS Dr Friedrich

Schönthaler. He had just opened a field hospital, but if the wife of Himmler needed an inoculation against smallpox and then fell ill, the doctor treating her had better be good. Frau Himmler had confidence in Schönthaler because he had good bedside manner. Unfortunately, that cannot be said of every treatment that SS doctors dispensed. Frau Himmler grew a little worried, as she had had a number of visitors, including General Ostland the Generalleutnant Braemer General der Kavallerie Walter Braemer (this is all one person). Frau Himmler also mentioned he was an SS-Brigadeführer; a Mrs Jost and Dr Grawitz visited three times. The worrying visit she said had come from the Bishop Köln. Frau Himmler was not very clear in her diary, whether this was Archbishop Josef Frings, who was certainly not a friend of the Nazis, which might have caused her that concern.

THE NEXT FIVE WEEKS
JOSEF HUGO DISCHNER

11 Transports with 11,176 Deportees
4 September 1942 – 9 October 1942

Deppner changed command with Sturmbannführer Josef Hugo Dischner on Tuesday, 1 September 1942, the third anniversary of the Nazi invasion of Poland. Within minutes of driving through the gates, anyone who got close enough to Dischner could tell he had a problem. Deppner had managed to calm things down, after that first train, and people were more compliant about getting on the transports. There had been a problem with the Jews who had turned their backs on their God and become apostates, joining the Catholic Church, among others. But Deppner saw this as a political problem for his masters to come to terms with. He had applied the Nuremberg Laws to determine who was a Jew, and the fact that a Jew changed religions did not stop their being a Jew. Dischner arrived with the one intention that his job was to fill the transport quotas. He did not care how that was carried out, but it would be done.

Dischner's appointment coincided with a change of tactic concerning the "round-up." His appointment was not a rushed one but a conscious decision on someone's part – quite an inspired one, but completely insane if looked at from the point of view that transports should go smoothly. A slight problem existed with this thinking: Dischner had been working for some time in the East in the General Governorate for the occupied Polish Region. Hans Frank controlled this area, and brutality was the norm there. Death came swiftly to those who got in the way, often because they lived somewhere needed in the German's plan for the East. Six million deaths of Catholic Poles in fact. Death was routine. Dischner came with this attitude towards the Dutch and German Jews and anyone else not Aryan. From Dischner's experience, Dischner's way of coping with his work was to imbibe. He seemed, nearly always, to have the smell of alcohol on his breath. This alone did not sit well with the Western Europeans he was now involved with. The Dutch and some Germans disdained his bullying tactics, but his sole aim was to instil fear into the Jews and other camp inmates.

Only a couple of weeks earlier, the local authorities had agreed to a "request" from Berlin to transport stateless Jews. Only one sort of stateless Jew existed in Europe at this time – the Jews from Germany who had been declared stateless by the Nazi Goverment. This had made it difficult for German Jews to travel. In mid-August, Wilhelm Zöpf, head of Jewish Affairs, summoned the commander of Security Police and Security Service in Amsterdam, Willy Lages, along with the head of the Central Office for Jewish Emigration, Ferdinand aus der Fünten. Zöpf gave the order, carefully in the name of Harster, for the arrest and removal of the Jews directly from their homes by the SIPO or Sicherheitspolizei, the Security Police, and Zentralstellen personnel. Lages and aus der Fünten both noted the chain of command before passing on the orders, solely to pass back any blame. The result was that the number of Jews reporting for deportation rapidly declined. This necessitated the use of raids. Armed with the addresses at which Jews could be found, the Amsterdam Police Battalion went out on the evening of Tuesday, 1 September 1942 to meet transport quotas. The lists had come from the Jewish Council. The raid was carried out during curfew hours when Jews would be at home. Any Jew found at the address was taken. The need to fill the quotas meant that raids started openly in broad daylight in plain view of all Dutch citizens. In just one night, on Thursday, the 3rd of September, the police were able to arrest 3,400 Jews who were then kept at the Zentralstelle, the headquarters.

The following night, on the evening of the Sabbath, the Jewish leaders met to discuss the numbers of Jews taken, which included young and old. A request by the leaders to exempt the elderly was turned down. They were simply told that the old were needed to make up the numbers. So what could they do? Not much. They knew that there was a number to be met, and they were there just to fulfil quotas. The Lippmann, Rosenthal & Co. Bank received a copy of the transport list of 715 people for Friday the 4th of September. The youngest – Marcus Nathan, eight months old; the oldest – Simon van Bever, 81. The bank was there to take "deposits" – in other words, to relieve the "passengers" of their money and then hand it over to the Reichsbank. That transport was quite a mix of Dutch, Germans, Estonians, Romanians, Poles and Slovaks. The money went partly to pay for their own murders at Auschwitz. This was a "special operation," and volunteers from the Auschwitz guards were never in short supply to assist. They received extra rations: a fifth of a litre of schnapps, five cigarettes, 100g of salami and bread. Dr Johann Kremer watched the operation, taking time off from the experiments intended to further his medical knowledge, which he felt would earn him a place in medical history. From Dischner's first transport, perhaps four people saw the end of the war.

By the time of Dischner's second transport on Monday, the 7th of September 1942, a pattern had been established. Raids were carried out to collect Jews and hold them at the Zentralstelle and at the Adama van Scheltemaplein in South Amsterdam; other Jews were held at the old theatre, now known as the Joodsche Schouwburg, the "Jewish Theatre." They would all be put on trams and trains to go to Westerbork, with money changing hands for each passenger, as well as 12.50 Dutch guilders for every extra tram. The Amsterdam police got a requisition of 10,000 litres of petrol a month to ensure they were able to assist the German forces. Selections were made before reaching the camp. Foreign nationals were exempt from transport so they could be exchanged for Germans. Kept back from transport were Jews who did not fit the classifications, such as the Portuguese Jews who were Sephardi, apostates, mixed-marriage Jews and Jews working in the armaments and diamond industries.

All this mass of people was heading towards Westerbork, and Dischner was expected to make the arrangements according to status.

Let me tell you about little Elly Frank. She was born Esther Jeanette Antoinette Frank 19 December1937 and died 17 September 1942. Her story comes along at this point to meet with that of Westerbork. Elly was four years old and had been abandoned purposefully by her parents, Hartog and Jacoba. How they lived with that I do not know, but they honestly believed the child would be safe with their maid under German occupation. Many parents had done this, erroneously thinking that their children would be safe if left with friends. Hartog lived until 1969, and Jacoba died in 1987, aged 88. At first, Elly was safe until orders came from Himmler's office that children were to be included in operations. Himmler's reasoning for this was that these young Jews would grow up and ultimately seek retribution against the Nazis. Elly came to the attention of the mayor of Lienden, Cornelis Kamp. Rather than hide the girl away as he was asked to, he notified the German authorities about the Jewish girl. Kamp remained Burgemeester until 1954. Harster's office, probably Gertrud Slottke, gave instructions for Elly to be sent to The Hague. Kamp complied immediately. Elly was transferred to The Hague and from there to Westerbork where Deppner asked Kurt Schlesinger to find her a place. Schlesinger found Maurits Broeks with his wife and thought it best for the two of them to "adopt" the little girl during the transport. Elly was just a number and as much held the same value as an adult did. Maurits was classified as a convict because he had refused to hand over his money at "the bank" and had hit a cashier. They set off on Monday, the 14th of September and passed through Bremen, Berlin and Oppeln. The train stopped at Cosel (Koźle) for a day. Heydebreck-Cosel was in Silesia, an area with prisoner of war camps and labour camps. Some five kilometres to the east was a sub-camp of Auschwitz called Monowitz. As with previous trains, the able-bodied men were whipped and beaten off the train and separated from their families left on the train. These men squatted by the tracks while the train departed, the noise of the engine drowned out by howls and screams of anguish. They then met Sturmbannführer Heinrich Lindner, a beast of a man, in charge of slave labour. With him was "The Merchant" Henschield. While squatting they were told that their wives and children had gone away to be gassed at Auschwitz and that they would work until they dropped. They were to be part of Organisation Schmelt, named after SS-Brigadeführer Albrecht Schmelt. He organised many camps in these industrial areas to support factories, such as one belonging to the large arms manufacturer Krupp. Maurits vowed not to drop, no matter how long. He was one of eight who survived the war; Elly was murdered on arrival along with 624 other innocents. SS and police leader Hans Albin Rauter was able to inform Himmler that by 24 September 1942, 20,000 Jews from the Netherlands had been deported to Mauthausen and Auschwitz.

* * *

Wednesday, 9 September 1942 – Open fire pits were used at Auschwitz, and 107,000 previously murdered victims were exhumed to be burnt.

Saturday, 12 September 1942 – The German Army reached Stalingrad.

* * *

In a six-day period in September, Dischner saw the camp grow from 4,000 to 20,000 inmates. As the camp grew, so did his temper. Always by his side was his riding whip, which he did not keep to himself. He was liberal with beatings and whippings of those who were not eager to go. Yet volunteers, those wishing to accompany their families, had to sign papers before being allowed to do so.

Literally everything was recorded. The lists would pass through various hands as people were assembled for transportation. The numbers continued to grow. Inmates saw 12,000 deported in October alone. Food was drawn for the transports, but the deportees got one loaf among seven people – if they were lucky. A bucket in the corner of the truck served as a latrine, and there was no water. A father, carrying an empty bottle, sought water from a guard for his young twins. The guard took the bottle from his hands and then smashed it against the train. No compassion. Dischner was a man without a heart.

* * *

Friday, 8 September 1942 – The food rations for Jews in Germany were reduced. This indicates that although food had been confiscated from other countries now part of what was called the Greater Reich, no new produce was entering Germany. The army had extended itself as far as it was going to. Hitler invaded countries to garner new resources to continue his war. Resources were now becoming limited, so Jews would have to go without.

Saturday, 16 September 1942 – The Nazis capitalised on Jewish possessions confiscated at Auschwitz and Majdanek: All currency was sent to the Reichsbank; gold and jewels were sent to the SS Headquarters of Economic Administration; watches, clocks and pens were distributed to troops at the front. Admiral Dönitz awarded U-boat captains with gold watches, which he kept in a tub and said, "Help yourself."

* * *

This story was told by a member of the Flying Column, men in brown overalls, who assisted deportees onto the trains: Dischner was at the embarkation, and the numbers were short. A little way off was a group of women meant to join their husbands in the camp. Dischner decided on the spur of the moment to make up the numbers with these women. When they realised what was happening, a great cry of resistance arose. Dischner was whipping right, left and centre, and some of the Dutch guards joined in with kicking and beatings. The noise reached a crescendo to attract the husbands from the camp. A few women escaped into the camp, but those with children were forced onto the train. When the men arrived, they volunteered to join some of the women, and a sort of calm was restored. On that transport, the men were separated at Cosel, and 1,414 were murdered upon arrival in Auschwitz and pronounced dead by Dr Johann Kremer.

Aad van As witnessed this departure, and he never wanted to see the likes of it ever again. Two thousand transportees had been herded into two barracks, no beds and no mattresses – in fact, nothing to make their stay bearable – and then the numbers were not enough, so Dischner had whipped those waiting to come into camp onto the train. Naturally this occurred after they had been registered. Someone sent a report of this incident to a superior officer, and a replacement for Dischner was sought. One more transport for Dischner and then he could return to Poland where Hans Frank showed more appreciation for Dischner's approach. A total of 2,224 people were aboard that train.

* * *

Monday, 5 October 1942 – Himmler ordered all Jews held in concentration camps in Germany to be sent to Auschwitz and Majdanek.

Monday, 5 October 1942 – In Dobno, Ukraine, *Einsatzgruppen* killing Jews was observed by Hermann Graebe, a German engineer and his foreman. Graebe later wrote a book about his experiences. Baron Axel von dem Bussche-Streithorst, a highly decorated officer, who also bore witness to the massacre, joined Count Claus von Stauffenberg's resistance as a result, even planning to act as a suicide bomber to kill Hitler. The baron epitomised the "Aryan" look and was chosen to model new uniforms for Hitler. This plan was thwarted when the uniforms were destroyed in a bombing raid. A second attempt failed when Bussche-Streithorst lost a leg in combat and could no longer serve as a suitable model.

* * *

Friday, 9 October 1942 – Catharina and Jacques Frank entered Westerbork. She was a nurse and assigned to Barracks 58, bed number 60.

* * *

The same day, 9 October, 26 train cars with 1,713 people on board left Westerbork. Representatives of the Lippmann, Rosenthal & Co bank copied the list and sent it on to Hans Fischböck, general commissioner for Economic Affairs in the Netherlands. The bank was accountable to him and noted his requirements very carefully. One-quarter of the deportees were under the age of 18; the oldest was 86. And the youngest? Four months. As time went on, the age became younger. Can you believe that? Younger than four months! The depravity of the human race reached a new low with this transport.

Upon arrival at their destination, some were admitted to the camp for labour; others, including the baby for sure, went to the gas chambers. Even Dr Johann Kremer recorded that the scene was ghastly. What happened? Franz Hössler, the SS officer, for some reason wanted the whole group in one chamber. He had them crammed in until there was not enough room for one last man. So he shot him, there and then, closed the door, and they were all gassed. Louis Menist was one of four to survive. He was separated from his wife, had his baby torn from his grasp and was pushed into the camp, along with Mozes Aldewereld who cried as he described what happened that Sunday morning on 11 October 1942. Louis's last sight of his wife was of her on the back of a lorry with their child in her arms.

It was Dischner's last transport. The calm of transports had been shattered. How would those who had witnessed it want to go on a transport? He was relieved of duty on 9 October 1942 the same day and succeeded on an interim basis by Polizeiinspektor Bohrmann.

* * *

Friday, 4 September 4 1942 – 714 transportees. Survivors – four.

Monday, 7 September 1942 – 930 transportees. Survivors – ten.

Friday, 11 September 11 1942 – 874 transportees. Survivors – ten.

Monday, 14 September 1942 – 444 transportees. Survivors – six.

Friday, 18 September 1942 – 1,004 transportees. Survivors – two.

Monday, 21 September 1942 – 713 transportees. Survivors – one.

Friday, 25 September 1942 – 749 transportees. Survivors – none.

Monday, 28 September 1942 – 610 transportees. Survivors – none.

Friday, 2 October 1942 – 1,014 transportees. Survivors – four.

Monday 5 October 5 1942 – 2,224 transportees. Survivors – 29.

Friday 9 October 1942 – 1,713 transportees. Survivors – four.

Dischner played his part in those five weeks. His record was 11 transports and 11,168 deportees, of whom 70 saw the end of the war – just 70 out of more than 11,000. The odds of surviving were 160:1 against.

THE GENTLEMAN KOMMANDANT

ALBERT KONRAD GEMMEKER

October 1942

Gemmeker was no gentleman. Etty Hillesum said he liked to play the
gentleman, but although Deppner and Dischner's hatred was out in
the open, Gemmeker kept his total disregard for Jews hidden. He
took everyone for fools. He did nice things for some people at certain
points in their lives, but did they have time to think how he had
duped them when they were herded into the gas chambers? Of course
they could not come back and call him the names they would have
liked to. They could not return and throttle the life out of him or claw
his face and pound him to pulp. No, they could not do that, and after
the war, such things were not allowed. Those souls, who had built up
a picture of the man, who had done nice things, could not possibly
have known about the horrors. It was the fact that they had said these
things that protected Gemmeker. He was a gentleman and not like
the others. But he was. You know that now, right? You know exactly
what he was like. When justice had the chance, however, he smiled
his way innocently into a short prison sentence and eventually into
early release, almost a repatriation. The kind officer gentleman, one
who just followed orders. No, *he* did not know of the horrors in the

East. Look and see, listen and hear how that man sent nearly 80,000 people to their deaths.

Hauptsturmführer Ferdinand Hugo aus der Fünten, head of the Central Office for Jewish Emigration in Amsterdam, was 33 years old and had a problem. He had been given the problem by the head of the Department for Jewish Affairs in the Netherlands, Wilhelm Zöpf. Aus der Fünten was responsible for overseeing the deportation of more than 140,000 Jews out of the Netherlands, but that was not his problem. His problem was Westerbork, the transit camp, where near riots had taken place, disrupting the smooth departure of Jews to the East. But that was not really the problem either. The departures would take place; however, locking up 20,000 people in one place and keeping them calm before shipping them out was the problem. Westerbork was one of his camps. Two Kommandanten, loyal Nazis to the core of their very beings, had messed things up. They could deal with insurgents, or Soviet POWs and whole populations in occupied Poland, but they had no idea how to handle Western Europeans and the Dutch population, who quite often sided with the Jews. Eastern tactics would not work here in Amsterdam. Aus der Fünten knew that. He needed someone who could charm the deportees, someone who could convince them to get on those trains and someone to keep them quiet before they went. Once on the train, it did not matter, just as long as they got on those trains. He needed someone who could lie every hour of the day and get away with it. He needed a façade of decency, someone who could manipulate, cajole and coax, someone who could make an order sound like a request. The Jews would see it as a caring attitude. He ran his fingers through his hair. He needed that man now! Today! Even yesterday! He was thinking. He had a whole bureaucratic system at his command – subordinates to do this for him.

This is how it could have happened – turning to Hassel, a young *Untersturmführer*, aus der Fünten thought to give *him* the problem. Surprisingly, Hassel knew the answer already. He knew Albert Gemmeker from Düsseldorf. He was his friend and knew he had a comfortable position at a camp where the prisoners entertained themselves and were no trouble at all, and Gemmeker let them get on with it. There was never any problem at Sint-Michielsgestel camp. Fünten pushed the paper on which he had been doodling across to Hassel who then picked it up and read the list of attributes. Hassel leant across the desk, picked up a pen and neatly wrote one name on the paper: Untersturmführer Albert Gemmeker. Fünten looked at the name and took the pen from Hassel. He scored through Untersturmführer and wrote Obersturmführer.

With one swift and deft action, Gemmeker was promoted, moved from Sint-Michielsgestel and found himself entering Westerbork only to be greeted by his old friend Hassel and other junior officers, with lots of heel clicking, outstretched arms and shouts of "Heil Hitler." The two old friends agreed that this was a fortunate time for them both; indeed they agreed these were the good times. Those walking in the vicinity of the main gate or on the Boulevard des Misères as the quick tour took place watched the new man. Another German to lord it over them, the Jews thought, to make them do this and that, and doff their hat and be careful to do everything with a smile and humility and doubly quick.

* * *

Monday, 12 October 12 1942 was the day Westerbork entered a new chapter with a Kommandant who carried no whip and no big stick and spoke quietly with authority. Gemmeker had arrived in more ways than one. He knew he had arrived. This was his day! This Westerbork was to be his success, he thought. A model for everyone to follow.

Aus der Fünten would have briefed Gemmeker: "Keep the trains rolling in and out. Keep moving the Jews and they will not expect what awaits them at their destinations." Fünten had attended briefings and noted what was said and not said. This note was passed to Gemmeker, a man he would come to know well on his visits, at the parties and soirees that would follow, the good times, at the expense of the inmates. The camp that would prove lucrative for all those involved, except for the deportees, but that went without saying. Top brass visits and other visitors would reflect on aus der Fünten and his choice of Gemmeker.

Gemmeker had been in the camp a few days. He had wandered in unannounced to have a look around and to get a feel for the place. He wanted to know what was happening, what he could improve, what he would keep and so on. He watched people as well. He saw their approach to the Jews. He may have spoken to some of them, asking what it was like at the camp. He had already made up his mind to continue his considered approach.

Gently smiling, he walked around. A smile invokes calm, but in this case, it was fixed and cynical. Gemmeker had never been to any camp training school before taking up his post. His career had been with the police. Besides, his first camp had operated smoothly: In fact, he had not had to do anything at all there. The camp had run itself. He found that the Jewish administration practically ran this camp, too. Perhaps he would leave it at that. The Jewish administration picked the names for the transportation lists. He would leave it at that; if a thousand were needed, the Jews could find the thousand. All he needed to do would be to authorise the list and to make a few adjustments. If he were not to do the sorting, the hate and fear would be directed against the Jewish administration. In this he was right. He walked around or cycled on his bike, like the friendly face of Nazism. That would be it; he would show the Jews the best face that Nazi Germany had to offer. Life in Westerbork could be good for Gemmeker. His own modern and spacious house, with a cook and a maid. Ellen Danby, the figure skater, would remember cooking for Gemmeker and his words of appreciation. Gemmeker would play the role of the benign "English Country Squire," as described by Etty Hillesum, respected and loved by all. His mind wandered to President Teddy Roosevelt and how he liked the West African proverb about speaking softly but carrying a big stick. Well, those diamonds on his collar patch and the whole of the SS were his big stick; all he had to do was to talk softly. The rest would follow.

It was the first transport for Gemmeker, although he did not have much to do with the organisation. He walked along the track, where there were mountains of luggage waiting to be thrown into the baggage car. People hurried up and down; here and there men in brown suits helped an old lady or man onto the train. Orders were shouted. The sounds from the steam engine and the smell of smoke and steam drifted along.

Some 1,711 "passengers" were to be put into the 24 carriages. All milled round, children looked tearful, parents looked distraught and the old, weary. A great deal of shouting with raised arms from Sergeant Major Albert de Jong, commander of the Dutch Military Police, the Royal Netherlands Marechaussee, at Westerbork, caught Gemmeker's attention. He noted this and sent a junior officer to tell him to desist, or de Jong would be on the train himself. Gemmeker must have already decided, it seemed, on his modus operandi. There would be changes. Some like de Jong may not have liked it, but as a Dutch military policeman, he had to take his instructions from the Nazis and acquiesce, or indeed he would be going "somewhere." Too late for today but the following transports would be different. Gemmeker would see this little scenario involving de Jong as indicative of many things happening in his camp.[1].Violence was not good, and Gemmeker knew it. In the long run, things would get easier. He started to walk up and down the tracks, speaking softly and encouraging people to get on the train. They were going to work in the East; there was nothing to worry about. They would meet up with family members who had gone before. The other Nazis would immediately follow Gemmeker's lead. The train was ready. Gemmeker gave permission for it to leave and, looking directly at the faces in the windows, began to wave the passengers off. As each carriage passed, they would see his smile as he waved them away, just like a Sunday School party going off for their annual treat. The train meandered away and Gemmeker may have given it a final wave for the benefit of the Jews in the camp who were watching. And it was thus that the deception encouraged by Gemmeker began. Here he was on his personal stage, playing his part and encouraging confidence in himself. His plan was to make fools of every single one of those Jews he would see off in the years to follow. It was a pretence that he kept up for the next two years and beyond, when arrested and challenged. The naïve Kommandant who had been duped by aus der Fünten and Zöpf, oh, and even by Eichmann and in his turn Hitler. Yes, he had been duped by all of them into doing their evil work. Did Gemmeker send those people to their deaths unwittingly? Let's see.

The smoke from the train filtered away, leaving Gemmeker with his officers. Hassel could well have suggested that they could go to the Kommandant's house and he could settle in. The train was no longer Gemmeker's concern. Not his concern that it would take until Wednesday to reach Auschwitz. Not his concern that on the way, German soldiers taunted the Jews, with slashing actions to their throats. Not his concern that upon reaching Birkenau 1,291 went straight to the gas chambers. He would not have felt any remorse if Louis Franschman had described to him how those from the old people's home in Rotterdam were carried to the lorries and then from the lorries into the gas chamber itself. Louis and his brother Salomon could have told Gemmeker that they with six others survived from his first transport from Westerbork. I can imagine his response if he had met them again, the pitiful denial that he knew what was happening. There was one from his first transport who would like to have met Gemmeker again, Simon Louis Toncman, the accountant. He lived to tell his story about his arrest by the Dutch police; his incarceration in Westerbork; and his time in Cosel, Bobrek, Blechammer, and Groß-Rosen; and finally what it felt like to be released from Buchenwald. Many Dutch civil organisations, even the Civil Service were still in place when the Germans had invaded. They were soon pretty much assimilated into Nazi requirements.

* * *

There were four days until the next transport, four days to make changes and communicate his expectations to the men under his control. Some did not like the changes, so Gemmeker used his authority, charm and that smooth tongue to make the men understand that his changes would make life in the camp far easier. Far easier he added, than being on the Eastern Front. You see. The fear of the East. Men on leave were meeting cousins, brothers and friends and speaking in hushed tones. They exchanged details about what was happening. Undeveloped film from cine and still cameras were being sent home for development and seen by families and friends. The Wehrmacht soldiers recorded what they saw as if it were some everyday thing, which to them it was. These films and photographs were seen by those back home and were an accurate testament as to what sons and brothers were seeing on the Eastern Front, or even taking part in. Some brazenly wrote home about their special tasks, but also making the rounds was the news as to what happened to lone soldiers if caught by partisans or Soviets. Other things were coming out, such as that the war was not going as well as it had been a year ago. It was generally agreed that the posting in Westerbork was quite good after all. Gemmeker started to use his organisational skills to mould the camp routines and the approach of captors to inmates. This change was needed because throughout the Netherlands there had also been a great deal of activity.

Hans Rauter, from his office as head of police, had sent another letter to inform Heinrich Himmler that 5,242 Jews in 42 work camps across the occupied Netherlands would be sent to Westerbork for deportation. He felt satisfaction that Himmler would be pleased and pass this information on to Hitler. Operation Harster had been going well. *Politiebataljon* Amsterdam Chief Sybren Tulp had left his office and led the operation personally in Amsterdam. But then the chief of police fell ill at the beginning of October and not everyone was so eager to carry on with the vigour that Tulp had demonstrated.

* * *

Wednesday, 14 October 1942 – The mass killings of Jews from Mizicz Ghetto, Ukraine, took place.

***

On Friday, 16 October 1942, Gemmeker was at the train to witness a smooth departure. The actions he had been instilling in his men for the few days since his arrival seemed to be having some effect. The names had been read out by barrack leaders early that morning. Gemmeker, asleep in his purpose-built house, had not heard the cries of those selected. Nor had he heard the relieved shouts of those left behind. He had not seen the busy activity of people arranging their few possessions; he had slept soundly. So by the time arrived to oversee the loading of the trains, he was dressed and must have felt that he cut rather a dashing figure in his uniform. He may have admired himself in the mirror in the green-coloured house. As he walked with his officers along the train, some recognised him, but others only knew he was the Kommandant from his rank of insignia. The more diamonds, the higher the rank, and if it were silver leaves or some such, they could see how lower ranks jumped. But to the prisoners, Gemmeker was just another German who did not like Jews. The train had 26 carriages this time but almost the same number of deportees as before, just one less, 1,710. Gemmeker saw a few of them, but he did not know how many children where on the list he held and looked down with Hassel. There were 358 for this trip. That top number was the most important – the names that went over various pages, of thin paper, with each person having a number. Gemmeker may have read the name of Henri Andriessen, but Henri was nothing more than a number. Henri could later have told Gemmeker all about the journey if he had wanted to listen and be reminded of the days he had sent the children away. Hartog Soep, the musician, could also have reminded Gemmeker of those days. Hartog was 25 years old when he reached Westerbork. He stayed two weeks before he was deported, taken off at Cosel, transferred to Bobrek, in March 1944 to Blechhammer, in January 1945 to Groß-Rosen and then on to Buchenwald in April, and finally to a small camp in Bissingen-Spaichingen, where he was released, but as many as 6,000 had died. Jeremias Sametini also survived Cosel, as well as Malapane, Blechhammer, Groß-Rosen and Buchenwald. He was 28 years old when he left Westerbork; after three additional years, he did not look 31.

Stepping out and putting on an act that would become oh so familiar as Gemmeker walked among the deportees. It was an excursion – everything would be sorted at the other end. Alfred Käsewieter may have approached Gemmeker, and both may have saluted with the mandatory greeting for party members of "Heil Hitler." Day in and day out, possibly 100 or more times a day, it was "Heil Hitler." They were but two men doing their duty for the good of the Fatherland. Alfred would introduce himself to Gemmeker. They would speak for a few minutes, exchanging personal information, career so far, that sort of thing. There was a sort of quietness that had descended. The noise of the engine could be distinctly heard. The shouting and excited hubbub had given way to quiet chat along the length of the train. The throng and mass of people had dissipated and distilled down into men in uniforms. The noise of the deportees was contained by the carriages, locked from the outside with windows that were permanently locked. A flurry occurred among the officers, and Hassel scurried along towards Gemmeker. He saluted his friend and informed him that the train was loaded. Gemmeker turned to Käsewieter, who saluted and then shook Gemmeker's outstretched hand. Käsewieter may have recorded and informed his superiors that this was one of the most efficient loadings. He turned smartly and ran to the carriage with the German police. Gemmeker stepped forward and waved his hand towards the engine. The driver waved in return, and the whistle gave a piercing blast signalling departure. Smoke, noise and steam issued from the engine as it lurched into motion; the carriages clanged as they took up its momentum and moved forward.

In his office at the *Nederlandse Spoorwegen,* Jan Smits was making out an invoice to send to Wilhelm Harster for today's transport. Payment would follow the agreed-upon delay.

Henri Andriessen, third time unlucky, had been woken in the early hours to join this transport to make up the numbers. There was to be no more grabbing people at the last moment and forcing them on the train. Some young single men were kept on standby. This time Henri made it to the train and settled back in his seat. He was not aware of the misfortune that had just befallen him. It would have come, sooner or later. He later marvelled that people were standing at the side of the tracks, waving to them at various points of the journey through the Netherlands. Some wore yellow stars; some did not. But they were waving to them. Waving them adieu. Henri wondered how they knew the train would be passing. German efficiency and German predictiveness answered that. In Germany, their reception committee was a member of the Hitler Youth who shook his fist at the train. That one small incident indicates how widely it was known that the trains were taking Jews to the East. Couple that with the experience of the previous train, where the soldiers made gestures of death – it was commonly known why the Jews were going east. Personnel at the Dutch Railways also spoke out of turn about the transports and handed on details of date and times.

You may think that people with little keep it for themselves. Yet I will tell you, the people on this transport shared their last pieces of bread with Soviet POWs working on the train tracks. That generosity was an unknown kindness to those Soviets.

In the evening, Henri's compartment organised a sort of cabaret to entertain themselves. He sang and won some bread, and a ten-year-old girl sang a song called "*Nederland*." Some older people on the train had come straight from their homes, and their cases were full of food.

Another survivor, Isaac van Dam, told how the train stopped several times and food was distributed, but there was little water. Meyer van Dijk said that when the train stopped at Cosel, it was usually the same story: Men were ordered off the train in a brutal fashion. There was some argument over the name of the man who made the selections for labour, Henschield, Hauschild or Hanschild. But they were all agreed as to what he was – *Le marchand de bestiaux, Der Viehhändler*, the limping Cattle Merchant. He selected those he wanted as slave labour, and all those over 50 years of age were sent back to the train. He had his quota. Always at Cosel, those from Westerbork were to experience for the first time the ugliness of the way in which Jews were to be treated. This was the East, where Nazis were masters of life and death. A place where a Jew was worthless, where Poles and other nationals were worthless. No one asked a question if a Jew or non-Aryan was shot, murdered or kicked to death. Those who ended up in hospitals were by far the worst treated, rotting flesh hanging off in strips. Most Jews from the Netherlands did not survive the winter of 1942 to 1943. The train had continued to Auschwitz, now in shock, with everyone fearful as to what was to follow. Thirty people survived this transport and can tell you that 116 women were admitted to the camp and that 1,024 went straight to the gas chambers.

* * *

Gemmeker was getting worried in October. Owing to the local actions, Westerbork was overcrowded. It was not built to accommodate the nearly 10,000 inmates. Gemmeker knew exactly, down to the last child, how many were in Westerbork – 9,799 people. The facilities could not cope. He was told that it had been worse. The rush to send 12,000 or so east had meant tremendous activity in the camp. Even the Germans were rather shocked at having to work in these conditions. Gemmeker wanted a large train to reduce the overcrowding, and it was on this train that Hartog Stempel and Isaac Grootkerk were deported, two months of age and 83 years old, respectively, along with the de Vries family of Clara, the trumpet and band leader, with both her mother and father, Arend and Betje. Another 1,619 people including an additional 166 children left on Monday, 19 October 1942.

I will tell you something further about this train. Earlier I told you that the soldiers did not really want to lose their positions here and get a more active posting, and before that, I mentioned that Westerbork was a profitable place for many Germans, but not for the

Jews. The Nazis were wonderful record keepers, and their records bear out what I am about to tell you. There were three survivors of this train. It is a real number and stands for three human beings who went through untold misery, solely with the intention of surviving. This is what they told – on the train they received bread. Yes, I know what you are thinking. Bread, they usually got bread. I have not told you yet. The Nazis requisitioned food for 1,500 people bread, butter, jam, vegetables and substitute coffee and not for one day, or the three days the trip was expected to take, but for 14 days – two whole weeks. It was issued. If the deportees did not get it, who did? Well you know before I tell you. The Germans got it. You do not need me to tell you how much that amount of food was worth on the black market, and if it were done so openly, there were many important people benefitting from the fraud. This included the Royal Netherlands Marechaussee, who was heavily involved in smuggling and extracting money from the inmates.

A survivor, Emmanuel Halverstadt, recounted that he had been placed in Barracks 60 and that one morning the military police entered and sealed the barrack. They were told to pack, as they were to leave for Auschwitz. On the way the train stopped a few times, and 297 were taken off at Cosel. Once they got off and they were guarded by police in green uniforms who wanted their watches and jewellery. The train stopped five kilometres from the camp. The SS beat them out of the carriages, and they were walked to Auschwitz. Some 497 men were admitted to the camp, and the rest, 830, were murdered after their arrival on Wednesday, 21 October 1942.

Thursday, 22 October 1942 – The Nazis stifled a revolt at Sachsenhausen by Jews destined for Auschwitz.

The inmates at Westerbork did not get much good news, but starting with whispers, then rising to an excited state, it filtered through the camp. On the 22nd of October, the Politiebataljon Amsterdam Chief Sybren Tulp died. Someone quipped that perhaps "the Golem" had got him and that he should have stayed in his office. It was hoped his replacement would also have such a long life. Three days before, Haring Tulp, Sybren's half-brother, had died in Buchenwald. Haring had been a member of the Communist resistance. He had been distributing communist literature such as "Het Noorderlicht," the Northern Light, and "de Waarheid," the Truth. He was arrested on 18 May 1941 and imprisoned in Amersfoort. His brother must have known about the arrest, but it appears he did nothing. In July, Haring was deported to Dachau, prisoner 31169, then sent to Buchenwald in September, and exactly a month later he was dead.

Jews like any other people have their great and their good. One new inmate to Westerbork was just such a person. Shortly before the news about Tulp, it went very quickly around the camp that the Chief Rabbi of Amsterdam Lodewijk Hartog Sarlouis had arrived. Many were amazed that he was being treated the same as everyone else was. There was an explanation, of sorts. The Queen had made a speech on the radio to the Dutch. It was regarded by the Nazis as a pro-Jewish speech, so Queen Wilhelmina had to be taught a lesson in her safe and comfortable surroundings in England. The twisted German logic was to imprison the chief rabbi and not only that, but to put him on the next transport on 23 October the first day in the month of *Kislev*. That would teach her a lesson. Yet the Nazis could not openly admit that the chief rabbi had been sent to an extermination camp. This was 1942, and news did not leak out until the end of the year, but even then, it was thought to be too unbelievable to be true. Typical of Nazi retaliation, it never hit those it was aimed at but usually an innocent third party.

* * *

Friday, 23 October 1942, yet another transport and again the same rations were drawn for this train, enough for all those people for 14 days. Yet the Jews got none of it, save the bread. These trains did not leave exactly from Westerbork; everyone had to walk to Hooghalen. This included seven-month-old Saartje Bromet and 87-year-old Zacherias Buitenkant as well as a teenager called Abraham Soesan from Amsterdam who was only 15 years old. He managed to survive Cosel and St. Annaberg, Klein Mangerdorf, Ludwigsdorf, Auschwitz and Dachau. Then there was Salomon Fresco, who went on to St. Annaberg, Fränke (Groß-Rosen), Wiesau, Bunzlau, Buchenwald, Mittelbau Dora and Bergen-Belsen. I nearly forgot Abraham Cohen. He went on to St. Annaberg, Klein Mangersdorf, Neurkirch, Liegnitz, Auschwitz, Groß-Rosen, Dachau and Mühldorf. And did I mention Hartog Polak? No, I did not. He too went to numerous camps; how he remembered them, I shall never work out – St. Annaberg Klein Mangersdorf, Omansdorf, Hirschberg, Dornhau, Ellenburg and then back to Dornhau. I hope you are forming a picture of how many camps existed. I will tell you the number in a few pages. These were just some of the names.

Gemmeker was not there to wave them off this time on Friday, 23 October 1942. Hartog Tertaas added to the story of this train that when it stopped, the military men were given water by the German Red Cross, but the Jews did not get any. The train made its usual stop at Cosel where 170 men were removed for slave labour. They had all been lined up and beaten while the men between 15 and 50 went through selection for slave labour. Fifty-three got into the camp at Auschwitz, and the rest were murdered, 935 souls, including Saartie, Zacherias and the chief rabbi with his family.

* * *

Friday, 23 October 1942 – The British counteroffensive at El Alamein started.

* * *

Saturday, 24 October 1942 – Catharina Frank was issued with a late pass because she was a nurse and needed to travel around the camp after curfew.

* * *

Towards the end of October, Westerbork was terribly overcrowded. It had a stable population of 2,000, yet 12,296 Jews were added to this by the various special operations that had taken place across the Netherlands. Westerbork was not just for Amsterdam Jews. Things were bad. Gemmeker gave orders that the Jews were to sleep on the floor until things could be normalised. It was not a situation of his making; he was just following orders. Naturally, the food was also insufficient. It always was, but even more so in those days. German efficiency at its best. For the transport planned for Monday, October 1942, there was disagreement over the numbers being sent east. Now the number of Jews did not matter, so long as they were moving away. So who would you listen to on a day like this when you were arguing over numbers? Who would you trust with numbers? Your banker? Most likely. The daily report stated 820, but the Liro Bank recorded 994 in a letter sent to the general commissioner for Financial Affairs one month later. The number of names on their list was 994; these people handed their money over for safekeeping. Not all of it was handed over. When their clothes were searched in *Kanada*, it was found sewn into seams, along with jewellery and other valuables. Canada? How come they were in Canada? Canada to the Jews represented a land of plenty, so the clothing shed at Auschwitz came to be called Kanada. It was a bit like South America being sunny and a land of smiles. There was even a German song about Venezuela being a happy land that Jews could dream about. Jacob Salomon Cats was 19 when he was put on this transport. He was already a slave labourer and had been for the last ten months since the start of 1942. He escaped transportation from Westerbork, initially by hiding, but what are friends for but to let you down? He was denounced. In those years you found out what people were capable of. Your best friend would do something awful to stay alive.

Jacob and his wife were put down for transportation. He lost his wife and her father during the selection at Auschwitz but later met up with his father-in-law at Auschwitz I. They entered the camp to the strains of music from the camp orchestra. How bizarre, he said. You have to agree? Hell on earth yet you are greeted at the door, not by Cerberus, but by notes penned by Beethoven but never ever by Mendelssohn. Another survivor was Izak van Dam. He later confused his dates; he thought he had left the day before. Is it any surprise that people became confused? He had already been in Staphorst, a work camp, before reaching Westerbork on the 20th. He was moved around quite a bit – St. Annaberg, Malapane, Blechhammer, Reigersfeld, Groß-Rosen, Buchenwald and Theresienstadt, where he was released one day after the war ended in the East, following the surrender to the Soviet Union on 9 May 1945.[2]

Did anyone ever escape? Oh yes, of course, sometimes with ghastly repercussions. Salomon Jo Braaf escaped. He woke up in the early hours of the morning, climbed over the fence and went to his old workplace. He returned that evening to the camp. You must realise that without papers, where was he to go? If he had papers, that large red J in his passport would have been something of a giveaway. So he went back. Then what did he find out? His name was not on the list for rations! If the Nazis did not get you one way, they got you another. Retaliation was meted out on those left behind if someone escaped. About 200 escaped in total from the camp, but when they did, it was like being in an alien land for many. The whole of the country was occupied, and safe houses were mostly full already, not only of Jews but escaping soldiers or downed airmen. There was a sort of peace in being within the barbed wire that permeated throughout the camp. Better to be in the camp than going east. Some believed that they were still in control of their own destiny, like the man who volunteered to go on this transport. His attitude was that it was inevitable that he would go east, but he would choose when.

* * *

Monday, 26 October 1942, the train left on time and stopped several times on the journey. Surprisingly, they could leave this train and have water. Leonard Neuburger was on that train with his wife and their ten-year-old daughter. He found out that his wife and daughter had been arrested and volunteered to go with them, completing the relevant paperwork. They reached Auschwitz on 27 October. One hundred and three men were taken off at Cosel, and the rest of the train had continued to Auschwitz; 429 men and women were selected for work, 412 went straight to the gas chambers, including Miss Neuburger. I have mentioned what the three survivors related. There were no others, none that I have been able to find anyway.

* * *

Tuesday, 27 October 1942 –Prior to the Wannsee Conference, if a Jew had married a non-Jew, the Jewish partner had been exempted from transportation. Now marriages of these people were no longer protected. Their children were called *Mischlinge* or "mixlings."

* * *

Wednesday, 28 October 1942 – This was the start of transfers from Theresienstadt to Auschwitz. I will mention Theresienstadt later, as there are a few sad tales that need to be shown the light of day.

* * *

Gemmeker oversaw one more transport on 30 October 1942. It was the ninth that month. I read that it was about 12,000 Jews who were deported that month from Westerbork. It was, sort of. Some 11,168 were transported out of Westerbork. Of course, there were others who did not pass through Westerbork, such as those who were sent directly to Auschwitz from other centres. I do not know how many of these there were. You can get a little upset by being a number off because that number is a person, a child, a baby. And do they not need to be remembered? Gemmeker passed sheets from one hand to another, names and numbers on those sheets of flimsy paper. They were never people to him. This month of October would never be repeated as "successfully" again. I am sure that this was a disappointment to someone like Gemmeker. No letters to Berlin, claiming another record broken. No congratulatory telegram in return to be kept in the pocket and shown to all you met, a telegram of congratulations from the Reichsführer Himmler. It was like an Academy Award for an actor – it got you into places. If you were a friend of Himmler, everyone wanted to be your friend. If you were a friend of Eichmann, others wanted to be your friend. Hence the little group of mutual sycophants grew in Westerbork.

Bob Cahen saw this train leave, on the last day of October 1942. He bemoaned the fact how they were becoming used to the transports, something that they should not do. Life in Westerbork was cruel. If someone were slow, they were told to hurry up. He said how they all hurt inside for the job that they had to do. Although Bob was not a nurse, he had a good knowledge of First Aid and worked in the hospital. He saw many heart-breaking things. He saved someone's life, from suicide only the next time he saw the man he was going to occupied Poland. He remembered a baby boy he cared for who had hydrocephalus. He hoped that the boy's fragile neck broke on the way to Sobibór or Auschwitz.

More arguments about how many were on this last train in October. The LIRO Bank said 652, other agencies record 959, Jacques Op den Berg, a member of the Flying Column, estimated 900. This time about 200 men were taken off at Cosel and 20 were put on the train. No one knew who they were, just 20 ragged souls, whose lives were already extinguished, walking dead. Op den Berg saw this happen, as did Alfred van der Zijl. They were two of the 11 survivors. Another was Mozes Hartog Waterman. This was to be his first camp. He survived St. Annaberg, Königshütte, Johannsdorf, Kochanowitz, Börssigwerke, Blechhammer, Groß-Rosen, Buchenwald and Schörzingen, a sub-camp of Natzweiler-Struthof, the only German run concentration camp on French soil. The rest of the train resumed its way to Auschwitz where it was recorded that 659 people went straight to the gas chambers.

* * *

Gemmeker's first month had come to an end. In the space of a few weeks he had disciplined his troops into a seemingly kindlier pack. They cajoled under trying circumstances huge numbers onto the trains. There was no riot. Gemmeker saw to it that it had gone quite smoothly. Congratulations from Berlin would have been the cream on the top of his real coffee. Gemmeker looked around. The camp was becoming well-ordered now that the overcrowding was decreasing. Everything was appearing purposeful but for Gemmeker, the best thing was a house of his own. It was a modern-built house with running hot water and central heating. It was wooden, green and white with spacious rooms and a lovely modern kitchen. A friend to confide in, whose estranged wife seemed attracted to him. He would cultivate Elisabeth Hassel. In fact, she was almost offered up to Gemmeker by his subordinate Hassel, who was probably pleased to offload her onto someone else.

Gemmeker oversaw the deportation of 7,759 people from Westerbork in October 1942. Of those 5,294 were murdered upon arrival at their destination, 2,396 died later from disease, overwork, malnutrition, disease, shooting or beating. Only 69 survived. October 1942 had a survival rate of 0.89 percent. The odds of survival were 112 to 1.

NOVEMBER 1942

SEVEN TRANSPORTS WITH 5,440 DEPORTEES

November 1942 – mass killings of 170,000 Jews took place in Bialystok.

* * *

It had been decided earlier at the suggestion of Schlesinger to Deppner that there should be 2,000 people on the permanent workforce at the camp. This did not mean the same 2,000, but 2,000 at any one time. Any over the 2,000 could be transported as not needed. Gemmeker carried on with this practice. Sometimes new inmates were admitted to the camp to replace those who had gone beyond their "usefulness." Gemmeker took pleasure in exempting people, the term was "sparing" them. Sparing them from what, if not death? At the very least, Gemmeker saw transportation to the East as a punishment for some or even retribution for bad behaviour. It gave him God-like privileges also enjoyed by many others throughout Nazi-occupied Europe. Perhaps you would like to guess how many camps there were. I told you a few pages ago that I would tell you. Think of a number. You will likely guess too low unless you know the actual number. Perhaps you will start in the hundreds, 100 across Europe? Two hundred? Three hundred? Keep going... 1,000? More –

keep going: 3,000, 5,000, 10,000, 20,000? Double it. There were about 42,000 camps that detained people. Not all were concentration camps; they totalled only 938. Only 938, I cannot believe I said that. Nice precise number, isn't it? There were 1,830 forced labour camps and transit camps, of which Westerbork was just one. There were 559 larger POW camps with tens of thousands of smaller ones. And what about the death camps? Guess! Start small; you can perhaps name them if you are interested in this or have read about it. Six, that is right. Chelmno, Bełżec, Sobibór, Treblinka, Majdanek and Auschwitz-Birkenau. Many camps had gas chambers to deal with small numbers. But these six were the largest killing centres. In November 1942, they were all working. Chelmno was the first. It used gas vans. People were forced or tricked into the back of one of three vans where the exhaust fed into the back of the van. The van drove off to a burial site, and by the time it reached the destination, the people, men, women, children and babies were all dead. Over a period of just four years, almost 300,000 Jews were murdered in this way. Local people could tell what was going on, and some assisted in rounding up the Jews. They saw the trucks, they heard the banging on the sides of the vans and they knew where the death pits were. Other people were also murdered, people who tend to be forgotten, such as the Sinti and the Romani. In the 1920s and 1930s, the Germans loved their music. All the big bands played "Black Eyes" or "Gypsy, You Have Stolen My Heart." At the bigger camps, the *Zigeuners* were encouraged to play and sing his music until it was time for them to go. Five thousand Sinti were murdered at Chelmno, equal to a whole town. The numbers were far greater at some other killing centres. Every camp could be a killing centre. Even Westerbork had a crematorium to dispose of the dead but no gas chamber. Executions did occur, but in these six death camps, the process was industrialised. Chelmno was so efficient, that only three people survived, representing 0.001 percent of the total sent there to be killed.

By March of 1942, the details from the First Wannsee Conference were being enacted via the building of Bełżec, Sobibór and

Treblinka. Three months after this "Himmler's Brain" Reinhard Heydrich was dead, assassinated by Czech soldiers. Retribution saw the destruction of Lidice and Ležáky. Ležáky tends not to be remembered, but both villages were razed to the ground, and all males over the age of 16 were murdered during the action. The women and children were sent to the various camps. Eleven children were sent to Chelmno, where they were gassed in the summer 1942, with one girl from Lidice. Not many from Lidice and Ležáky lived to return to the villages after the war. This action of wholesale slaughter affected some Sudeten Germans, something that they could not come to terms with.

The chairman of the Wannsee Conference was dead, but the secretary still lived. Working from his office in Berlin, Eichmann oversaw the transportation of all people among the various camps.

A field telegram was sent containing information about Treblinka, Sobibór, Bełżec and Majdanek. It was intercepted by British Intelligence and decoded, as all German wireless communications were being intercepted and read. Forget typing errors; the numbers are quite clear for 1942. It is a large number, so if you are not good at reading large numbers, I will spell it out – one million, two hundred and seventy-four thousand, and one hundred and sixty-six. Again, these are exact numbers. Nazi efficiency. Treblinka in 1942 was the largest killing factory and accounted for 713,555 deaths, thus far. I say thus far because Auschwitz would quickly overtake the capacity of Treblinka as new gas chambers were being designed.

When you consider all these numbers, you can see that Gemmeker was but a small cog in this vast killing machine. But without all those small cogs, the machine would not have worked. Small cogs like the police that made the arrests, guards in towers, train drivers, guards on the trains, camp staff, cooks, accountants, and engineers – all of them were small cogs, whirring and enabling the machine to function. "I was following orders" to make the killing machine work.

Gemmeker may well have been feeling pleased. He had been informed that in the future, trains could depart from the camp itself.

The timetable from the Dutch Railway Company indicated that the first train was to leave from the camp and not from Hooghalen, which had necessitated walking. The only problem was that the track was in the middle of the camp, where everyone could see what was happening. Everyone would need to stay in their barracks until the train had departed.

* * *

Monday, 2 November 1942, the Liro Bank put the number at 973. The bank should have known; the staff had a list of everyone on the train and took their money into safekeeping. Abraham Jonas Walg, Jacob de Wolf and Coenraad Rood were all on this transport. Walg and Rood had been arrested. Walg was a member of the Jewish Council, so for a time was spared. De Wolf had joined his parents when they were taken to Westerbork. I find it odd that Walg was selected, as he was a member of the Jewish Council before admittance to the camp. The list for each transport was put together by the Jewish administration in the camp. It selected Walg. De Wolf and his family had been kept at the Joodsche Schouwburg in Amsterdam where they were registered before coming to the camp. The theatre had hosted the Nelson Troupe, Herbert and Rudolf Nelson, and as they became more famous, they began to organise displaced Jews into performing cabaret in Amsterdam. They were later joined by Willy Rosen, Max Ehrlich and many more from a similar revue at the Lutine Palace. The latter were known as the *Prominenten*. These people properly enter the stories, in a short while.

Thousands of people were registered at the theatre. It served as a holding and registration point but had once been a place of laughter and entertainment. It now had become a place of Nazi brutality perhaps gave an indication of what was to follow. The dehumanising process began there. But some children were fortunate enough to escape from there. Parents "threw" their children over a wall to waiting Dutch hands that secreted the children away. One child

43

rescued from the day care centre in 1941 was Salo Müller. He was then moved around Amsterdam one step ahead of the Nazis. Thousands though just passed through the Schouwburg, their first registration before transportation. Most ended up in Westerbork, like Salo's parents who were transported east.

Coenraad Rood had been in Westerbork just a month when his name was put on the list. He said how violent some of the Dutch military police were, including Sergeant Major de Jong, who beat prisoners, forcing 17 into a space meant for eight. Rood described the beating as savage. Walg was appointed wagon leader and was tasked with the collection of water.

It was again Gemmeker who indicated that the train could leave.

Abraham Jonas Walg, Jacob de Wolf, Coenraad Rood and Luis van der Kamp survived. They were able to tell how they were taken off at Cosel as slave labour while the rest of the train travelled on to Auschwitz. Of those who had left Westerbork on the 2nd of November, 654 were dead two days later. In all, 14 from this transport lived to tell their own story about Gemmeker and the other Nazis. It may seem impossible to believe, but if you were taken off at Cosel, you stood a better chance of surviving than if you travelled on to Auschwitz. When the trains ceased to stop at Cosel, survival rates tended to drop. Men were taken off at Cosel, so there are more men among the survivors. At the time, this was not known. If you were a man, you stood better odds of surviving, not because you were stronger, but more men were used for labour. So who was worse off in terms of survival? Mothers, children and the elderly.

Ask yourself where you fit. What would your chances have been? I mean, do not kid yourself; you would be safe if you were not Jewish, right? That did not matter to the Nazis. Some British went to Auschwitz. Allied soldiers went to Auschwitz. If your face did not fit, you went to Auschwitz. If you were in a certain place at a particular time, just by coincidence, you went to Auschwitz. You could have been rounded up as a hostage. It did not matter. Anyone was at risk, and it did not have to be Auschwitz you were sent to.

You have seen how many camps existed. If you were in an area where the resistance was active, you stood a greater chance of being rounded up. The people in Lidice and Ležáky or Oradour-sur-Glane in France had not done anything, yet they paid with their lives. They never knew why – a reprisal, a punishment for something they had not done. It was like this across all those occupied countries throughout Europe and North Africa.

The Germans themselves did not escape the Nazi horrors either. They were governed by strict, open-ended laws ripe for interpretation. Protective custody meant that you could be taken off the street at any time. There was even a law forbidding malicious intent. Let me dispel a misconception. Do you think that the Gestapo was some huge organisation? There might have been 20,000 working for the Gestapo, but only 3,000 of those were Gestapo officers. They carried a metal disc stating their position. They did not have to tell anyone about themselves unless it came as a direct order from a superior. They were indeed a law unto themselves seemingly could appear anywhere. The other 17,000 were involved in the bureaucracy. They did not need huge numbers of officers in the field, for they relied on informants. One can only guess how many of those there were. Your neighbour could have been an informant. Your own son or daughter could have been an informant too. You could be reported for listening to the wrong radio stations, for spreading something you had heard on the radio, or for telling a joke that was against the regime. You could have been an informant yourself. People who wanted to settle an old score could watch and wait for you to do something that could be reported. It would be filed, and someone in an office would decide whether you needed a visit. You had to be guarded at every turn, every day, all through the day. How about when you had been drinking and told a joke about Hitler? Depending on the maliciousness of the joke and the fact that you were drinking, you might have gotten off with a few days' correction. Yet people were executed and sent to the camps for telling jokes, especially towards the end of the war. There was no getting away from the war in occupied Europe. You lived your life through it and around it. You were in it, completely. So how would you have kept yourself out of the camps? Plenty became complicit and joined in, hoping to avoid arrest or involvement. The worst? Perhaps Jews who turned Jew hunters. They were paid a bounty for every Jew they brought in. Next in line, nationals who joined the Nazis did their dirty work for them or signed up to join the SS. There were a few Dutch who did that. Even a small number of British who were caught up in the war were recruited from camps.

I have already mentioned how some of the Dutch police collaborated with the Nazis. It was the same in France. The Nazis utilised local police to detain Jews and to deliver them to holding camps, just like Westerbork. In the Channel Islands, on Guernsey, the British police did the same. A small number, three Jewish women, but they were taken. There was no local outcry, unlike when the Nazis wanted the Freemasons residing on the Islands.

A feeling in Britain exists that had the Nazis successfully invaded there, things would not have occurred as they did in the rest of Europe. It is one opinion. Another is that it would have been exactly the same way. Before the declaration of war, there had been an active fascist movement, which was led by Sir Oswald Mosely. He was not just supported by thugs and criminals; he had great support among the aristocracy. Many elevated persons had supported Mosely. There were the Mitford girls, Lord Rothermere and *The Daily Mail* along with others who actively supported appeasement and many who were vacationing in Germany right up until September 1939, including relatives of the King. One can ask why the Duke of Windsor met Hitler. Jews were expelled from positions in aristocratic households. The Nazis had a list of all those who were to be imprisoned after the invasion, and no doubt there was another list of those who could be relied upon to assist the assimilation of the United Kingdom into the Reich. There would have been informers to hand over resistance fighters and Jews along with volunteers to join the SS against Bolshevism; some were recruited from POW camps in Europe. So the British police would have been the same, driving around the Germans and British Bobbies, posing for film and photographs with

Wehrmacht soldiers. I see no difference between the expected reaction to the Nazis in the United Kingdom and other subjugated countries in Europe. Yet as in other countries, there would have been resistance, just as great as in the Netherlands, France and elsewhere.

Yes, some resisted and paid the price, and some resisted passively. Some hid Jews. All praise to them. And you, what would you have done? Plead ignorance? Not your concern? What if your neighbour or friend had been taken? What then? Would you have kept quiet? Protested? Admit it; you do not really know how you would have reacted until you were forced to face things. You might like to think, you would... Would what? Speak out? Protest? Or turn your back and walk away? I pray that you and I never face such a time. But there are times it comes to us all one way or another. Do you take issue with someone who shouts out about Jews or calls them a name or makes false generalisations? Do you tell them it is not acceptable? It does not have to be Jews. It could be Muslims, as the Nazis were too lazy to work out the difference between Jew and Muslim, both being circumcised. It was communists, gays, gypsies, Jehovah's Witnesses, priests, teachers, pacifists, theologians, authors, singers, film stars, comedians, children and babies. Do you tell them, the ones with foul mouths, to be quiet? If we do not, chances are we would be quiet when the persecuted were put on the lorries and taken away.

* * *

On the following Friday, 6 November 1942, the train was not quite so large, and only 476 souls were sent east. In case you doubt this, then Fred Schwarz could tell you what it was like. He had already been in the camp for nearly two and a half years together with his brother. The barrack leaders had called out the names to the anticipated shouts of joy and dismay. Men, women and children carried their luggage to the train, which was leaving from within the camp. It was not a proper station; a track went down the middle of the camp with wires on either side. It had been laid by camp inmates and employees of the Dutch Railways. There must have been some sort of perverse satisfaction for the Nazis that the Jews had helped build the camp, had laid the train tracks, and chose who would go and were also responsible to get them all onto the trains. It meant that the Germans did not actually need that many staff to operate the camp. Yet there was never any large-scale resistance or uprising. Just sad resignation. In among the crowd were the Jewish camp staff organising everything for the Nazis and the people in brown overalls. These were the "Flying Column" who helped people onto the train. The nurses from the hospital were accompanying the sick to the train as they were carried on stretchers by the men in brown. There was a fully staffed hospital at the camp along with a camp dentist, Wolf, who ensured everyone left with cared-for teeth. The train had come in from Hooghalen, another smaller camp, and was waiting for the people from Westerbork to board. The Jewish Council claimed that 425 had been sent to Germany, but the Zentralstelle's list had 476 names on it – actual names, with date of birth and occupation, not simple numbers. Lipmann Rosenthal & Co copied the list for bank purposes, and then it was passed on to the general commissioner for Economic Affairs. This was Hans Fischböck, a Brigadeführer newly arrived from Austria where he had been on the council overseeing the joining of Austria and Germany in the Anschluss. He was an ardent Nazi convert of two years' standing and was responsible for, among other things, the "Ordinance to Eliminate Jews from German Economic Life." The title says it all, and here he was helping to literally eliminate Jews from *all* life. He had come up with a perfectly diabolical scheme to charge the Dutch for the occupation of their country, some 400 billion Reichsmark. He was another one who escaped warranted retribution. He managed to get to Argentina, using the Catholic Church's ratline, an escape route initially intended for those escaping the Nazis, where he was given Argentinian citizenship, even returning at times to Austria and using his real name. Actions by states to bring about amnesty and reconciliation resulted in his escaping trial, although the Austrians did refuse to give him back his Austrian citizenship and confiscated all his wealth. Some sort of justice but hardly recompense for the untold misery his actions and laws caused.

Let's go with 476 people on this train from 6 November 1942, of which 101 were under the age of 18. This next illustration of madness aptly highlights the Nazi mentality. Among these children was a newborn. Born on that morning, the infant, along with the mother, was deported. Do not let anyone call Gemmeker a gentleman. He sent the baby, the two-year-old sibling and the mother, recovering from labour, to the East. Somewhere in among the 13 carriages was also a 91-year-old: Jacob Levie from Zuidland. He was born 14 July 1851 and was to die three days later at Auschwitz.

Simon de Vries and his wife are on the train. She was taken from the hospital to the train. Israel de la Penha was on the train, too, classed as a criminal. He had escaped the camp and when returned was beaten up by Sergeant Major de Jong and thrown into a cell. The very next day, he found himself on the train. At Cosel, Israel and Simon were taken off the train to work in the labour camp. On the 7th of November 1942, the train arrived at Auschwitz; 366 people were murdered immediately, including the baby and the 91-year-old, as well as mothers and children. Only Simon, Israel and one other lived to see the end of the war.

* * *

On Tuesday 10 November 1942, 748 people hurried to get into 12 carriages, among them a seven-month-old baby and a 90-year-old man, fresh from celebrating his birthday. They had been brought from Amsterdam late Saturday night and had spent an additional two nights in the camp. The people were frightened, some quiet and some noisy. Those with exemption stamps were particularly annoyed that they were being deported with everyone else. Struggling along with the others was Mozes Vischjager. He thought it odd for the train to be leaving on a Tuesday, as it usually left on a Monday. The trains left either Monday or Tuesday. In that month, they alternated. In two days' time, Mozes would be sporting a black eye. He would make the mistake of waving goodbye to his family when he joined the other

176 men under 50, getting off at Cosel to become part of the labour detail. On 12 November, 758 Jews arrived at Auschwitz, of which 517 were sent to the gas chambers, and 48 women and three men entered the camp as slave labourers. None of them survived. Gemmeker had waved off another train to hell.

* * *

Train number four was to leave from inside the camp. Gemmeker would have noticed the smoothness of the operation as he walked up and down the side of the train, chatting with his officers and acknowledging prisoners when they wished him goodbye. By this time, Alfred Käsewieter and the men under his command must have spoken to the camp guards and officers about their journeys guarding the trains from Westerbork to Auschwitz. It was becoming common knowledge among the camp guards what happened to those sent east. But they were all under strict instructions to keep quiet about it. And they did, even after the war. They smiled for cameras in the camp and smiled at the inmates and each other. Sick, perverted smiles. Gemmeker was perhaps already cultivating the eventual defence that he did not know what happened to those he sent east. The local populations were starting to know in every town and city throughout Germany; why else would young boys stand next to train tracks and make hanging gestures at trucks carrying Jews? Children asked questions of parents about the people waiting for trains at the train stations. Parents, if honest, said they were Jews going east and that they would not be coming back. Those who lied claimed they did not know. And what did the Jews say? They carried on with the belief that they were going east to start a new life, even the 90-year-olds. What would have happened if they had told each other the truth, that they were going to be murdered. Why would you tell someone you loved such a ghastly thing? When the trains reached Cosel and they saw how they were treated, the panic set in. And the knowledge that what they had thought and hoped for was not true, that others must have been wrong and that they would in fact be murdered became a grim reality. The truth was so terrible that they could not contemplate it.

$$* * *$$

Monday 6 November 1942, 763 people followed the instructions as to which of the 14 carriages they were to sit in. The three-month-old baby with the mother was in this carriage, the 86-year-old grandfather in that carriage. Nineteen *Häftlinge* or prisoners were here, all together, under guard. If you had tried to escape arrest or the camp, you were a criminal. This train had one *Freiwilligen*, a volunteer. He had filled in the correct and proper papers to allow him to go with his family. Then at the last minute, there was a flurry of activity. It had been decided that seven others would be added to the transport. They were called *Nachtrag*, the addendum. They were found spaces, and if there were no available spots, room was made. One hundred and six were under the age of 18, off on a great adventure, into the unknown. If they were lucky, the boys aged 15 to 18 would get off at Cosel, about 80 kilometres from Auschwitz. And if they were lucky again, they would survive the harsh regime of beatings, executions and starvation as they worked for the Fatherland. And if they were very, very lucky, they would be one of the three men who survived to be released at the end of the war.

Ninety-eight percent of those sent east by Gemmeker died. The odds of survival were 50:1 against. While those boys were still alive at Cosel, their mothers and younger brothers and sister were already dead. Six hundred and sixty-three died within hours of arrival at Auschwitz. It was best these boys did not know. Some never got to know, but those who survived wanted to know whether their families had survived, too. It was a longing ache and futile hope that somehow someone had survived. It could be years later, actually 1951, getting on a bus in Tel Aviv, and recognising the bus driver as your son or the elderly passenger as your mother. "Moishele" had found his mother. Want to calculate the odds? It is impossible.

No one was coming back from Auschwitz to say what it was like, so no one assumed the worst. I will tell you later about one who returned but remained silent for fear as to what might happen but was kept in isolation. I will return to this later. In fact, somehow "favourable" reports were coming back. Post cards came from those deported. The Nazis spoke about conditions, and the Red Cross workers were not taken to those camps. The Dutch became used to the deportations, and the Jews felt reassured and again started to report for deportation.

* * *

Thursday, 19 November 1942: The Soviet counter offensive began at Stalingrad.

* * *

Even before I tell you about Abraham van Spier, you most likely will be able to guess his story. He was deported with his family on the train that left for Auschwitz-Birkenau on Friday, 10 November 1942. Of the 724 deportees on that train, which included his wife and ten others of his family, only five survived. Can you imagine what it was like, what it is like, to lose 11 members of your family, including those nearest to you? What if you sit now and count off 11 of your own family and imagine that you will never see them again. Abraham lost his wife and two-year-old daughter. He asked himself why he alone survived. Many survivors felt guilty that they had survived, a burden that they had to carry with them for the rest of their lives that out of their whole family, they were the lone survivor. Abraham carried that with him. He carried their loss every day for the rest of his life. What sort of torture is that? Many did not cope well and punished themselves in various ways, even to the point of taking their own lives. Others were determined to survive to make a statement. Survive at all costs. Abraham was one such man. There were hundreds of thousands of other men like him with their families who travelled that same road. Abraham was the one who remained to tell of their story to be a witness for those times. If you have been noting the Nazi's actions concerning trains going to Auschwitz, you probably can work out how Abraham survived that journey. He was destined for Auschwitz in late 1943; so few survived from that time, but those who did were usually the young men who left the train at Cosel. This train left Westerbork with 724 deportees and arrived at Auschwitz with 726. Yet Abraham said he and some others got off the train at Cosel. It must be that the train picked up exhausted slave workers to be sent on to Auschwitz for euthanasia. Abraham did not say, and if this were true, none of the workers joining the train would have survived, as they were all *spent*. You remember how one witness did say at the end of October that he had seen 20 men put on the train at Cosel? Eighty-two men and women were admitted to Auschwitz to work, but none survived to confirm whether others got on the train at Cosel. Abraham thought he was alone in surviving that train, but he did not know about the tailor Mozes Engelsman. He was removed from the train at Cosel and later moved to Buchenwald where he was liberated. In all that confusion, it is no wonder that Abraham did not know about Mozes, 19-year-old Samuel Jas, Siegfried Parsser who reached his 30th year the month before, or Louis Schuitevoerder who was only 17. They did not know each other. They did not raise their eyes to see who else they knew; they did not want to draw attention to themselves.

* * *

Tuesday, the 24th of November, still only 1942, and 779 people were milling around the train, waiting to be told where to board. Others of the 2,000 camp workers, encouraging the people like Lemmings, got aboard with the food issued. White uniforms among the multitude helped the sick and infirm, who were denied by Gemmeker and the other Nazis the peace of dying in bed. Infants and children were there, too, 103 of them this time. The youngest was born in July, and the oldest grandparent was 88 years old. There were about 80 in each of the ten carriages. This was the Auschwitz train, so it drew to a halt 80 kilometres from its destination at Cosel. "The Beast" made his selection of 70 younger men to work until they drop. If you are quick at maths, you have already worked out how many were murdered immediately. From that train, 667 went to the gas chambers. These numbers. Please do not become inured to them, as we are only in November 1942. Almost another two years of death remained. One member of that Cosel group survived to see a day when he could decide at what time he got up, what time he went to work, and what sort of work it would be and what he would do with his life rather than having some lower member of humanity decide for him.

The Nazis never realised that it was they who were the *Untermenschen*, not the Jews or Slavs or Poles or Gypsies and all the others. The Nazis had descended below what is required to be counted among the ranks as members of humanity; that they needed a human streak never occurred to them. Some survived by telling themselves they were misled or were only following orders and that if they had said "no," they would have ended up in the gas chambers. Whom were they fooling?

They had volunteered for this work; they were paid with bribes to do it. They queued up for the chance to receive extra cigarettes, drink, food and long rest periods, including "prostitutes". They wore happy faces in the photographs, and they referred to it as the "good" or "happy" times. The most damning evidence is that no one had forced them to join the SS. It was for volunteers who could prove they were pure German without any Jewish ancestors in their family back to 1800. Officers did not have any Jewish blood in their families as far back as 1750. By 1940, nearly all the requirements, including no dental fillings or glasses along with height restrictions, had been relaxed. They were also recruiting from nationalities once regarded as inferior, such as Ukrainians and Slavs as well as Muslims. And their leader, a fine example of manhood, who never graced the front pages of any health magazine, Heinrich Himmler vomited when splashed with the brains of a Soviet prisoner being shot as a demonstration of Himmler's orders being carried out. This had brought about the Wannsee Conference, and a more humane form of murder, not for the victims but for the executioners. That was how the conversations had gone and been recorded by Eichmann.

* * *

A Monday was the last day in November of that year. Nearly 1,000 people were due to be deported to Auschwitz. Gemmeker had approved the list and had made a few alterations to prove a point. He could do that. He was the Kommandant, and it was his right to take someone off or put some unfortunate on the list.

A few days earlier, in the middle of November, events had taken place that influenced the makeup of the train's list. If someone asked you what Amsterdam was famous for, how far up on the list would you find diamonds? Quite high up the list I imagine. You would probably say canals or art, even bicycles. Let me give you another. How about raincoats? The Hollandia-Kattenburg factory, in the northern part of the city made raincoats, famous throughout, well, Amsterdam for one. They were good raincoats, and the Wehrmacht placed many orders. So anyone working there was exempt, spared from arrest, as it was war work for the German Army. Now this was an irritation to the Nazis in the SS, as many of the workers were Jewish. This irritated Hans Rauter. We know how he liked to send reports to Himmler about the perfect execution of his orders, but that was not easy when there were so many he was expected to leave alone.

Hitler encouraged competition among those close to him, often giving departments the same task to perform. This had the effect of Himmler, Goebbels, Göring and all the others at the top vying for Hitler's attention. This was mirrored further down the pecking order with various department heads vying with each other to please their chiefs in Berlin. Good news about targets met were important. A telegram asking for an explanation about incomplete quotas was not. This struggle for recognition and assertion of power in Amsterdam was no more evident than with the Jewish Question. The Jews were actually in demand, first to work for the war effort and second to be deported to the East. Or was it the other way around; first for deportation and second to further the war effort?

Hans Rauter was struggling with how to fulfil his quotas of expected numbers for deportation. He had long wanted the Jews in the Hollandia-Kattenburg factory but could not get his hands on them. Then came a reason, well, an opportunity for an excuse, which would fulfil his quotas and get one over on other SS leaders in Amsterdam. These *Rüstungsjuden* were annoying Rauter. But the *Rüstungsinspektion*, the department for completing Wehrmacht orders for clothing and anything else they needed, wanted to hold onto them. Rauter was looking for something to put the department in its place, which came with the arrest of Martha Korthagen. The whole of the Zentralstelle was aware of Rauter's intended need, an inroad into that factory. Poor Martha suddenly found herself the centre of attention. She had been arrested on suspicion of being a member of the Dutch resistance. We all know that there was not any need for a reason to arrest someone; they could be held in protective custody, which did not afford any rights at all to the person in detention. Thousands upon thousands were in prisons and concentration camps in such protective custody. Although permission to execute a German citizen needed approval from Berlin, that was not extended to any other nationals. Martha was in a very precarious position, especially when she mentioned that she had once worked at the factory close to Rauter's heart. Rauter took an interest in Martha's case. Orders were issued, and the uniformed *Orpo*, the *Ordnungspolizei*, and the regular uniformed police with Willy Lages of the Sicherheitsdienst and head of the Central Bureau for the Jewish Emigration in charge surrounded the factory. All the non-Jewish staff were sent home, which coincidentally included any member of the Dutch resistance, the *Nederlandse Volksmilitie*, who therefore had a lucky escape. All Jews at the factory were arrested and taken to the Euterpestraat where they were then made to pass by a booth that hid Martha from sight. Martha pointed the finger at 130 Jews as being resistance members. They were transferred to the Scheveningen penitentiary. Dutch humour referred to it as the

Orange Hotel, as it held so many loyal Dutch people. The other "innocent" Jews were sent to Westerbork, but one managed to escape. The 130 received brutal interrogations before being sent to Westerbork themselves. They were put in the criminal barracks; five were tried in Nazi courts. Two of these were executed at Westerbork, and three were sent on to concentration camps. It did not end with the arrest and deportation of the workers. All their families were arrested as well and sent to Westerbork, too. The Nazis were always good at noting where orders came from, and it would put them in good stead later. They somehow knew they were doing wrong. If Germany did not win the war and they had to justify their actions, they were ready with their defence: "I was following orders." In this case, Lages and aus der Fünten both claimed they were following the orders of Herbert Johannes Wölk.

* * *

The train that left on that last day of November in 1942 consisted mainly of the factory families. There were nearly a thousand, 996 to be exact: 104 children, the people who were arrested and a few other "criminals" in the "S" carriage at the end of the train.

It was a cold day, but surprisingly the heating was turned on as the train left. We get the story from a young nurse who was aboard train. She said that letters and post cards were thrown from the train as it reached the Dutch border. They were waved adieu by the usual crowd, who knew the train timetabling. She stated that the German soldiers or Alfred Käsewieter, the train commander, acted appropriately, but that food – bread and jam – was not distributed until the morning of 1 December. It was a snowy day, and later the train stopped as usual before reaching Auschwitz. One hundred and seventy were taken off the train and sent into the Sakrau Camp, at Cosel. The selection did not include many from the "S" carriage. Yet one man managed to beat expectations and survive. When the train stopped, Jacob de Boers slipped out and joined his wife in the other part of the train. There he was selected for slave labour. Jacob's journey was not over at Cosel; he was moved onto Blechhammer, Groß-Rosen, Buchenwald, Natzweiler-Struthof, Bissingen and finally Dachau-Allach. Herschel Goldberg was also a survivor from that train. He was 19 when he arrived at Cosel. When the train arrived at Auschwitz on 2 December, 247 survived the next few hours after the arrival, but 749 did not. They went straight to the gas chambers.

News began to filter into Westerbork of the Nazi defeat in North Africa. Any Nazi setback brought a smile, behind closed doors, to the faces of those imprisoned at Westerbork. It gladdened their hearts and blew and ignited the flame of hope held in their hearts.

Moshe Flinker did not rejoice over the news about Tripoli. While others believed their salvation was drawing near, Moshe, aged 16, thought that the end was not near. The end would be when almost the whole world was destroyed, for salvation would not be delivered by the Allies. It would be from God because nearly the whole world had tortured the people of Judah.

November 1942 drew to a close, and Gemmeker as Kommandant had transported 5,440 people out of Westerbork. Of those, 4,256 were murdered at the end of their journeys, 1,150 others died of other causes and only 34 saw the end of the war. There was a survival rate of 0.63 percent for this month. The odds of surviving were 160:1 against.

DECEMBER 1942

THREE TRANSPORTS WITH 2,495 DEPORTEES

"Happy Chanukah" should have been heard all over the camp from the lips of every Jew in Westerbork. It was Friday, the 4th of December 1942, the first Friday in the month, Kislev 25, the "Holiday of Lights." There were small groups that kept the holiday, and photographs were taken to mark the occasion. Happy faces, crowded in together, sitting on their bunks, outdoor coats to keep warm. Happy faces, if that was possible, in this miserable place? Two candles were lit today. Six places still awaited lit candles. Some were perhaps there who would not get to see all eight lit on the 10th of December or celebrate the 11th.

Rudolf Werner Breslauer would take a photograph of another group with all the candles lit. The light was shining and reflecting from their faces. Was there ever a time such as this? Yes, in many places throughout the Reich where Jews were forced together there would be the spirit of Chanukah and remembrance of the rededication of the Temple in Jerusalem when Judas Maccabeus stood against the Greeks. Who would stand for them against the Nazis? Where were the modern-day Maccabees to fight their cause? Such was the question asked again and again, all through what should be a joyful holiday.

It was a Friday, one of the normal transport days, with the Sabbath celebrated on a moving train. The old passenger train drew into the camp. The Dutch Railways were not intending to use their newer rolling stock to transport the Jews, but that did not stop them from charging the Nazis the going rate. It saw their profits increase, even in time of war. There was always someone to profit from another's misfortune. There were 12 carriages today, enough space for the 811 people on board who were cajoled and coaxed yet again into the compartments. Most on this train were older. You might not think of 55 as old, but by the time you had been through arrest and time in the camp on poor rations, you looked old, and you behaved as if you were old. Above the age of 55, you had outlived your usefulness to the Nazis. The selection at Cosel did not need anyone over 55, as they would not have lasted long in any slave camp. How old are you? Although some children survived, the youngest were also superfluous to the needs of the Reich. On this train were 114 "vapid" children. The children could not contribute to the work of the Reich, but they counted towards the number needed to fill a train. It does not seem logical, but to talk about logic with the Nazis makes light of the fate of those poor souls who were destined to die. Death watched and waited to receive them like all the others, without exception or compassion.

I am guessing it was a miserable journey, like all the others. No one survived to recount what happened from the Jewish side. How many got off at Cosel is not known. If anyone did, their stories are gone, completely gone. There is nothing to remember them by, except the names next to a number on a piece of flimsy white copy paper. Auschwitz recorded that 16 men were taken into the camp to work, perhaps even to process those who had accompanied them to the camp. Some 795 were put through the routine of undressing and walking into the shower. This process was watched and had been timed previously, so it was already known how long it would take; 795 bodies were then to be disposed of by the work detail.

At this time, the Jews were taken to the Little Red House, a converted cottage with an opening where the gas pellets were thrown in. The earlier chamber inside the camp was in sight of Höß's office, and sounds from there reached Höß's office. For those reasons, this building gradually ceased to be used. The Little Red House and then the Little White House were thought to be well away from the main camp and out of sight. A distance away from those two houses were the pits where the bodies at first were buried, then dug up and burnt later upon Himmler's orders as the Red Army approached. The gassings took place at night so that the victims were disoriented and less likely to run, as they could not see where to run to. The next morning, the *Sonderkommando*, a work party made up of Jewish inmates, would bury the bodies in pits. From this transport, 16 men were employed in work at the camp, but not one survived to have their story told. Shortly before the Westerbork Jews arrived, on the 1st of December, 532 Norwegian Jews had been processed; 186 men were registered, and 230 women and children had been murdered. That number may seem small, but each number was a life, remember?

I have mentioned Norway. Have you heard someone referred to as a "Quisling"? Quisling was the infamous Norwegian collaborator. Let me take you away from Westerbork for short time while I answer a question about the rest of Western Europe where men prided themselves on being civilised. Let me put the Netherlands into its European context.

WAS IT THE SAME IN WESTERN EUROPE?

The Jews in Norway numbered 2,173. Of these, 775 were arrested, and many fled to avoid arrest. The Norwegian resistance smuggled 900 out of the country. The total Jewish dead in Norway was 765 – a smaller number compared with the dead of the Netherlands, representing 35 percent killed of the total Norwegian Jewish population. In the Netherlands, the number was nearly 75 percent of the estimated 140,000 Jewish population. The Jews in France fared better than those in the Netherlands. There were more than twice the number of Jews in France in 1940, 340,000. Of those, 75,000 were deported to the camps, where nearly 97 in every 100 died. France was divided into the occupied northern part, which resisted, and the southern part, which kept a form of French government. Jews were encouraged by the Nazis to go the unoccupied part of France. The Vichy Government, so called as it was based in Vichy in southern France, complained about this, but the protestations were derided by Joachim von Ribbentrop, the Nazi foreign minister. The Jews in Vichy France were interned. In November 1942, all of France came under German control. French public opinion turned against the harsh treatment of Jews, and the arrest, centralisation and deportations were then mainly overseen by Germans. But there were still French people, especially the *Milice*, who aided the Germans in deporting the Jews. The deportations to Poland started in March 1942, with just one that month. Then in June 1942, there were four trains. In July 1942, a further eight, and in the last two weeks of that month, trains left every Monday, Wednesday and Friday. A similar pattern held in August and September and then only four trains until the end of 1942. The whole of 1943 saw no set pattern to the 17 departures. In 1944, there were 11 deportations, the very last being on 11 August 1944 from Lyon to Auschwitz. The vast majority of the trains bound for Poland went to Auschwitz, 69 of the 73.

There were about 75,000 Jews living in Belgium. By Dutch standards, they could have been deported in a matter of months. Most of these Jews were not of Belgian nationality but were other nationals seeking safety away from Germany. As early as October 1940, laws were passed against the Jews by the military government. The Nazis began to seize Jewish property, but suddenly Flemish collaborators burnt two synagogues and pillaged the house of the chief rabbi in a pogrom in Antwerp. In 1942, as in the Netherlands, the persecution worsened, and Jews travelled through Mechelen, a transit camp like Westerbork. From August 1942 to July 1944, some 25,000 Jews and a smaller number of Gypsies, 350, were sent to the camps in Nazi-occupied Poland. The Belgians as a whole were unhappy with the treatment of the Jews and resisted by hiding almost 30,000 from the Nazis. Many of the Jews joined the resistance and took part in raids, even raiding a transport train to Auschwitz, releasing Jews and Romani. Unlike in the Netherlands, the Belgian police refused to round up Jews: Many Jews owe their lives to this fact. Nonetheless, 31 trains left Belgium, 27 to Auschwitz, one to Ravensbrück, one to Bergen-Belsen and two transfers to France.

And in Luxembourg? At the start of the war, there were 3,500 Jews in the country. Many of those were from other countries, but when the Nuremberg Laws were enforced in Luxembourg, more than 70 percent fled the country. They were the fortunate ones, as they stood a better chance of surviving by fleeing to France. Those who fled to the Netherlands did not fare too well. There were about 1,000 Jews remaining in Luxembourg. By the end of the war after trains had travelled to Auschwitz, Theresienstadt, Łódź, Lubin, France and Moravia, there were only 36 left alive in all of Luxembourg.

For those of you who know something about the Holocaust in Western Europe, you may already know about Denmark. It had a Jewish population of 7,500. Some of these were Jews from other nations who had gone to Denmark to learn agriculture and were bound for Palestine. This agricultural training was similar to that of the pioneer group at Westerbork. The Jews in Denmark were accepted into Danish life. They were respected, and for a time, they were left alone by the Germans. They regarded the Danish as sort of Aryan, so they did not want to upset their sensibilities by deporting the Jews. This is what happened when a large enough group of people stood up against the Nazis. The Danish government had not required Jews to register, nor were they required to wear the yellow Star of David, and when some Nazi sympathisers tried to burn the synagogue in Copenhagen, they were foiled in their attempts twice, once in 1941 and again in 1942. They not only were foiled but also were arrested. The Danish authorities refused to discriminate against Jews, and the King spoke out in support of them. Oh, you might have heard he once wore a yellow star, but that is not true. Nice thought though that King Christian would have done that. Things changed in 1943. There was resentment that the Germans were there. Strikes and civil disobedience against the Germans did not go down well, with the Nazis. Then the Danish Government resigned on August 28, 1943 after they had been told that the German Military courts were to try their own people for disobedience and sabotage.

On 29 August 1943, the Danes awoke to a different regime when the German military commander, General Hermann von Hannecken, declared "martial law" to have the army rule the nation according to army laws. All Jews in Denmark were arrested. Telegrams flowed between Karl Rudolf Werner Best, the *Reichsbevollmächtigter* and civilian administrator in Copenhagen, and Hitler in Berlin. This resulted in permission for the Jews to be rounded up under martial law. It was at this point that *SS*-Obergruppenführer Dr Karl Rudolf Werner Best got cold feet. He foresaw that there could be great civil unrest if all the Jews were suddenly arrested. He thought about how this unrest could be avoided. Best spoke to German Naval Attaché Georg Ferdinand Duckwitz and a few others for good measure. Now there was nothing odd about that, telling officer colleagues when the round-up was planned for, except that they told Danish officials, who then told others, who told Jewish leaders, who spread the word around the Jewish congregations. Within a short time, everyone knew the secret. Time was short, and it would prove difficult to get 7,500 Jews out of harm's way. They were put into hiding and into safe places, and when the time came for the round-up, the Germans found very few Jews. The Danish police stood their ground and refused to allow German soldiers to force entry into Danish homes. Quite often when the police did find Jews, they left them in hiding. The Nazis managed to find about 470 Jews. The others were secretly manoeuvred towards the coast and smuggled over to Sweden, including an additional 700 non-Jewish relatives. One Danish policeman, Knut Dyby, was instrumental in saving many Danish Jews. Knut hid many people and then arranged their escape from Denmark. Something like 1,888 people owed their survival to Knut. He then went into the ports and arranged with fishermen to take Jews and others escaping the Nazis to Sweden, which accepted them as Danish refugees. The Nazis then proposed to deport the 470 Jews, mainly German, out of Denmark. Well, that was the intention. The Danish Red Cross made such a noise that the Germans had a rethink. They decided these Jews from Denmark would be sent to Theresienstadt. At Theresienstadt, which also had the slogan *Arbeit macht frei*, "Work brings freedom", above its gate, the inmates could receive parcels and send post cards. The *Reichssicherheitshauptamt*, Reich Security Office, had to agree to a Danish Red Cross representative to a visit in June 1944. There the Danish Jews stayed until released in 1945. Of the 470 Jews who went to Theresienstadt, nearly all of them returned. Out of 7,500 Jews in Denmark, 120 died. This is a small number compared with the deaths in the Netherlands and the Holocaust as a whole, with millions involved. One hundred and twenty is a small number, but still that number refers to human life; it is the population of a small hamlet or village. The refugees in Sweden all returned. But what did they return to? In other countries, they returned to find people living in their houses, their property and businesses gone to others. In Denmark, they returned to find everything intact, just as they had left it. While they were away, it had been protected from the Germans and their collaborators. A Danish Jew faced a survival rate of 63:1 in favour, unlike any other country in German-occupied Europe.

What have you learned from that? I hope you have seen that the answer of some countries was more responsive to the plight of the Jews than that by others. If we had been a Jew in Germany, where might we have turned? I posed that question previously. We now have the benefit of what we know now about the Nazis. Perhaps we would decide to would keep out of it? Keep our heads down? Would we complain if they came for our neighbour, friend or family member? What would we have done? And what would we have done if we had been asked for help?

* * *

Let me tell you a story I have heard told by someone who was told by someone close to Himmler's entourage. In fact, I have heard it twice as slightly differing variations of the same story. In one, it was overheard by a telephone operator listening in on a private conversation, and in one, it was on Hitler's birthday, whereas in the other, late in 1942, but the gist is the same. Let me put the two together.

It was Hitler's birthday or some other notable anniversary, and Himmler telephoned to wish Hitler a "Happy Birthday" with some good news that 50,000 Jews had been exterminated. The call was taken by Martin Bormann, Hitler's private secretary. Bormann let it rip at Himmler, literally – they were only "evacuated, evacuated, evacuated" and put the phone down on the *Reichsführer*. The other version has Bormann reminding Himmler that news of that sort must be delivered by courier, not over the phone.

* * *

On Saturday, 5 December 1942, Himmler issued a directive that all Jews in Germany who had been arrested since the previous deportations were to be sent to Auschwitz and Majdanek. I do not suppose it took him long to make that order. It probably only took a dozen words, uttered to a subordinate to take action. Fate sealed. Could not be revoked. Done. Marga Himmler complained in her diary, a week earlier, that she was alone so much, but then she had the Christmas shopping to keep her busy, and entertainment such as watching a fashion show. In fact, she went to two fashion shows; one she described as being "ugly". The second had 200 models with "beautiful clothes". Professor Benno von Arent, the *Reichsbühnenbildner*, did well that day. The Reich designer also knew what was happening away from Berlin. As a member of Himmler's staff, he got to see things others did not. I wonder whether he talked to Marga Himmler about those things as he demonstrated the cut and sweep of a dress.

* * *

On Monday 7 December 1942, Moshe Flinker was writing in his diary about the great question. It is a beautiful diary, written by a teenaged Orthodox Jew. The entries usually end with a sorrowful prayer. The language portrays Moshe's roots founded in the Hebrew language. At 16, he knew you could be a Jew yet many other things, too. His family had come from Poland many years earlier. He was born in The Hague, and he celebrated his birthday every 9th of October. Moshe was a Jew and Dutch. He was Dutch and a Jew. His beliefs were strong. He knew of the difficulties that Jews were facing. His family could no longer eat kosher food, they wore the "Star of Shame," he walked for 90 minutes to get to his Jewish

67

school, and he no longer owned a bicycle nor could travel on public transport. These things he mulled over, and he shared his personal thoughts with the reader. The great question? Why was God letting all of this happen to the Jews? Moshe concluded that it was because they were being punished as they were in the past. Yet God had not revealed their transgressions or error of their ways. Moshe's only salvation would come from God. It would not come from the British or the Allies. In his prayers, he did not pray for British victories against the Germans. The British and Americans would not save the Jews; it would be God and God alone who did. In some ways, God's salvation would come when it could get no worse. At the very point that the Jews were lost, then God would intervene in a dramatic way and save them. If the British and Americans were scoring victories against the Germans, in some ways, this was prolonging their punishment by God. If the Germans achieved supremacy, then God would redeem the Jews. He believed that their salvation would come when everyone acknowledged that the Germans would be victorious. The intervention of the Allies would prevent the situation from reaching its zenith and therefore postpone God's intervention. This was not a defeatist attitude, far from it. It was the belief of a devout Jewish teenager in an impossible situation, trying to make some sense of it all through the lens of his religion. The moral high ground of the British was not to be acknowledged. In Moshe's eyes, others were just as bad as the Germans in the way that they treated the Jews.

It was Tuesday 8 December 1942, and the train was ready to depart on Gemmeker's signal. It was his little piece of theatre, his little way of demonstrating his power, his little display that he was in control. The deportees had been selected and informed, packed what they could, had shared goodbyes and had been escorted and helped to the train. There was noise, tears, confusion and order with one ending only: Departure with 927 people to the East. All expected to be accommodated in 11-year-old carriages. A total of 796 adults and

131 children boarded. Heels clicked, and "Heil Hitler" was said. The Kommandant gave the signal; the train responded with a shrill scream and hiss of steam. The wheels turned slowly, then caught. The carriages clang and struck each other. The train left. There were waving arms and sad, despondent faces pressed against the windows. Among the lost was Gerrit Jas. He alone lived to tell his story and, with it, snatches of tales from those who slid into oblivion. He told that the train stopped at Cosel. He and 59 others were selected to die a slow death from exhaustion, beatings or starvation. Gerrit's parents, Hartog and Klara, had died at Auschwitz almost three months earlier, on Thursday, 24 September 24 1942.

The train continued to the main camp at Auschwitz. It arrived on the 10th of December with 927 people on board. Again, it could be that, as it is the same number that left Westerbork; 60 were put on the train at Cosel. Only 42 people survived the next few hours; among the 39 men was Hermann Kluger. The other 885 people? They went to the gas chambers. Hermann survived by chance. He was not removed at Cosel because he had been classified as a criminal. He was a musician the Germans had accused of simply knowing members of the resistance, although not an active member himself. He was put in the penal barracks at Westerbork, as he would not co-operate. As a convict, he continued from Cosel on to Birkenau where he was selected with 38 other men for work in the camp. Another man who had been selected to work asked why he had to walk to the camp and was offered a place on one of the trucks, which then took him to the gas chamber. Hermann's musical skills earned him a place in the camp orchestra. He played while the Sonderkommando extracted gold teeth in the crematorium and while other prisoners were hanged. No one else survived from that group of 38.

* * *

That was the last train that stopped at Cosel to feed the Nazi factories centred around Zakrzów in Southern Poland, about 80 kilometres due west of Katowice. Simon Tonckmann had arrived last October, and he lived to describe the horrors of the camps. With 32 others, he lived to commit his testament to paper for those who did not survive. Sakrau was a "dismal" place, on a hill overlooking a valley among the trees "that swished in the wind." It was about 18 kilometres from Cosel. Originally, it had been populated by Polish prisoners, but these were replaced by Jews from Westerbork, Drancy and Mechelen. Passing through the first gate, they walked between the Kommandant's residence and the guards' barracks. They found themselves in the work area where there were smithies and carpentry shops. Through the next gate they would find themselves in the prisoners' barracks.

The camp leaders were found among businessmen like Willi Drobeck, a café owner from Breslau, and Kempinski, a hotel owner from Groß Strehlitz. As at Westerbork, the internal control was run by Jews. Drobeck was regarded as a bad man, whereas Kempinski was regarded as quite good. The camp taught the prisoners how they should behave before moving them on to work in other camps, such as Spytcowice, Zeybinia, Seibersdorf, Klein Mangerdorf, Sackenhoym, Annaberg, Reigersfeld and Blechhammer. The camp at Sakrau was "owned" by the Kallenbach company from Berlin. Sakrau was a *Zwangsarbeitslager* or a forced labour camp. Kallenbach also had another camp at St Annaberg in the Landkreis Groß Strehlitz. It subsidised the costs of those camps, as did thousands of other firms using slave labour. Drobeck's camp became a camp for the sick from January 1943 until it closed. The first 100 to arrive had frozen limbs and were losing fingers and toes. A doctor would arrive and select those unfit for work who would then be sent to Auschwitz. The camp shut down 22 May 1943.

* * *

Thursday 10 December 1942: German Jews arrived at Auschwitz straight from Germany.

* * *

A copy of *Blue Band Nieuws*, extra edition, circulated throughout Westerbork. The handwritten newspaper-style sheet composed by Werner Löwenhardt from Dortmund had the lead article entitled *"Binnenlandsch Overzikt,"* Domestic Overview. Werner was an artist like Leo Kok and made drawings around the camp. His skills meant that he was exempt from transport. He was 23 years old and spent another three years in Westerbork. His father and his eight brothers had all served in the German Army during WW1. Only Werner and one brother, Heinz, survived.

* * *

The last train in 1942 left on Saturday, the 12th of December. Gemmeker saw to it that 757 boarded the train. For some reason, a large number of "convicts" was on this particular transport – 200 of them. My entry for this train is short, and you may know the reason for this already – no one survived to tell what happened. It went through Cosel but did not stop for anyone to get off. Auschwitz recorded that 121 men were taken into the camp, and 636 were murdered upon arrival on 14 December. No other trains came from Westerbork until January of the next year.

Auschwitz dealt with an average of one and a half trains a day, so some days more, and on other days none. Let me state the obvious, evident to many: if there had not been trains, then the number of those murdered in the Shoah (Hebrew word for Holocaust), the Porajmos (Gypsy Holocaust), Polish genocide, Soviet and Slav genocide, and the persecution of religious groups and homosexuals, along with Muslims, political prisoners, criminals, asocial prisoners, mentally ill, alcoholics and drug addicts, vagrants, pacifists, beggars, conscription dodgers and prostitutes would not have been so vast. The railways enabled the Nazis to pursue their persecution of all those people.

I will go further and say that without the co-operation of non-Germans, the degradation and murder would have drained the Wehrmacht of so many men, Germany would not have been able to pursue the war to the extent that it did. If Jews had refused to run the administration of camps, it would have necessitated employing others, possibly Germans. Can you imagine what might have happened if the Germans had not declared war on all those groups? The number of men available to fight in the German army would have been greater. Perhaps the outcome may have been different. But that is a question of little importance. From the outset, Hitler nailed his flag to the flagpole of hate, hatred of all those groups as well as whole nations, such as the Poles. I will leave that one for proper historians to argue over.

By the spring 1943, Auschwitz had four huge crematoria. Each crematorium had gas chambers for the killing and ovens for disposal of the bodies. There were 46 ovens, which could process 4,500 people a day. Auschwitz was staffed by SS soldiers. There were 7,000 in total over the years, with only 840 of those later facing a court of law at some time in their lives. The trains from the Netherlands were quite small in comparison with trains that later arrived from Warsaw or Hungary. Some trains held as many as 7,000 prisoners, when the capacity of the wagons was doubled, 100 persons per wagon, an average of 5,000 per train of 50 wagons. Obersturmbannführer Eichmann had to balance all this with the capacity of the killing camps and the labour requirements over the whole Reich. The "passengers" were "charged" from their bank account with Lipmann, Rosenthal & Co the equivalent of a first-class one-way ticket, but the SS paid the *Reichsbahn*, the German railways, only for a third-class ticket. It amounted to something like 240 million Reichsmarks. That is quite a figure.

Recently, I read that the Reichsbahn stole the equivalent of $664,525,820.34. Can you believe this sum? The German railways has admitted complicity but has not apologised. The *Nederlandse Spoorwegen* apologised only recently for its part in the deaths of so many Dutch and other nationals. Salo Muller was instrumental in bringing this about. It did not bring anyone back and was done with a great deal of prompting or even demands, and most likely those who had co-operated in any way no longer worked for the railways. The French Railways, the SNCF, allowed people to search their records and has set up displays about transportation, especially about the children. The railways also made financial restitution to those in the United States who sought some sort of recognition and recompense through the courts.

Towards the end of 1942, a letter was sent from Willi Zöpf, head of the Department of Jewish Affairs in The Hague, to Berlin that 42 trains had deported 38,606 people to the East. It was hoped that by the end of the year, the Netherlands would be *judenfrei*, free of Jews. This included the plan to send 8,000 ill Jews and their families to the East. They would be removed from nursing homes and hospitals, starting early in 1943. It had also been decided in late 1942 to rescind the exemption orders placed on certain categories of Jews. They would be arrested and kept at Vught concentration camp or other camps in Barneveld. In December, Himmler wanted all able-bodied prisoners sent to concentration camps, and to facilitate this, Heinrich Müller, the Gestapo chief, decided that 3,000 Jews would be deported throughout January 1943.

* * *

Many miles away in London, it was made public what was happening throughout Europe. News was reaching the outside world that Germans were systematically murdering Jews and others. It seems strange that this gave the war a purpose, if it did not have one before. Up until then, the Allies were fighting German aggression, but on 17 December 1942, every combatant fighting for the Allies or everyone resisting oppression in occupied Europe was fighting Nazi ideology that legitimised the murder of people in the name of the state. Sir Antony Eden, the British foreign secretary, stood up in the British Parliament and made a statement to confirm the rumours – that the Nazis were fulfilling Hitler's often-made threat to exterminate the Jews of Europe. To leave the Germans in no doubt, US President Franklin Roosevelt declared that the crimes would be avenged. Every German knew that after the war they would be called to account and that they would try to hide what they had done or been party to, enabling it to happen.

A thousand miles away from London in Auschwitz, people were asking where those were who were going to help them.

CHRISTMAS 1942

There were no deportations between 13 December and 10 January 1943 because the Germans were celebrating Christmas. The rolling stock was needed to transport German troops to their homes for the holidays. It was a short respite for those at Westerbork.

Gemmeker took the opportunity to celebrate Christmas in his house. There were social gatherings. He seemed pleased and relaxed as he donned civilian clothes. He was pictured raising glasses with his mistress and secretary, Frau Hassel. The green house was decorated with garlands and a tree. There were more formal pictures in uniform with SS-Hauptsturmführer Ferdinand aus der Fünten and SS-Untersturmführer Hassel and with Mr Scheltnes from Lippmann, Rosenthal & Co in civilian clothes. They all enjoyed looking through a book with Gemmeker turning the pages. Maybe it was a book of photos Breslauer had taken.

Rudolf Werner Breslauer was a professional photographer, and Gemmeker had use for him. Breslauer could take photos to record Gemmeker's first Christmas in Westerbork: Gemmeker with his mistress and Untersturmführer Hassel – posing as happy families, Gemmeker playing the bon viveur with his superiors, Gemmeker posing as he lights the candles on the Christmas tree in the officers' mess, and Gemmeker on the "top table", surrounded by the officers and invited guests for a proper Christmas meal, everyone tucking in and making pleasant conversation. Pleasant conversation, while elsewhere others were hungry, or cried or mourned. No doubt Gemmeker enjoyed the photos, perhaps he even thanked Rudolf. He would have another use for him later, but for the moment, he could continue taking photographs for Gemmeker to enjoy. As long as Breslauer was useful, he, his wife and their three children were safe.

It has been said that the festivities at the end of 1942 included a social evening to celebrate the deportation of the 40,000th inmate east. By the end of 1942, the total number of deportees was 41,099 of which Gemmeker had transported 15,694. It was therefore a rather perverse celebration and another insight into how Gemmeker's mind worked, a *Danse Macabre*. The Jews were literally just numbers on a sheet. Humanity had no place here.

* * *

Thursday, 17 December 1942: The Allies condemned German mass murders.

* * *

Monday, 28 December 1942: Women at Birkenau were sterilised in the first experiments of this sort.

JANUARY 1943

FIVE TRANSPORTS WITH 3,264 DEPORTEES

In this year, the number of Jews killed by Einsatzgruppen and reported to Berlin surpassed one million.

* * *

The Christmas respite ended on 11 January for 751 men, women and children in Camp Westerbork. Again, there was a high number of convicts: 194. It was a cold Monday morning when before sunrise, people made their way to the train. Gemmeker may have felt a little annoyed that it was back to work, but he enjoyed the deference shown him.

Every survivor was able to point the finger at him. Every survivor had a horrific story to relate. Every survivor stared death in the face and cried, shrunk in fear, their feelings, dragged up from their primeval being, the instinct to survive and live through what ever happened and to arrive on the other side alive. Every survivor would be a nail in Gemmeker's coffin to remind him of the evil deeds done. How could one think that murdering innocent children was the right thing to do? Himmler knew. The children would seek revenge for the deaths of parents, so they all had to go.

Maurits Wolder, 20 years old when liberated lived to point the finger. He and seven others. Maurits had been arrested by the Gestapo and imprisoned in Amsterdam. He made friends with Juda Toff, also arrested, and the pair made up their minds to escape. Maurits was 17 then. They both arrived in Westerbork on the ninth of the month, time enough to join the train departing on the 11th of January. They told the others in the carriage what they were going to do. It was a risky thing to give others that information. Someone could use it to gain favour with the Nazis. At Haren, the train came to a stop, and they both slipped out. Maurits hid under the carriage and was helped by a Dutch farmer when the train had gone. Juda was captured and sent to Auschwitz. He did not survive.

Jonas Pront arrived in Westerbork on the 21st of December. He had been arrested by Dutch people in German uniforms. Ferdinand aus der Fünten gave instructions that Pront was to be given a good beating before getting on the train. The train took three days to reach Auschwitz. Five men, including Jonas, were selected for work when they arrived along with 176 others. First, they had to undress; the weather was freezing, and snow was falling. They got a hot shower and then had to run naked all the way to the barracks. They were given shirt, underwear and trousers and were kept in Block 8 for two days. From there they went to Kanada to sort the clothes of the prisoners. It was not unusual to find clothes belonging to friends or family members. Jonas and the others were alive. The 562 who had travelled with them no longer existed. They were just names on a flimsy piece of paper, numbers and statistics reported back to Berlin for the day's tally.

Among the 181 selected to enter the camp, four women between 19 and 34 were selected for medical experiments by Dr Eduard Wirths. They were taken away to be experimented on by any one of 20 doctors involved in such work at the camp. Among them were Horst Schumann (sterilisation and castration), Johann Paul Kremer (selection for experimentation), Eduard Wirths (chief physician), August Hirt (The Bone Collector), Emil Kaschub (wounds and infections) and Carl Clauberg. Clauberg first worked in Barracks 30, which was part of the hospital complex in the women's camp. Rudolf Höß, the Kommandant, then gave him Block 10 in the main camp. He kept between 150 and 400 Jewish women upstairs and experimented with sterilisation, using an irritant that closed the fallopian tubes. Then there was the one you are going to tell me I have not mentioned: Mengele.

Josef Mengele had a propensity to inflict pain on children, especially twins. He also assessed the incoming prisoners for life or death, as did all the doctors as part of their duties. They sent them to the left or right, to live or die. Mengele had volunteered to work in the concentration camp service. He collected twins, and he even introduced himself as "Uncle Mengele." He gave them sweets and showed kindness to keep them calm. He would amputate limbs from one twin or infect a twin with a disease. If a twin died, the other was murdered so that post-mortem comparisons could take place. Mengele also liked to experiment on pregnant women before disposing of them. Little wonder he was called *Todesengel,* Angel of Death.

The belief was that one man is superior to another by right and that invoking "survival of the fittest" to justify the "master race" mentality of superiority over others is perverse. Even if one has that mentality, what right does it give that person to treat another human in such a way – because they can? We see the manifestation of this "superiority" everywhere; people believe local people are better than newcomers or better than people who hold a different label. Why does man fail to acknowledge humanity in others?

* * *

Monday, the 18th of January, another transport was ready to leave Westerbork. Do I need to describe it? Gemmeker slowly processed through the crowd, reassuring everyone that they would be fine in the East. Lie. They would be looked after. Lie. They would meet up with old friends and family. Lie. He saw the loading of 44 "prisoners," poor unfortunates caught for some reason or another, doing something the Nazis objected to. It was decided that nine more should join them. There was plenty of room on the train for another nine when it suited the Germans and the forms were completed.

Seventeen-year-old Sophia Annie Jacobson went by the place where Gemmeker was standing with her parents to help her old grandmother find her place. There were some Jews who had been working for the German Army, irritated that their exemption had run out. They were the first Jews who had been sent to Vught Camp, another 450 from the Joodsche Schouwburg, sent to Vught, were also previously exempt.

Leonard David Frank looked at Gemmeker and his officers as Kommandant Gemmeker walked by. They did not know Frank. He had worked in the economics section of the *Joodse Raad*. Everything had been done, he felt, to prevent or delay his deportation; he bore no one any ill will on that count.

Max Levenbach was suffering from the cold in his 60th year, with yet another chess move swirling around inside his head, and he almost bumped into Gemmeker, but came to his senses just in time to stop himself.

Leon Greenman was with his wife, Else, and Barney, their two-year-old son, was there too. Also with Leon was his 83-year-old mother-in-law. Here is Leon's story, in brief, as he wrote about it in full. They had been arrested by the police, accompanied by at least one Dutch Nazi Party member in their black uniforms, distinguished by their caps, with the "S" shaped in the form of lightning and their uniform collars black shirts. Leon had difficulty recognising them as Dutch collaborators. Johannes Hendrik Feldmeijer was one, but he was too high up in the order for it to have been him; besides, he had a unit named after him: Sonderkommando Feldmeijer. Members of this unit included Heinrich Boere, Klaas Carel Faber and Pieter Johan Faber. Men like these thought nothing of executing patriotic Dutch men and women and rounding up Jews. It may well have been members of the Feldmeijer unit who arrested Leon and his family. They were taken from their home. You remember the Danish police thwarted attempts at this. They were taken to the main assembly site in Rotterdam, called Hangar 24, and then on to Stieltjesplein to board the train. The train travelled overnight to arrive at Hooghalen. Then they were all marched to Westerbork, even the elderly mother. Leon and the family were kept at Westerbork for more than three months. This was when Leon made it known he was British. Gemmeker saw Jew first, so he classified them himself as Dutch Jews.

Leon Greenman saw Gemmeker standing by the train, talking to Schlesinger. Leon had spoken to Gemmeker numerous times asking about his British papers. The previous day, Leon had been informed that he was to be transported with his wife, Else. Leon felt that he should not be transported and went to see Schlesinger at the administration building. Although Schlesinger expressed surprise that Leon and Else were on the list, I suspect he knew already. He said that he would speak to Gemmeker. When Leon noticed Schlesinger was speaking with Gemmeker, he asked Else to speak to Gemmeker about their papers. He would not do it himself because he knew Gemmeker was fed up with him. Gemmeker could be like that. He could take an instant dislike to someone, especially if they were "challenging." So Else asked Gemmeker about their papers and for their deportation to be halted. Perhaps she was holding little Barney, for Gemmeker could hardly make eye contact with this little family. With a twitch of his head, he informed them the decision had been made, and they are to go. Where would Gemmeker find four replacements at such short notice? Leon, Ilse, Barney and the grandmother all climbed aboard the carriage.

All boarded, clicking heels, Gemmeker handed control of the train to Alfred Käsewieter. Gemmeker's last action would be to wave the train off, giving permission to leave the camp. He was glad it was going. His feet were cold, and he tried stamping them in the hope it would restore some warmth to them. Striding across the camp he returned to his house and to breakfast, with real coffee. Gemmeker could afford these luxuries; he had his little "sideline" of keeping people off the list in exchange for some sort of remuneration, and this was paying good dividends. Others would receive their shares from this, but that still left plenty for him to enjoy life.

The train left between 10:30 and 10:45 am and made its way through the Netherlands. It stopped at the border with Germany to exchange locomotives with one from the German Reichsbahn. This engine took the train forward, through Germany to Poland and Auschwitz, a little-known destination.

Leon told what it was like on the train. They had sat in compartments in the carriages that held eight people in two facing rows of four. All they could do on the journey was talk. They talked for the whole 36-hour-journey to Poland. They talked about their work during the week, how they would all meet on the weekends and how they could return after the war. People were compliant since they believed (or wanted to believe) that it was only a temporary arrangement. They would be working for the war effort. There were others who were conscripted, ordinary Dutch people who had been selected or even volunteered for work in Germany, but not in such great numbers. The train stopped various times. They could not see outside, as the windows on this train were covered. They could not get out, and there was nothing to eat or drink for anyone. Babies cried, and children grizzled.

As the train was travelling across Germany, Heinrich Himmler in Berlin felt irritated by the slow movement of things in general. When the person at the top is vexed, everyone in the pecking order needs to be vexed. It is like the old story about how the "slap" travels down the pecking order until it reaches the least significant at the bottom. Himmler thought not enough Jews were being transported and wanted good news to pass on to Hitler. The numbers had fallen during the Christmas period. Himmler spoke to Eichmann who confirmed that the trains were running again, but there were simply not enough of them. The transports were at full capacity, Eichmann told Himmler. Himmler wrote to Albert Ganzenmüller, the undersecretary of State at the Reich Ministry of Transport, on the 19th of January. When you got a letter from Himmler, it would first freeze your blood. If you read it and it was good news, your blood warmed, but if it were bad news, your stomach turned over. Albert Ganzenmüller reached and blanched. The letter from Himmler asked for his help and support. It was not a request; it meant that the recipient was not helpful and was in fact hindering Himmler's plans. Himmler wanted to "wind things up," to use his words, and he needed more trains. He and Eichmann would get more trains, no matter where else they might have been needed. The transports to camps were to be the number one priority. There had been discussions before between Ganzenmüller and the SS. He offered a half-price deal for trains carrying more than 400. The SS crammed as many as they could onto the trains. Himmler's insistence about his need for more trains for deportations and the movement of artworks across the Reich influenced the outcome of the war, hence troop movements and supplies were hindered.

Train number 44 from Westerbork arrived at Auschwitz the day after Himmler wrote this letter. Leon Greenman remembered that day, especially the shouting. He saw a pile of suitcases covered in snow. He wondered why they had to leave their blankets. Were they not going to be needed? They were separated into two lines: men on the left, others on the right. A woman cried and wandered from her line to join her husband. A guard brought down a club onto her head, and she dropped. The guard walked away with the same club and tapped 50 men on the shoulders. They were selected to go into the camp. The other 698 went to the gas chamber, including 102 children. By the 21st of January, there was no evidence that those people had existed; there were just names and numbers on lists. The lists were preserved, somehow. How do we remember them? As a number? One of 713? A name on a sheet of paper? A name on a suitcase? Who were they, except known unto God? Well, if he remembers them, it does not excuse us. Can we research every single one? Can we say where each came from, their age? Who was in their family? Oh, for some we can, those who had to be accounted for, but the millions killed, where they lived? Gone. It is an impossibility to know them. These are the ones we do remember by numbers. They are numbers who lived in a town or village, who were taken out and murdered, dumped in a pit without the proper rights carried out by the *Chevra kadisha*. Without any preparation of the body, *Tahrah,* and without a *tallit* to wrap the body in for burial, without burial and without natural decomposition. There were no mourners to make *Keriah*; there was no eulogy, *Hesped,* and no person to say the *Tziduk Hadin* prayer. Millions were cremated against the Jewish law. There was nothing for those millions killed by sadists high on amphetamines and without any moral fibre. Leon's last view of his wife and Barney was of them on the back of a truck, heading to the gas chamber. Who said *Kaddish* for them all?

* * *

You remember how I told you how the Danish police did everything they could not to co-operate with the Germans? In contrast were instances of the Dutch police being trained by the SS. One such instance was the Schalkhaar Police Battalion. Schalkhaar is near Deventer. On the 14th of January, the police arrested the whole of the Jewish Council, and when the members were in custody, the police arrested almost every Jew at home, too. Some were later released, but the others were sent to Westerbork. The Sicherheitsdienst at Arnhem saw to their transportation. The same day in The Hague, 95 Jews were taken from their homes, of whom 59 were arrested and sent to Westerbork. The next day, 70 more people were arrested. Those employed by the Jewish Council, *De Joodse Raad,* were exempt from this roundup.

Throughout Amsterdam, another 450 were arrested over the same period and sent to the *Schouwburg* for processing. Then the sick and elderly were seized and sent on to Westerbork. Gemmeker did not see them enter the camp. If he had been interested, he could have welcomed them. The 430 persons were dealt with in the morning of the 19th of January by the Jewish camp police, the *Ordnungsdienst*. At the same time, 25 Jewish "criminals" arrived from Rotterdam. Is it not odd that the real criminals were imprisoning the innocent, yet calling them the criminals?

* * *

During the evening of 22 January 1943, the list of names was read aloud. There were sighs of relief and sighs and gasps of horror – a dreaded fear of your name being read out persisted. On the list were 516 names, of which 234 were men and 282 women, of which 38 were under the age of 16 and 353 people were over 50. There were 45 "criminals", of whom ten were from Rotterdam. Among them were 40 Jews from Germany and 20 Jews from Poland, a few came from Russia and one from Romania. The sick had left before on the trains, but there were also the seriously ill, 150 of them. Space was cleared for them to be able to lie down. They were carried on the stretchers. How do I know this? The Liro Bank provided all the information on the lists as it fleeced the prisoners prior to travel.

The train was ready and left at 8 am, or a few minutes later, on Saturday, 23 January 1943. Gemmeker would accept the slight delay. It was recorded as arriving at Auschwitz the next day. That was quick for a journey during the war, but it was a small train, so perhaps it was able to proceed quickly. Auschwitz recorded it as arriving on the 24th. From that train 496 went to the gas chambers on arrival. Nineteen were accepted into the camp. The only survivor was Levie or Louis Bannet, one of the "criminals". When he arrived, wearing an evening suit late on the Sunday night, he sat in the truck holding a violin taken from a dead elderly man on the train. The door made a noise like a drum roll as it slid open. A cacophony of voices greeted them. German voices screamed at them to get out. Large Alsatian dogs, as if on elasticised flying wires, jumped up and down, anxious to get into the truck. Children cried. Louis jumped down and came face to face with a man he described as Clark Gable: tall, handsome, clean uniform and whip in his hand. Louis thought he recognised Mengele, looking like Clarke Gable. But I think Louis is wrong, as Mengele did not transfer to Auschwitz until May of that

85

year. Louis heard shots. The man standing near him complained of the cold, and Louis gave him his coat. He got an odd look from the young man called Pieter who was from Amsterdam. Louis looked too formal in his evening wear. He explained that he was arrested for playing the trumpet.

There was already a train that had recently arrived from somewhere in Poland. They all had to line up – men separate from women. Louis and the others walked towards a building from where screams were coming. Inside they saw naked men being hosed down with freezing water. Louis undressed and was forced against a wall and hosed down. His ear was causing him great discomfort, as it was frost bitten. The hose was switched off, and a prisoner came in carrying uniforms similar to the one he was wearing. They were told to put on a uniform and to take a pair of clogs, ones like farmers wore in the Netherlands. But these were aimed at removing dignity, as they were one size fits all. Louis went with the others to receive his new identity, his tattoo. The tattooist spoke to him in Dutch, and they started a conversation. His numerical artist was Hein Frank, a fellow musician. It was a wonder that Hein was still alive. He had arrived in Auschwitz on 8 August 1942, together with Edith Stein, St. Edith Stein or St. Teresa Benedicta of the Cross. She went to the gas chamber wearing the clothes of her religious order, those of a Carmelite Nun, not having been allowed to give up her Jewish identity. And yet here was Hein, still alive after five months when typically the life span in the camp was about six weeks. He told Louis he needed to get into the camp orchestra. Louis thought that Auschwitz was just for mud and the dead, but he managed to secure a job in Kanada, sorting clothes, and then had a terrifying audition for the camp orchestra. The two other musicians at the audition, Jan de Leve and Herman Pons, could not play a note because their lips were too cracked and their fingers frozen. They were described as in need of a "trip to the showers" or "two for the ovens." Louis had managed to warm his hands at a stove where he had burnt them and yet was able to play the opening notes of "St

Louis Blues." He joined the orchestra, playing as trains arrived or when the inmates marched off to work. Some months later, he was awakened in the middle of the night and thinking the worst. He was then taken to a large house together with a drummer and a violinist. He realised it was a party for Mengele. Louis played in the orchestra until the camp was liberated. Hein died almost exactly a year later, on the last day of January 1944.

* * *

It was the same routine as before. A list was used by the Zentralstelle, provided to the Lippmann, Rosenthal & Co. bank, to note who deposited how much money "so that it could be returned to them, at a later date." We all know now where it went: into pockets and banks all over the place, finding its way to Switzerland and South America, any place other than back to whom it belonged. By the time the Dutch Jews arrived at Auschwitz, they would have been deprived of all valuables. But some did not trust the Liro Bank and had money and jewels sewn into their clothes. They secreted jewels inside their own bodies. In clothes, all would be found in Auschwitz's Kanada. Other jewels and, of course, gold would be found shortly before the bodies were burnt. If they had left valuables in bank deposits back in Amsterdam, these would be identified and raided by the Nazis.

Unterscharführer Oskar Gröning knew how the system worked. He was an SS squad leader at Auschwitz. He had always been a bookkeeper and had volunteered to join the SS. He lost his easy desk job when it was decided that fit, young men could be utilised better and allow injured veterans to feel useful sitting behind a desk. Gröning went to Berlin and was given some training. He signed an oath that he would never reveal what he was about to do.

Now, if you were asked to sign on your honour to never ever to reveal what you were going to be asked to do, would you not be a bit suspicious? If the Germans thought they were doing the right thing by liquidating the Jews in the whole of Europe, as Hitler said, why would they keep it quiet? It seems to me that they were not entirely convinced that what they were doing was the right thing.

Gröning was given instructions for his journey and told to report to a place called Auschwitz. I believed him when he said that he had not heard of it. Anyway, he arrived at Auschwitz and settled in. He was surprised how much food there was when it was mealtime. In 1942, Germany was hardly a land of plenty for everyone. The next day after his arrival, Gröning was taken by a more senior officer and told his banking skills would come in handy, showing him the barracks where money was sorted and bagged. Gröning was amazed by the various sorts of money from all over the world, literally. At this point, Gröning was naïve. Then he asked where the money came from. Jews. Is it being kept for them? Negative. Will it be returned to them? At this point someone probably told Gröning exactly what Auschwitz was.

He then saw for himself what sort of place it was. As he walked around, he saw children being shot who had hidden in the trucks and elderly left on the ramp who did not move because they had been shot. Then an incident occurred that could leave him with no doubts. He saw a baby who had been left on the ramp. People intent on survival will make sacrifices, even that of their children. An SS man picked the baby up by its feet and smashed its head repeatedly against the side of the wagon, until it stopped crying. That told Gröning how his fellow SS colleagues acted towards Jews and anyone else on the death list. Gröning tried to claim he asked to leave Auschwitz after witnessing these things. Perhaps he did, but perhaps he did not. All we do know is that he stayed. He himself said he settled into the routines. One night late in 1942, he joined a group of SS that was trying to find some Jews from a transport who had run off and were hiding in the woods. Gröning and the other guards went to the Little White House and saw bodies of at least half a dozen men who had been shot. Gröning and the others were told they could leave. Of course they did not. They hung around on the edge of the woods, in the darkness, waiting to see what was going to happen. They could hear a low murmuring coming from inside the old farmhouse. They watched an SS man don a gas mask and then empty a tin of something through the hatch in the side of the building. The murmuring was replaced by screaming, which continued and then subsided. Another SS man showed him the pits where the bodies were burnt, and a trusted Jewish worker, a *Kapo*, a *Funktionshäftling*, prisoners with a "function," told him about the process and gave details as to how the bodies burned.

Gröning claimed he tried to avoid witnessing the worst of the horrors, but like the others, he profited at the cost of the Jews. He would slip the odd banknote away from those he was sorting. With these notes, he bought himself a fancy revolver from a "fence" and placed his new possession in his locker. Gröning was trusted, and it was his responsibility to transfer the money to the bank. On one of these trips, he returned to find that his locker had been sealed, so could not open the door. Those high up in the SS, away from easy pickings at the camps, had ordered that an inspection be carried out, as it had been reported that SS personnel were stealing, not from the Jews, but from the Reich. What they found was displeasing: some members of the SS were looting. While Gröning was away, his locker had been sealed. He knew that inside was incriminating evidence of his profiteering from the Jews. With some help he pried open the back of the locker and retrieved the incriminating evidence. If Gröning had made it known he did not agree with what was going on in the camp, he would not have had friends to help him escape the SS investigation. The fact that he did seems to indicate that he kept his mouth shut and went along with everything. Gröning, unlike the Jews, lived to see another day. He was later transferred and placed in a fighting unit in the Ardennes during the Battle of the Bulge and was captured by the British but kept quiet, lied about his service record and said he had worked in an administrative department that was nowhere near Auschwitz or any other camp. He was sent to England where he was well looked after and then returned to Germany. He remained quiet for years, but in the end, he spoke out on television and was seen around the world. He wanted to speak out against denial of the Holocaust. It was one of his last acts before being tried for his part in the murder of 300,000 people. He confessed his guilt to stealing but did not see how he was complicit, like so many other men and women, in facilitating murder.

There were thousands like Gröning who all knew of or had taken part in genocide. It was a new crime, crimes against humanity. Hubert Zafke and Reinhold Hanning were at Auschwitz at the same time as Gröning, and they were also discovered in later life. If you asked Gröning whether he thought it was wrong to profit from the Jews, he thought it was not. Millions were dying, not just the Jews. Millions were in fact dying, but not all were murdered in gas chambers at a camp where he worked and pocketed things for his own use, things that had once belonged to Jews.

* * *

Leon Greenman had been at Auschwitz more than a week and was possibly in places that Gröning avoided. It was Leon and his wife who had lost their British passports, and when papers did come through, proving British citizenship, Gemmeker decided to ignore the papers and had the two classed as Dutch Jews. Gemmeker needed them to make up the numbers.

On Friday, 29 January, among the 659 people being guided onto the train were 114 children, a baby girl of three months and a 90-year-old man, to which an extra 49 were added at the last minute, plus 33 "convicts." There were some foreign nationals on this train. Anyone who knew their football would have spotted Eddy Hamel. He was American with Dutch parents. He had returned to the Netherlands and played for AFC Ajax until 1930. He was so well respected that his fans would always swap sides by walking around the pitch to be on "his" wing. His wife, Johanna, and he had twin boys, Paul and Robert. Eddy was helping them into the train. Later they would be separated at Auschwitz. Eddy was not to know that his wife and two boys would be murdered within a few days.

Shouting was heard all the time: "Get on the train!" or "Return to barracks if not travelling!" A lot of ill people (71) were transported that day, so 30 additional men were needed to carry them. Money was handed over, and all deportees embarked. The signal was given, and the train whistled and rolled down the tracks of death to Auschwitz, where 590 would be murdered upon arrival.

There was excitement in one compartment because an escape had occurred. Nathan Wijnperle had been arrested but separated from his mother, Elsa, but they had met again at Westerbork and had boarded the train together. As the door to the carriage was being shut, Nathan had pressed his knee against the carriage door so it did not lock properly. When the train stopped during that first night, Nathan and his mother jumped from the train. They survived with the help of a Catholic priest. After the war, Nathan did not return to the removal company Abraham Puls because it was the workers there who had handed him over. Puls, a member of the Dutch Nazi Party, was sentenced to death after the war for his collaboration. His removal firm turned up at vacated Jewish properties to seize furniture and possessions. This action gave the Dutch a new word: "pulse." An estimated 29,000 houses were stripped by the Puls Company, but the death sentence was never carried out.

Eddy never told Leon Greenman whether he had seen Johanna and the boys. They died in the early hours of Monday, 1 February 1943. Leon Borstrock had also seen his own family taken away, his wife, Roosje, his son of six months, Jacques Jules, and his daughter, four-year-old Frederika. Leon Borstrock had been born in London, so like Leon Greenman, he too was British.

The story of Leon Greenman and Eddy continued. Some months later in April, Eddy and Leon were standing in line. Eddy told Leon that he had an abscess in his mouth. For Eddy, that was the end. In another camp, if he had been a hostage, it might have been treated, but not here in Auschwitz where he was just a Dutch Jew. He was murdered on Friday, 30 April 1943.

Alfred Käsewieter may well have done his duty. He served as train commander when the train arrived at Auschwitz. He was not even aware two people had escaped. No need to hang around; he had seen what happened often enough. He wandered off to get something to eat and to warm up. He had only a short time in which to do this before the train would be on its way again. It was needed urgently on Himmler's orders. Käsewieter did not care much what happened; some 590 went off to the gas chambers, including, Joanna, Paul and Robert along with Elsa, Barney and the grandmother. Taken for slave labour were 67, including Leon, Eddy and Leon Borstrock. Only the two Leons survived the war. They were two London men, married to Dutch women, who were in the Netherlands when the Germans invaded. Do you not want to ask them why they did not return to Britain before the Nazi invasion of The Netherlands? They had little idea as to what would happen. They had their reasons for not leaving; who are we to question?

* * *

By January 1943, the work of the Einsatzgruppen was being scaled down in the East. Nazi records show the number murdered by these death squads had exceeded one million. Himmler had a special unit to do the number crunching.

Stalingrad was about to be retaken by the Soviet Army. It was the beginning of the end, and Himmler now knew that. A new army had just materialised on the Soviet front. It was well-armed and could fight in the winter conditions. It had arrived from Siberia, released when the fear of invasion by Japan had receded. Himmler was worried. He gave orders that Jews were to dig up all those bodies that were buried and burn them; no evidence of mass murder was to fall into the hands of the Allies. He did not want to be incriminated, not if he were to survive and be part of a new German government after the war. The Soviets, however, meticulously recorded every atrocity that they came across with film and photograph, which included the murder of their own civilians and soldiers. They took witness statements but did not share all of this with their allies, so very few knew about this aspect of Soviet witness.

The Einsatzgruppen operated in the Netherlands, but without the freedom that they had had on the Eastern Front. Whatever happened in the East would influence what could happen in the Netherlands and Western Europe in regard to transports to the camps. Eichmann had to balance everything like a chess grandmaster, ensuring that the murder camps could handle the average of one and a half trains a day.

FEBRUARY 1943

FOUR TRANSPORTS WITH 3,666 DEPORTEES

February, the shortest month, yet Gemmeker managed to deport more than in January. This was transport 46, leaving on 2 February 1943 with 890 deportees. Included were seven "convicts" and one lone soul added at the last moment. In among these poor sentient beings was one confused *Geisteskranker*, a mentally ill person. The Germans had been killing the mentally ill for years. They were in fact among the first to be euthanised in Germany itself. Parents who had sent their children to be cared for in mental institutions expected them to be given the care that they could not afford them at home. First it had started with the sterilisation of all mental patients as early as 1933. There had been much talk about euthanasia or "mercy killing" before the Nazis came to power. Hitler himself had said that, in a state of war, euthanasia would be used for the incurably ill. He judged the German psyche rightly; it would not stand for this approach in peace time, but it would be enforced in time of war. His decree was dated 1 September 1 1939, the day Germany invaded Poland. On medical notes, a red "+" meant death. But even during the war, some parents raised concerns about how many of their children were dying of various ailments. The first experimental gassings had involved the mentally ill. Prior to that, lethal injection had been use, but the mentally ill presented an opportunity to try out

94

fake showers with fake nozzles that poured out carbon monoxide instead of water. These data were useful at the Wannsee Conference. This "Aktion T4" was carefully documented. There were six killing centres which murdered 70,273 mentally ill patients.

At Hadamar near Limburg in Germany was The Hadamar Euthanasia Centre, *NS-Tötungsanstalt Hadamar*, known locally as the "House of Shutters. The town children of Hadamar came to know what the large grey vans were actually doing as they toured the countryside, pumping carbon monoxide into the back of the van, full of patients. The children taunted each other by saying how they would end up in the Hadamar ovens, which spewed thick smoke into the sky from the crematoria. A celebration was held in the crematoria itself at Hadamar when the 10,000th patient had been processed. The deception was discovered when patients died from appendicitis when the appendix had in fact been removed years earlier. Relatives saw through fake death certificates or found a female hairgrip in among a son's ashes. Some complained to the church. The Bishop of Münster Clemens August Count von Galen protested the T4 killings in a sermon on 13 August 1941. Karl Bonhöffer, a leading psychiatrist, and his son Dietrich, a theologian, protested the deaths as well. Their evidence was collated through talking to parents and relatives. The secret was out. Two weeks after the sermon, Hitler ordered cessation of Aktion T4. The result was that the gas installations were dismantled and sent to the concentration camps. Also sent were the doctors to help sift out those who did not contribute to the German war effort, in all, probably about 250,000 "useless eaters." The fact that one person was sent from Westerbork illustrates the wider programme of euthanasia of the mentally ill.

Somewhere among the many adults were 85 children. All died, 83 upon arrival and two teenagers a couple of months later. Date of birth for the youngest was 30 April 1942, so not yet even a year old. This was Marcel Alexander van Rijk; This poor little mite is an illustration of the Nazi obsession for record keeping. He along with Louis Bloemist-Kaas, born in 1849, were the youngest and oldest on the train, ten months and 93 years of age, respectively. Gemmeker had the hospital emptied again. It was not one or two ill patients; there were 120. These mainly came from the Jewish psychiatric hospital at Apeldoorn, taken on 2 January 1943. Some people were sent from Westerbork to clean and tidy the hospital, and they came back the day the train left. The scene of the train leaving was pitiful, as usual. Gemmeker was walking about as if seeing off a church outing.

Although they did not know it, 3,300 km to the east, 200,000 Germans had been lost at Stalingrad. Two days before, newly appointed Feldmarschall Friedrich Wilhelm Ernst Paulus had surrendered his army to the Soviets. On the same day as the train of Jews was departing east, 235,000 German, Italian, Romanian and Hungarian soldiers were being marched into Soviet captivity, with a chance of one in 47 of survival.

* * *

Tuesday, 9 February 1943, the train stood ready to depart, yet again there were many infirm on this train. About 220 Jews from convalescent homes were on this train set for this deportation among the 1,184 transportees. They arrived that day from Borneokade freight station in Amsterdam. Also milling around under guard were 98 prisoners, Jews who had been caught doing something or other they were not supposed to, like being out on the streets past curfew.

Andries Kollem was able to describe what had happened at the Hospital at Apeldoorn. He went on this transport but survived. He had been arrested once and sent to Dalfsen but had then released. Unfortunately, he got a job as a painter at the Apeldoorn Hospital. You might ask why getting a job there was unfortunate. He got mixed up with all the other staff who were sent to Westerbork and found himself incarcerated for a second time, but this time with the hospital staff and any Jews who had lived in Apeldoorn. Out of the prisoners, three survived. Jacob Rabbie had been arrested for going to the cinema; Jews were not supposed to go see films. He had been crammed with ten others in a single man's cell at Amstelveenseweg and had been in Westerbork since the previous December. With these two in the last carriage were Jacob Fresco, who had jumped from a transport and for this reason was a prisoner. He said he did not get any food on the journey. Everything was boarded up, so chance of escape was slight to impossible. Another survivor, Adries Kollem, said that they got bread, jam and sausage on the journey. Prisoners got nothing. Jacob Fresco said the train travelled to Auschwitz via Bremen.

The train arrived at Auschwitz on the night of 11 February, and they were kept waiting until 6 am on the following morning. Peeping out through the boards, they could see the lights of Birkenau. The doors were opened by the SS and Käsewieter's men, the train guards. They saw men in striped uniforms. Everyone was told to leave everything, as they would get new things later. They helped each other down, and men aged between 18 and 40 were ordered to the left. Everyone to the right was destined for the gas chambers, unless reprieved. Men and women totalling 179 were led off into the camp – 1,005 were led off to their deaths and cremation. Of the children, three went into the camp. Two only lasted until April, but the third survived until February 1945.

The Jews who survived were taken to Monowitz, Camp 3 at Auschwitz. David Lutraan related the terror they felt when their *Lagerälteste*, camp leader, told them of the horrors within the camp.

* * *

Gemmeker seemed a bit peeved at the escapes from the camp. He gave a *Lagerbefehl*, a camp order, to the effect that as retaliation for anyone escaping, ten people from the escapee's barracks would be deported, and action would be taken against the barrack leader. This was Camp Order number 5. Everyone considering making an escape now knew that Gemmeker would order retaliatory action. It did not stop escapes, and Gemmeker kept his word, often going beyond his threat of deporting ten.

* * *

Friday, 12 February 1943: Heinrich Himmler visited Sobibór.

* * *

Tuesday, 16 February 1943, about noon: 1,108 tearful people, awake since the early hours of the morning, had been told that they were due to be transported to the East, into the unknown, from where no one had returned. The weather was quite mild; 1942 had been quite a severe winter across Europe, but a warmer day was hardly the sort of thing that was of any cheer to those being transported. This was quite a long train with 25 carriages and with more people than usual, including 207 children. The youngest had been born exactly seven weeks earlier.

I guess no food was provided for the baby on this journey since none had been provided on any other train. You can say that it never occurred to Gemmeker to ensure that there was food for everyone. He knew that babies went on the transports – he saw them embark. Would a caring man not have ensured that the babies would have food to make this journey across Europe? Is this not an indication of how heartless this man was towards the Jews?

At least 200 children were born in Westerbork between July 1942 and April 1945. Most of these babies were then murdered at one of the death camps. During the time that Gemmeker was at Westerbork, 20 children who were born in 1942 were dead by the time of the liberation. From 1943, some 90 never reached their first birthday, and 53 born in camp never saw their second birthday, while five more were murdered in their second year. Ten children born in 1944 did not get to their first birthday. A total of 178 children were born and murdered on Gemmeker's watch. This does not include babies who came to the camp; these are for births in the camp. If you want to check, you can do this through Yad Vashem in Jerusalem. Similarly, you will find more than 1,000 people died at Westerbork camp; now the need for a crematorium can be understood. Did

Gemmeker's family accept that he did not know what happened at the death camps? Some Nazi children, such as Niklas Frank, acknowledged the crimes of fathers. Niklas was the son of Hans Frank, the successor to Heydrich.

Here is what Samuel Herzberg said about the transport of 16 February: He sat in a carriage of people from Westerbork who had held various jobs. He did not know the route but recalled Breslau. The train had stopped once when one member of each carriage could go and collect water. When they got to Auschwitz, he said, just as the others reported, that they had to leave their baggage where it was. Men were separated from the women. He found himself standing among men between 18 and 40 years old, on the left. The others he thought just disappeared into the night on lorries.

Elkan Speijer was unlucky and got caught hiding on a farm near Zutphen. He was better at hiding in Westerbork. He had arrived in the camp with the expectation that he would be deported within two days. Elkan was having none of that and hid. He remained in hiding in the camp, nameless and numberless until Gemmeker insisted on all prisoners being re-registered. Elkan travelled with the green-uniformed regular German police and said that they were not bad. As leader of his carriage, he had to go get water the several times that the train stopped. He had seen a food car attached to the train, but he said that they did not receive any food. The train arrived in the dark, and Elkan saw the same men in striped uniforms and the SS with dogs. Five people survived this transport out of the 261 who entered the camp. More than 800 went immediately to the gas chamber: 315 men and boys and 532 women and girls.

* * *

On the last Tuesday in February, the 23rd, 1943, another train was lined up within the camp. Again, more than 1,000 people were headed to the East. Let's get the number right: 1,101. On that Tuesday, the 51st transport from Westerbork and Gemmeker's 21st, departed. Exactly ten percent of the train was made up of children.

The youngest was 14 weeks old, and oldest adult was just coming up on 91.

Ruth Stein-Issen was on that train with her half-Jewish husband. That was important to them, as they applied for exemption, which was of course refused. She described that when they arrived at Auschwitz, the SS were waiting with large clubs and that they were beaten off the train. In fact, her husband was struck just for helping someone else. She had watched as lorries left. A woman near her said that they were going to be killed straight away. A Nazi guard had said that the people in the lorries were going to a nursing home. After the slow ones had been beaten off the train with clubs? Still the Nazis kept up the pretence. At this point, Ruth did not know how lucky she had been.

On that train were also Moses Leman and his family. He had been running his father's butcher's shop in Hardenberg since 1932. He had married the same year, and Ottillia and he had three children, Sientje, Mathilde and Liepman, who was named after Moses's father. They had all been in Westerbork since October 1942, Moses in Barrack 84 and the others in Barrack 40. In November, they were all together in Barrack 58, but now they were on the train to Auschwitz. In a few hours, they would all be dead.

Out of the 1,101 on the train 1,014 went straight to the gas chambers. Only 87 went into the camp. Ruth and three others survived from that transport. She said she did not know about the other three, not that it comforted her much. None of those three were her husband.

The following Friday on the 26th, the Romanies started to arrive in Auschwitz. Fighting in the Wehrmacht did not mean exemption. Gypsies who had been serving in the Wehrmacht were sent in uniform with citations in hand to the special camp at Birkenau. Can you believe that? As Jews found out, previous military service counted for nothing; the best you could hope for was a spell at Theresienstadt. Gypsies and Sinti were treated abysmally. Deaths from beatings or malnutrition were higher than for other groups. I am told there is disagreement about numbers, but 20,000 Gypsies, Sinti and others from a traveller background found themselves in Auschwitz, where few survived. One little Sinti girl will become known to us later.

This was how February came to an end: with four weekly transportations to the East, all leaving on time, with the correct numbers and with little trouble. Gemmeker would see that his approach to keeping a calm atmosphere at the camp was working for him.

* * *

At some point in February 1943, Dora Gerson, the German cabaret singer and film star, was transported to Auschwitz with her husband, Max Sluizer, and their two children, Miriam and Abel. She died on 13 February – the whole family was killed together. They were most likely killed upon arrival, as there was no room for children in the camp. There was a third-class train and the 47th transport (IIIL) that left Westerbork on Tuesday, 9 February. It was recorded as arriving at Auschwitz-Birkenau on Thursday, the 11th with 1,184 transportees. It is doubtful that the killings would have been held over to the following Sunday. This transport coincided with the commencement of the deportation of Jews from Drancy in France. One train from France, with 1,000 deportees, arrived on the 11th of February, the same day as the transport from Westerbork. The total number of Jews arriving that day would have been 2,184. Of those, 323 entered the camp, leaving 1,861 to be murdered. The previous train had arrived on Thursday, 4 February, with 950 Jews from Berlin. From those poor souls, 663 were gassed. When we examine this information in cold analysis, we see that the gas chambers had been unused for nearly a week. The killing capacity of Auschwitz at this time would have been able to handle 1,861 murders and would not have held any over until Sunday, the 14th of February. Dora and her family most likely died on the day they arrived, within hours of leaving the train between 6 and 7 am on the 11th of February. There is no record of Dora's entering the camp as one of the 66 women.

MARCH 1943

FIVE TRANSPORTS WITH 6,684 DEPORTEES

I have sought information as to why there was a change in destination for the trains leaving Westerbork from Auschwitz to Sobibór. It was not made on some sort of whim; there would have been a calculated reason for the change. Some 7,240 Jews from Skopje, Štip and Bitola in Yugoslavia were sent to Treblinka. However, the first of 19 trains from Greece were sent to Auschwitz, as were 1,500 Jews from Berlin. The Romani were also being murdered at Auschwitz. It was perhaps that Auschwitz could not accept trains from Westerbork, as the camp did not have spare capacity. Eichmann would have known exactly the reasons, but although he came to the camp, it is doubtful that Gemmeker would ask such a direct question of him.

Gemmeker obeyed orders. He obeyed them extremely well, which is why he stayed at Westerbork for so long. It seems like he was not someone who thought outside of the box. He had found a natural style and stuck to it. He was quiet and methodical, probably why he had found it so difficult to be accepted into the SS. His style suited Westerbork, and everything basically found a place, but he did not seem to have any master plan. He copied what he had found at his previous camp, had not changed it and brought it with him to Westerbork. Orders said Sobibór. Gemmeker did not know where it was – it was just another of these places that popped up out of nowhere. He knew someone must know what they were doing and that it was not a mistake. Perhaps he thought to ring Eichmann's office for clarification, but he would have just been told that it was correct. He did not need to bother himself. It would be reported to Eichmann, who might even tell Himmler that Gemmeker was asking too many questions. Gemmeker decided to keep quiet, like so many others had. The Minister of Transport Albert Ganzenmüller worked out the timetable. Well, not personally, but he and Eichmann agreed on the schedule, so if there was a mistake, it was made higher up and was not Gemmeker's fault. He could breathe easily. It was best to keep quiet. And he preferred it that way; he appeared soulless, without emotion, never angered, never shouted. He must have had some emotions he kept to himself and Elisabeth Hassel, who was his antithesis. She strode around the camp like a queen and expected deference from all who she felt were lower in life. To Gemmeker's superiors, she was efficiency, sweetness, giggly and the soul of the party, careful not to contradict Gemmeker. Outside of her circle, within the camp, she was known as "Gemmeker's Evil One." Probably some of the camp guards agreed, as she could be short with them too. As much as she might have liked to, it is not known that she ever hit anyone. Rather, if you crossed her, it was not unusual to be put on a train going east. For all we know, she may well have been the power behind the throne, but Gemmeker was the same every day, so perhaps not. Rather than tell you here, I will mention at points where Gemmeker allowed his visage to slip. It might have been triggered by Frau Hassel on occasion.

SS-Sonderkommando Sobibór was located in the Second Polish Republic occupied by Germany. It had been built as part of "Operation Reinhard," and it was secret. It was where Jews were to be sent to be suffocated by gas from large petrol engines. It had opened in April 1942. Jews had been sent to that area to turn it into a new agricultural area to be populated by colonists who were ethnic Germans. When this idea was dropped, Hans Frank and others discussed what to do with all the Jews in that area, which came to some 95,000. They agreed that there was only one thing to be done with them, and Sobibór was built to a design by Richard Thomalla, who had also designed Bełżec.

Stangl from the T4 operation was the first Kommandant. Between May 1942 and October 1943, the camp was operational. The *Gasmeister*, the man in charge of the gassings, would have a good idea as to how many died there. Erich Bauer put the number at 350,000. This is more than double the lowest estimate. He told others, who repeated it, that he had overheard a conversation between Franz Stangl and the two officers Karl Frenzel and Gustav Wagner that in the competition between Bełżec, Treblinka and Sobibór, their camp came last. It was famous as one of the few camps where not one but two organised mass uprisings occurred against the guards. Sobibór was a death camp, so chances of survival were slim. Anyone on these transports to Sobibór would later regard their survival as a miracle. From the Netherlands, 19 transports were sent, which took 34,213 to intended death; of those, only 19 survived. The deportees arrived, they stripped, the women had their hair shaved and they went straight to the gas chambers. A few Jews were kept as workers, and when they were of no further use, they joined the other Jews in the gas chambers. Those that did survive only numbered 58 in total, and they told of the brutality of the guards, the degradation and the cheapness of life. There were enough of them to see that some retribution was ultimately meted out to those who inflicted the misery. After the war, Samuel Lerer bumped into Bauer, the Gasmeister, at a fun fair in Berlin. Bauer expressed surprise they were still alive. This chance meeting resulted in Bauer's arrest and conviction. It seems Bauer who denied everything had a change of heart in prison and admitted everything, unlike the Jews at Sobibór, he escaped the death sentence because Germany had abolished it.

For those who have an interest in train routes, I cannot tell you much other than the trains may have travelled through Hamburg and Berlin and passed south of Warsaw to Sobibór. Those who survived Sobibór were unaware of the route taken to that place of death.

* * *

Tuesday, 2 March 1943 was when the first train left Westerbork destined for Sobibór. The train guards knew that it was a place of death with hardly any selection; those sent were of little use to the Reich. I know it is an awful epitaph for a 95-year-old grandmother and an infant of just two months, but they could not work, so they might as well be sent to a death camp. This was quicker and more efficient and may be the reason the train was going to Sobibór and not to Auschwitz. Auschwitz, Birkenau and Monowitz were factories and needed labour, patients, nurses and doctors from mental institutions. The old and young did not fit that category; they would be "food eaters" and therefore a drain on resources, which by this time were becoming scarcer. The Germans had used up resources from the various countries that they had invaded, and the majority of the produce was taken from every nation the Germans occupied. Produce was then sent back to Germany for that "feel-good" factor that things were going right and as reminder of the "happy times'. But there were no more countries to invade. The Germans were losing ground, so the screws on the subdued nations had to be tightened. Everyone was now making sacrifices, even in Germany. The *Lebensunwerte Leben* or the "Lives of those unworthy of life" were to be eradicated.

The first transport to Sobibór stood ready; 1,105 people were aboard what was to be one of the last trains to be made up of carriages. These poor confused souls had only spent a few short days in Westerbork before leaving for the East. Those who had mental issues had been treated abysmally by members of the Dutch National Socialist Party, who were working alongside of the German security personnel and the Dutch police. At the rear of the train were the shaved heads and blue uniforms of the 72 "prisoners." Upon arrival at Sobibór, it was a matter of undressing, shaving heads and going into the showers. Among these were Jud Simons and her family. Jud had won a gold medal with the Dutch gymnasts at the 1928 Olympics. With her were her husband, Bernard, her five-year-old daughter, Sonja, and her three-year-old son, Leon. All were murdered. From the orphanage were Salla and Lotte Auszenberg, two children out of 149 on this train. Salla and Lotte had been sent to the Netherlands for safety with Max and Josef. They became separated as they were moved around and ended up in Assen where 500 children were sent to Westerbork the previous October. Josef had already been sent to Auschwitz in October and was murdered upon arrival. Max survived and joined his parents in England after the war. What anguish those parents must have felt.

Out of this transport, 13 were selected to work, but not one of those survived the war. On the 5th of March, they had arrived and had been told to write post cards about how good things were. The cards were stamped at Lublin Airfield and arrived in the Netherlands six months later, all simultaneously on 7 September 1943. Two more cards arrived in the new year sent from Auschwitz.

I can tell you a little something about this transport when it arrived at Sobibór. As it was the first, it stuck in the memory of Dov Freiberg from Warsaw. He was amazed to see the staff and patients from a mental institution in the Netherlands. An absurd scenario took place: The senior medics set up a field hospital; they checked lists and gave out medicine. Nurses helped patients into the camp, and the hospital directors asked the Germans for various items. Within a short time, everyone had been duped into entering the inner camp and was dead. Dov lived to stare Eichmann in the face and to tell the world his story in Jerusalem in 1961 and to stare at the faces of his captors at Sobibór in Hagen in 1965.

* * *

That same day, Frau Himmler was writing in her diary. Himmler had been home for a visit. These visits were not regular, for as she recorded, he worked "so hard for Germany." She was also aware that other times, when he was not working hard, he was visiting his mistress, Hedwig Potthast, his secretary. Although very few outside of Himmler's circle knew of Potthast, Marga Himmler had known for two years by this time. Potthast lived near Ravensbrück Concentration Camp for Women, which might explain why Himmler visited the camp so often. When visiting, Himmler would explain to Marga the current situation facing Germany in some detail. She was therefore aware that things were not going well and was reluctant to write too much in her diary about it, as she felt low. She noted that Himmler was in good health, even better than he had seemed in 1942. She busied herself with work in the German Red Cross, although she felt she was not always respected enough as the wife of the Reichsführer, where the other ladies were sometimes difficult.

It was the evening of 5 March· and everything was quiet at the orphanage at Pletterijstaat 66 in The Hague. Lorries drew up outside, and police and soldiers got down and entered the orphanage. They had come for the children and everyone in the building. They were all taken to Westerbork; among them were Feigel, Pepi and Esther Weiszbard from Berlin. They were to leave on the next available train, which was going in a few days' time to Sobibór. They had been separated but found each other again at the orphanage. Pepi was ten, Feigel was 13 and Esther, the oldest, was 17 and 8 days old.

After some days in Westerbork, 1,005 deportees were ready to leave. It was Wednesday, 10 March 1943. Gemmeker waved the train off as it disappeared out of the gate with all those who had been at the orphanage in The Hague. I guess he went off for a bite to eat and some coffee. I would not know what his coffee tasted like, but he liked the finer things in life, and he could afford it. It was most likely real black-market coffee, not that *ersatz* stuff made from nuts; the "replacement" stuff was served in the camp coffee bar.

The train rattled along towards Sobibór. Five days later as it neared the camp, it passed through a forest. On the train, the deportees perhaps thought the forest would be a good place to walk as they looked out of the carriage windows.

There were nurses from the nursing and mental homes who had followed their co-workers a week later. They were lucky not to have been selected the previous week, or they would have been dead by this time. Originally, because they worked at the hospital, they were exempted from transport. They were rounded up in the raid that I have just told you about. Cate Polk was one who survived and recounted how she was rounded up and ended up in Westerbork, where she had helped in the camp hospital. It was one of the best hospitals at that time, but she said that there were many sick there. She hoped she would stay there, but she was selected to be transported.

The train arrived. As Sophie Engelsman remembered it, the deportees got down and were beaten and hit as soon as the doors opened. Seventeen were selected and kept back as the rest moved deeper into the camp, many on trolleys, and disappeared from sight, memory and existence.

Of this group, four would die later, but 13 managed to survive the war, but not in Sobibór. They were transferred to Lublin. They had been the first selected because they were nurses, yet the previous week, all the hospital staff went to the gas chambers. Some doctors and male nurses were also selected and put in the front carriage of the train. Sophie and Cate were not allowed contact with them. They thought it odd when the Germans asked if they had diamonds. They might have laughed at this naïve question, thinking that all Dutch people had diamonds. At Lublin, they alighted from the train and were told to carry their belongings. They giggled at this, as most of their belongings had been left at Westerbork and the rest at Sobibór, so they did not have anything. Cate Polk, Sophie Engelsman and the others had no idea that the Germans wanted to kill Jews. They never saw the men again. Their visit to Sobibór had lasted two hours, yet they would relive it every day for the rest of their lives. Sophie had lied about her age to become a nurse. She admitted she did it to avoid transportation, yet there she was, leaving Sobibór. She would shudder each time she heard that name.

* * *

The following Wednesday, 17 March 1943, there was another train to Sobibor following the same routine. Gemmeker had checked the list of those being deported. He did not care that among the 964 names was Elias Cohen. His finger had not even paused as it ran down the sheet of crisp thin paper over Alex's name. Elias preferred to be called Alex, but the list said Elias, not that Gemmeker would consider using his familiar name. Gemmeker was not happy that day anyway, but he did not show it. Always that faint smile shone across his face. He could have read a death sentence with that same smile. That smile that was fixed on his face, but there had been some disquiet this morning when the train arrived. He usually waited to be told that the train had arrived and boarding was underway before joining the throng, which moved away from him as he wandered through – not like a magnet repelling a like pole, but in this case, like a leper ringing a bell. One of the junior officers had arrived at the office to inform him that the train consisted of cattle carts. They had all been expecting carriages, old carriages, but at least ones with seats and windows. Gemmeker had gone to see. Sure enough, there were the cattle carts, no seats and no windows. The travellers were unhappy about getting into these without any facilities. A bucket for water and a bucket for effluent. It took more than a little persuasion to get everyone on board. The Flying Column worked hard to persuade everyone to get on and walked along the edges of the crowd to stop anyone from running away. Already sitting in one of the trucks was Bernard Salomon Themans with his wife, Judik Simons. They were from Utrecht, where they ran an orphanage. They were deported with their own children and everyone from the orphanage. Gemmeker complained about the use of cattle carts for transport. He had noted the reluctance of the Jews to board such a train.

Elias Cohen could have told Gemmeker, had they met again, what had happened to them as the train disappeared from Gemmeker's view. The train stopped at Sobibor, and the Germans started shouting. Elias called them *moffen* (it is a derogatory term used by the Dutch when talking about Germans. The sick were thrown onto carts with agonised cries, and the women and children were herded through the gates, from the train station into the camp. The men were left behind. Elias related that they were asked whether there were doctors or nurses. He had thought about stepping forward, as by this time he had some idea of what was happening. He decided against it, as he would soon be found not to be a doctor. Then the German asked for all men aged 35 and below; when he did not get very many, he upped the age limit to 40. Elias stepped forward, stating he was a metal worker. I will never know how people like Elias survived. From Sobibór, he went Lublin, and from Lublin, he went on to Majdanek with about 35 people selected based on their skills. He operated machinery in the ammunition factory in Skarżysko-Kamienna where the poisonous materials and lack of protection killed most of the forced labour. Yet he lived.

On the 23rd of March 1943, 1,250 people started their journey east, ending at Sobibór. Their journey must have been hell. If it was hell indeed, then what was Sobibór itself? All perished at that place. Not one survived. How can a thousand human souls just disappear? Gassed and burnt, covered over, hidden, lost to all. In Germany, not one person was mourning their passing. Abraham de Oliveira, 62, was on that train, an Olympian from the 1908 gymnastics team. He died with all the others – of no value to the Reich.

* * *

The day before, on the 22nd of March, the Nazis celebrated the completion and opening of Crematoria Number IV at Auschwitz. The "processing difficulties" would be eased.

* * *

Tuesday, 30 March 1943, another train left Westerbork with 1,255 deportees for Sobibór. Cattle carts were used. A response had arrived about the cattle carts, nothing more than Gemmeker had expected. It was pointed out to him that there was a war on and that even soldiers of the Fatherland were travelling to the front in cattle carts, so the Jews were not to expect anything better. As was occurring elsewhere in Nazi-occupied Europe, Dutch Jews, too, would travel in cattle carts.

The train left after following the usual procedures. Within three days, all those on board would be dead. This was the fifth transport to Sobibór. What was left? Only hair, glasses, clothes, cases, gold teeth, prosthetic limbs, any jewellery and money, inanimate objects left to witness a life and to be recycled within the Reich. Elsa Keezer was among the deportees. A day after she had been sent to Sobibór, the camp received a call from the Jewish Council explaining that she was on the Barnveld List and therefore exempt. Too late for Elsa.

* * *

Sometime in March, Wim Loeb found himself in Westerbork. He was in a mixed marriage to Dina. He was given a choice. He would be going to a camp in the East to live, but he would be sterilised, castrated as he saw it. He got a message out to Dina his wife, through a cousin. Dina was horrified and jumped on her bicycle and raced down to confront Sturmbannführer Zöpf at his office. Furiously she explained to him what Wim had been told. After she had left, Zöpf picked up the phone and rang Westerbork. You can imagine Gemmeker jumping up from his chair and standing upright to take a call from one of the highest-ranking Nazis in the Netherlands. After a short and terse conversation, the deportation of "mixed-marriage Jews" ceased. Wim was allowed to return home to The Hague. He and Dina enjoyed the train journey home.

* * *

Wednesday, 31 March 1943 – The newly built Crematorium II opened at Auschwitz.

APRIL 1943

FIVE TRANSPORTS WITH 6,781 DEPORTEES

Sunday, 14 April 1943 – Crematorium V opened at Auschwitz.

* * *

Gemmeker did not like cattle trucks being used for transport, but he was not a humanitarian. His indignation was not because he wanted the Jews to have a more pleasant journey. Gemmeker wanted everything to fit in with his master plan. Everything had to appear normal. To this end, the whole camp, although a new phenomenon, had to appear to be normal, too. It was to present the caring face of Nazi ideology and show that although Jews were not liked throughout the Reich and not welcome in Germany or occupied countries, they were sent east where they could lead much more productive lives. The war meant that they were refugees and as such could be quarantined in a camp. Westerbork was a Durchgangslager for those awaiting transport to the East, a transit camp. Therefore, while Jews were here, they had to be treated in a way that would add to the deception and could cover up what Westerbork really was, a feeder camp for concentration and extermination camps in occupied Eastern Europe. If you were being transported, you would no doubt get on a passenger train more readily than if you were treated the same as cattle were.

What was the camp like? It was a muddy piece of heathland, 500 metres by 600 metres.

There were eventually 215 barracks of various sizes. Some were huts with a stove for heat and wooden bunk beds. Others had a small kitchen. They were far better than the huts in other camps, but there was still little privacy. Favoured inmates got privacy by being housed in small bungalows. In the winter, there was mud everywhere. There was a café where inmates could meet and a large assembly hall that was used for processing inmates. There was also a kitchen and a hospital, which was well-equipped and staffed by Jewish doctors and nurses. There were factory rooms where men worked, dismantling aircraft or sorting metals. In Westerbork, unlike in any other camp, housed a synagogue. Remember, everything was to be normal for the Jews. If this were a holding town for Jews, then it had to have a synagogue. There would not be a shortage of rabbis either. Every skill was utilised in some way or another. There was also a school where children were educated until they were 14. Each term the pupils got a report written in German. For younger children, there was a kindergarten and a barrack for orphaned children. Children born at the camp were kept in the maternity ward where they were cared for. Remember though that everyone in that camp was a number that could be called and sent east, more so if you were Dutch. Orphans were sent east, as were the sick, the infirm and babies.

The hospital was quite large, but remember we are describing a big town of sometimes 20,000 people. At its largest, the hospital could accommodate more than 1,500 people. It had seen 120 doctors and had employed 1,000 people. A job in the hospital meant that you were spared from the transport unless numbers were needed and Gemmeker removed your exemption. When actions against the Jews were taking place, the hospital would be crowded. It may have been well-staffed, but it did not always have enough plates to eat off or bed linen to put on the beds.

Etty Hillesum described one day of registration in the assembly hall: On the stage were the typists, recording everything. She recalled the day that the apostates arrived, the ones who had revoked their religion and become Catholics. Deppner had no time for these people. A Jew was a Jew. Many of these Catholic converts arrived on the same day following various raids. They were nuns and priests wearing yellow stars on their black habits, and they were totally bemused. A priest looked calmly around on his first day out of the seminary in 15 years. The same day came many who had been severely maltreated, shaven and beaten into submission; here was the first instance afforded them where they could take stock as to what had happened. Later that day, in the evening, the priests were seen walking in single file around the camp between the wooden barracks saying their prayers, their evening vespers, fingering the beads one at a time on their rosaries.

* * *

Don Krausz was able to tell what it was like as a child in the camp and how he wandered out of the camp and was ushered back in by the Dutch SS. He went to school with his sisters. They were Hungarian and were extremely lucky. He and his family were waiting in their barrack for the names to be read out. This was done at 1 am. There would be sobbing and cries of relief mingled together. There was a window of eight hours in which to pack, fill bottles with water and find food for the journey. Those selected had to reduce their baggage and gave items no longer needed to friends or relatives. Those not selected would in turn give things for the journey, spare food especially. The first time the family was selected, Don's father was ill, so they could not travel. His father was sent to the hospital, and after about three weeks was fit enough to travel. This was another way that Gemmeker sometimes showed care and concern, delaying the whole family's deportation gave this impression. The family was more relaxed that it would not be split up and could remain together. They were expecting to work on the farms and factories to replace the men who had been taken for the army. Don's father was well again, and they were selected to travel. Naturally, Don's father would do everything he could to keep his family together and safe. He knew it was safe in Westerbork, and he would try anything to keep everyone in the Netherlands. A doctor at the hospital was a family member named Dr Albert Israel Haas, aged 61. They felt he had some influence, no influence with the Germans, certainly not with Gemmeker, but with the Jewish administration. They were mostly German and Austrian, which suited the Nazis. Later inmates started to refer to them as the "aristocracy."Gemmeker gave the directions, and Schlesinger and his team carried them out. When Jews saw him riding along on his bicycle, they tended to hide. Only one other rode a bicycle through the camp, and that was Gemmeker. The complete administration of the camp was conducted by the Jews themselves. Although the camp was in the Netherlands, the Dutch had little to do with the running of it, as they had been eased out of positions of authority, which created some resentment. There were not huge numbers of German soldiers at the camp, and by now they were war wounded and no longer fit for active service. The council members were told that a thousand names were needed for transport, and they found a thousand. Each Jew was a number. So it was that Dr Haas and Herr Krausz went from official to official to get the Krausz family names taken off. It took them most of the night, but they did it. They were safe. I hinted about this story earlier, and now you know that it was Dr Haas whose name was put upon the list in their stead. It was not just his name but that of his wife and young child as well. They were on one of these trains to Sobibór, a name on a list, a number for extermination, a quota met. I cannot say who decided to put Dr Haas's name on the list. Perhaps it was some sort of perverse punishment for sticking his neck out too far.

How was the Krausz family lucky? Well, the family missed that transport, but there were only so many times that a person could be exempted or spared. They were Hungarian, allies of Germany, yet

116

Jews, so they had fled and ended their journey in Amsterdam. Back in Hungary, political changes taking place. Admiral Miklós Horthy de Nagybánya had been regent in Hungary for exactly 23 years. He had encouraged a strange alliance with Hitler. The Krausz family's selection coincided with a time that Horthy refused to co-operate too much with the Nazis, and the deportation of Hungarian Jews ceased. Don's father had kept their papers, so they were still regarded as Hungarian Jews. Other Hungarians who were stateless found themselves deported. When the mass deportation of Jews from Hungary restarted, the Krausz family were not among the murdered 565,000 in camps or the 15,000 shot by Hungarian Nazis in Budapest and dumped in the Danube. The Krausz family were lucky. The survival rate of Jews in Hungary was somewhere around 1 in 3. Without Wallenberg and others this would have been far worse.

* * *

Normality was Gemmeker's key. But as a German officer and as SS Lagerkommandant, discipline was to be expected. There was a punishment block. It seemed that one could end up there for the slightest offence. Jews who had run afoul of the smooth running of the camp were shaved and wore clothes denoting them as prisoners, whereas everyone else wore their own clothes. The prisoners lost privileges like letter writing, which were strongly censored anyway. It is like the old joke told in Germany of a man who meets a friend who had just come out of a concentration camp. When asked what it was like, he described it as a holiday camp, breakfast in bed, games, a lot to eat and that it is run by the nicest people one could ever hope to meet. The man expresses disbelief, as it was not what Fritz Schmidt had said at all; he had said it was an awful place with beatings and punishments. His friend informs him that this is why Fritz is yet again back in the concentration camp. Nothing bad was to be heard by anyone about Westerbork. An internal police force worked at Westerbork known as the OD, the Ordnungsdienst, also referred to as the "Camp SS." By the spring of 1943, 182 men were in the OD. They had started off life as the fire brigade, and that was still one of their functions. But they were not popular – they were spies in the camp. They reported infringement of camp rules, and everyone knew that this could mean a spell in the punishment block or transportation. The OD guarded and escorted prisoners when they were to perform hard labour outside the camp. It was the OD that had assisted when the Jewish psychiatric hospital had been emptied back in January. The commander of the OD was a Jew from Austria, Arthur Pisk.

Gemmeker did not want anyone to know what lay ahead for them. To prepare for their life ahead, they were offered organised training courses. One such group included those destined for Palestine. Jews had been allowed to immigrate to Palestine. The restrictions placed on them were great in regard to money and possessions. Their furniture was purchased from them, much below market value, and they could then buy supposedly similar items when they arrived in Palestine. Westerbork had a group of men destined for Palestine, and they were being given training in fruit growing and farming and everything they might need for work in Palestine.

There was also shop, the *Lagerwarenhaus,* where Jews could buy cosmetics, toys and even flowers, along with small household items. Not missing a trick, the Nazis had introduced camp money, which could be exchanged for bona fide money at rates biased towards a Nazi profit. Another form of distraction was the camp orchestra, the entertainment group and football. I have already mentioned one footballer who went east, but football proved to be a major distraction and was supported wholeheartedly and financially by Gemmeker. I will speak more of these later, as up to this point in spring 1943, these activities had not all been wholly developed.

* * *

Monday 5 April 1943, the sixth transport for Sobibór stood ready to leave, and 1,187 names were on the list and had been "loaded" into the trucks. All those anxious souls were aboard, some suspecting what might lie ahead, the rest trusting what they were being told and that they were going to the East to work, which included even the old and the young. The Jews were told that the old and young were travelling so families could be kept together. Within three days, no one would be left alive to tell their story; in fact, hardly a trace of their existence would remain. To the Nazis, it was best that they had never existed. No survivors. Not one. We have all seen the film of the Hindenburg disaster. News of the event went around the world within hours. People were horrified by such a catastrophic event. The world was stunned. Do you know how many died on the Zeppelin? Thirty-five and one member of the ground crew. All around the world it was news, and there was a great deal of sympathy. Yet, when 33 times that number of people died at Sobibór on 8 April 1943, not one person mourned their passing.

* * *

The very next day on the 6 April was Rosh Chodesh, Nisan, New Year's Day, and even more were waiting for their train to depart. That day there were 2,020 deportees on board. I can tell you about just two people on that transport. They saw Gemmeker by the train, with that smile across his face, calm and comforting or cynical and hideous. They did not know him, as they had not been in the camp long. Ursula Stern, 16 years old from Essen, had arrived the week prior. Urusla had been found hiding with the Pompe family. Mrs Pompe was sent to Ravensbrück for hiding a Jew. Ursula's parents had already been sent to Auschwitz. They were dead already, although Ursula did not know that then. Her father had also been a member of the resistance. Ursula had been a prisoner because she had been caught in hiding with her parents. She was imprisoned in Utrecht, then Amstelveen and then Vught near Westerbork. She described her journey as dreadful. I imagine she was stuck for words to describe that train and more so when she arrived at Sobibór. It would be at Sobibór that she realised her parents were dead. She was put to one side with the others on the opposite side of the platform. They went to the gas chambers. She too was given a post card to write to her family to let them know that she was safe. She wrote to her Dutch friends and was able to see the post card after the war when she returned. She described Sobibór as hell. We did not go there or to other such places, and we do not know hell. Although you could not get into *Lager III* from where Ursula was, it soon became evident to her as to what was happening there; that was where the gas chambers were. She worked in the sorting barracks in *Lager II,* about 300 metres away. Sorting clothes and so on did not mean she would be spared. She was told that every so often there was a "clear out" of workers who went to be gassed. Many committed suicide before they were to be murdered. Ursula was able to add to what I have been told already. So too did Selma Wijnberg, 20 years old, from Groningen. She had been arrested with her family and interned at Westerbork. Selma had used the name Greetje van den Berg, but she was still found. Selma felt she too had been duped into believing life in the East was all right. She had read postcards that had been sent from Wladowa in Poland. The postcards said that life was pleasant there, so she readily collected her shoes, clothes and food for the journey. Later she realised the prisoners had been forced to sign the postcards. Both Selma and Ursula escaped in the 1943 revolt at Sobibór, and we shall come across these two heroines again.

Catharina Gokkes was also on this train. Kathy was five months short of her 20th birthday. At present she was a secretary, but later she too becomes a heroine.

Train number eight to Sobibór departed Tuesday, 13 April 1943. On the train were 1,204 condemned men, women and children of all ages. Every one of them was condemned. Germany efficiency saw to it that none survived.

Monday 19 April 1943 – The Warsaw Ghetto Uprising started, and the Waffen-SS responded.

Monday 19 April 1943 – The Bermuda Conference meets to discuss refugees from Nazi Europe but did not agree on anything regarding the Jewish plight.

* * *

Tuesday, 20 April 1943, it was Pesach, the first day of the Passover holiday. Unlike the Israelites in Egypt, the Angel of Death did not pass these Jews by. He touched them. It was the ninth transport, and 1,166 lost souls stood huddled together in the trucks bound for Sobibór. The train rattled across occupied Europe. They deportees turns to look out the small window covered in barbed wire. Each time the train stopped, their hearts raced faster. Each time someone wanted to use the bucket, everyone knew. Some gave up and sank into a lethargic state, already lost to the world. Some spoke prayers, others swayed in time with the rocking motion of the train, shunting forwards and backwards as the brakes were applied or the train picked up speed. Dry mouths made silent protestation, and children cried. The sick baby lay still in its mother's arms, lifeless. The elderly were riddled with pain and gave up to the peace of death. And all asked, *Why is it them*? Night came and went, once, twice and for a third time, and with the dawn came a day of death.

Death stalked Sobibór, even for those not destined for the gas chamber. Franz Reichleitner was not to be seen greeting trains. He was the Kommandant at Sobibór since September 1942. He was 36 years old and a member of the Nazi Party since 1936. He had succeeded Franz Stangl who had gone on to Treblinka. He felt a little aggrieved, as it was he who had got Stangl a job in the first place in the Aktion T4, but he *had* received some acknowledgement when Himmler had promoted him to SS-Hauptsturmführer during his visit in February. Himmler seemed to like rewarding his managers of death personally and face to face. Reichleitner did not know it, but he only had less than a year to live himself. He was feared, always immaculately turned out and in gloves. He literally did not like getting his hands dirty; he had others to do that under his control.

Inmates felt sick when they saw him and knew of his temper. He was proud of the fact that a train never had to wait overnight to be processed; it was all done on the day of arrival. One of his subordinates was Karl Frenzel, 32 years old from Templin. Frenzel (the one who was joking about killing league tables) had also come from T4. He was in charge of the work camp and selected those who could work. Those he did not select were consigned to the gas chambers. He claimed he did not know what Sobibór was going to be like, but that did not stop his being one of the most brutal at Sobibór. On one occasion, he killed a prisoner who had failed at suicide. A Jew could not take his own life because it was the Germans who were masters of life and death. His punishments could be arbitrary. Once he saw a guard slapped by an elderly Jew who did not like the way he was being treated. Reichleitner witnessed it, pulled the old man to one side and shot him in front of everyone.

* * *

Tuesday, 20 April 1943 – It was Hitler's 54th birthday.

The orders were that any speech made in honour of his birthday had to mention:

- His battle against Bolshevism
- His struggle against Jewish power
- The Führer's great achievements in government and the economy
- A firm belief in the ultimate victory
- His far sightedness in building German independence in industry
- Only Adolf Hitler and his incomparable Wehrmacht can defeat Bolshevism.

* * *

Tuesday, 27 April 1943 was the last day of Pesach, the end of Passover. Transport number ten departed to Sobibór from Westerbork. Yet again, 1,204 haggard and tormented souls breathed listlessly in the rancid air of the cattle trucks. Yet again, there was no survivor. In among those being transported was one who Gemmeker would not have noticed or cared about if he had recognised him because although he regarded himself cultured, it was only skin deep and only oriented towards German culture. French and Dutch music were of little interest to him. He did not care to listen to "Les Six" from France – Poulenc, Milhaud, Honegger, Auric, Durey and Tailleferre. Nor was he aware that the Dutch disciple of these was only a few metres away from him. Leo Smit, aged 42, was at the height of his musical career as one of the foremost Dutch composers of that time. He had recently finished his "Sonata for Flute and Piano" but would not live to hear it played. The notes may have swirled in his mind as the strident first chord from the piano was followed by the soaring notes of the flute. Gone and almost forgotten. He was dead by the following Friday.

There had always been a camp orchestra, even before Gemmeker arrived. The *Gruppe Musik Lager Westerbork* was not allowed to play Dutch music or that of Jewish composers, as that was regarded as corrupt. But Gemmeker relaxed the ban as long as it was light music. The camp orchestra started to play nothing but works by Jewish composers. Light music would chase away peoples' cares. The orchestra was happy, as it gave them temporary exemption from being sent east.

MAY 1943

THREE TRANSPORTS WITH 6,819 DEPORTEES

Saturday, 1 May 1943 – Catharina Frank gave birth to her first son in Westerbork, and they call him Clarence.

* * *

Saturday 8 May 1943 – The leaders of the Warsaw Ghetto were killed.

* * *

Sunday, 9 May 1943 – There was excitement in Barrack 5 of the hospital. Betty Snatager-Polak had given birth to a son, Emanuel. Everything was done properly, and the birth was announced in the *Jewish Weekly Magazine* on the 21st. Father Herman was very proud. They had been at the camp since the 20th of January of that year.

* * *

Transport number 11 bound for Sobibór departed from Westerbork transit camp on Tuesday, 11 May 1943. On board with another 2,510 deportees was 27 year-old Jozef Wins from Naarden. He was doubly unhappy because he had been betrayed by someone he felt he could trust and was arrested on 12 March 1943. He spent a day in the headquarters of the Sipo-SD, *Sicherheitspolizei* and Sicherheitsdienst, the merged organisation of Security Police and security service. From there he was taken to the prison in Amstelveenseweg. He was left alone for eight weeks and then sent to Westerbork and straight into the S Barracks, the punishment block. He spent a long weekend there before joining the train on Tuesday the 11th. As a prisoner, he would be transported first. Jozef did not get any bread on the journey. At each stop, the SS made them hand over pens, flashlights, watches, rings and anything of value. Immediately behind the engine was a second-class carriage where the SS guards travelled. Käsewieter and his men would be posted here. On the fourth day, Friday, 14 May, the train arrived at Sobibór. Jozef thought it looked a pleasant place; such was the deception, with houses and small barracks with red roofs and gravel paths. But Jozef did not stop at Sobibór; he travelled on with other prisoners to Trawiniki, southeast of Lublin. It was a forced labour camp on the site of a sugar refinery. It had been meant for Soviet POWs but was later used for training the SS and Ukrainian auxiliary police. Here the workforce sorted mountains of belongings arriving from the concentration centres across Nazi-occupied Poland. All of these workers were destined to die in November 1943. Jozef was not one of them; he stayed there for only six weeks. He survived selections for murder and the beatings by the Ukrainian guards. Most others died from disease or starvation.

* * *

Sunday, 12 May 1943 – Samuel Zygelbojm committed suicide. Samuel was a member of the Bund in London and a representative to the Polish Government in Exile. Like all politicians, he had been receiving news of the atrocities being committed in Nazi Europe. He had the "Bund Report" which had come out of Poland. He had tried his best to inform everyone in any position of the plight of the Poles and the Jews. That day, he was told the last Jews had died in Warsaw.

Out of desperation, he killed himself. Like many Jews who did not go through the camps and Jews who had survived, he had a tremendous feeling as it related to having survived.

* * *

Thursday, 13 May 1943 – The German and Italian troops surrendered to the Allies in North Africa.

* * *

Friday, 14 May 1943 – Little Isaak David Levi Frank was cremated at Camp Westerbork after having died of pneumonia the day before. On Tuesday, the 18th of May, his parents were sent to Sobibór and were gassed the following Friday.

* * *

Tuesday, 18 May 1943 – Gemmeker waved off train number 12 bound for Sobibór. The train disappeared from view and with it, all 2,511 people on board.

* * *

On Wednesday, 19 May 1943, Berlin was declared to be *judenfrei,* free of Jews. This was not exactly true. Some 4,500 who were married to non-Jews and were left alone remained, as did 1,500 "Jewish Submarines" who had gone underground and disappeared from records. So what do we have here? Another lie. Two of the "submarines" were Marie Jalowicz and Larry Orbach. Now if there were Jews living in Berlin, the centre of the Reich, it was also true for other cities throughout occupied Europe. You do not need me to remind you about a particular Frank family; it comes into this account later. It was dangerous time to be in hiding. People were paid money to turn in Jews, and some even made a living from doing so. The worst of all and least understood were those who were Jews themselves, like Stella Goldschlag who worked in Berlin – to save her parents, she turned over other Jews. In the Netherlands, Anna "Ans" van Dijk informed on Jews in hiding. Ans turned over 145 Jews to the Nazis. Of course, those who were hiding the Jews were also punished. Hiding Jews was a dangerous undertaking. By this time in May 1943, Anna van Dijk had taken to collaboration rather than hiding Jews. Jozef Wins was angry, as he felt that he had been betrayed.

* * *

Tuesday, 25 May 1943, train number 13 and the largest yet to Sobibór transported 2,862 men, women and children from Westerbork. That morning, Catharina Frank had said goodbye to her husband, Jacques, aged 31. He was on this train. They had only arrived that month and had agreed that he would go on ahead and they would meet up later when she was in a better state to travel because she was at least six months pregnant. The last she saw of him was a face perhaps looking through the door before Hans Margules or one of the others closed it. By Friday, they were all dead or condemned to a life that would lead to death. They were dead as soon as Gemmeker held that list in his hand. It was a train of ghosts.

* * *

Moshe Flinker held his faith and confirmed it in his diary. His faith defined his whole life. It was something the Nazis never realised: they were trying to eradicate a faith, which was unassailable. They gave them numbers and a striped uniform, shaved their heads, made them wear ill-fitting clogs and starved them, but their faith nourished their soul and their very being.

* * *

Wednesday 26 May – Little Emanuel Snatager died at 17 days old. No one knows why, because he was quite a healthy baby, but he died at 7:45 in the evening. On the following Monday, he was cremated at the camp. His ashes went in an urn to the Jewish cemetery at Diemen. His mother, Betty, stayed on at the hospital until she had recovered.

* * *

In May 1943, an odd figure came to Westerbork. He was not striking to look at. He had round glasses like everyone had in those days and wore a suit that might have once fit a body that was prone to showing a delight for the best things in life. His face was round, his pate was definitely thinning, and he was just over average height and had eyes that twinkled. He liked hats and wore one, as did most men. But there was also an energy about him if you knew where to look for it. He was a drab shadow of his former self. People passed by him and did not give him a second glance. He had eluded capture with his wife and was looking around for faces he knew. Both he and his wife were registered at a desk in the great assembly hall. The man registering had given them more than a cursory glance, in fact his eyebrows had arched as if to ask why he was there. They had been found with his wife's parents in Amsterdam. Here standing before them was Willy Rosen. If you were German, Austrian, Dutch or spoke German, you knew this man. You heard him sing on records; you heard his music. He was perhaps one of the most prolific German composers and lyricists of popular music in 1920s and 1930s Germany. If you had been really lucky, you had seen him perform in Germany and Austria and in many other countries. This man was a star, and here he was in Westerbork.

It did not take Gemmeker long to find out that Willy Rosen was in his camp. He had heard he had been performing in the Netherlands, having escaped Germany, and wondered whether he might turn up in the camp. Gemmeker already had Franz Engel, Camilla Spira, Erich Ziegler and Max Ehrlich. Now another comedian, Rosen, was there to join them. Max Ehrlich was able to fill theatres on his own as a "Conferencier" - the man who told jokes and introduced acts. Willy

Rosen could do the lot, sing, tell jokes, write humorous sketches, and write music and lyrics. An idea began to form in Gemmeker's mind.

Sometime after Willy had arrived and settled in as best as he could, Willy having made himself known, Gemmeker sent for him and his wife. His reasons were selfish but would also, if it worked, bring more normality to the camp. What is more normal than a cabaret?

Erich Ziegler had already performed for Gemmeker at his house when he had guests. What better way to entertain your friends and impress your superiors than with Ziegler playing piano, especially his jazz version of "Beethoven's Ninth," late at night, after dinner? Erich had first performed on Sunday, 27 December 1942 in an impromptu evening concert.

Heaven knows what they thought Gemmeker wanted them for when they were told the Kommandant wanted to see them. You hardly saw him face to face. He smiled at them, but that did not relax them any further. He told them about wanting them to put together a revue and that they could use the large assembly room. It had a small stage which they could use, and he would get them a couple of pianos. One thing he insisted on – it was all to be performed in German. Ziegler, Ehrlich and Rosen knew they could fill a performance themselves but also knew that in the camp were other performers, some of them well-known Dutch entertainers. Any Dutch entertainer had to perform in German. They were told to start work immediately and to keep Gemmeker abreast of developments and requirements. He would even audition acts, including those of Rosen and Ehrlich. The main leads of this group found that they were moved to the bungalows and better living quarters. They became Gemmeker's pet performers. If they had a job, it meant they stayed at the camp and were exempt from transport.

* * *

On 30 May 1943, a 32-year-old SS-Hauptsturmführer arrived at Auschwitz. I mention this because some from Westerbork were to meet this "Angel of Death." He was appointed by *SS-Standortarzt* Eduard Wirths, the chief medical officer, to the position of chief physician in the *Zigeunerfamilienlager*, the Roma camp, at Birkenau. One would expect that the title of physician alluded to some sort of care. Yet it was where children and twins especially would remember Joseph Mengele. Mengele had requested a posting to the concentration camp service, and it was granted. He had heard about it from Dr Otmar Freiherr von Verschuer, a German geneticist with an interest in researching twins. Verschuer knew that Mengele would have real subjects to conduct research on and encouraged Mengele to apply to this branch of the SS. Some German doctors had sworn the Hippocratic Oath, yet they saw Jews as a diseased growth on humankind that needed to be excised. Since 1933, they had received lectures on racial purity. Many doctors in high positions of authority were ardent supporters of eugenics. The oath that they took as members of the SS was superior to any other oath they might have taken. They believed themselves to be right, and doctors who qualified in Nazi Germany did not take the Hippocratic Oath. Mengele was a doctor of anthropology and had been granted a doctorate in medicine in 1938. All his qualifications had been gained in the Nazi system. Wirths also qualified under the Nazi regime. Both men had been wounded while on active service and were unfit for any further active military service. Both held each other in high regard and both were Nazis.

Friday, 28 May 1943 – The 21-year-old Jacques Frank, husband of Catharina Frank, died at Sobibór. Remember his name for later.

JUNE 1943

THREE TRANSPORTS WITH 8,420 DEPORTEES

Tuesday, 1 June 1943. It was raining as they boarded the train, just over 3,000. We need to be exact. There were 3,006; someone said 3,017. There was one survivor: Jules Schelvis. Jules was 22 years old. He was from Amsterdam and had been arrested together with Rachel, his wife, and the rest of the family by the Germans on Wednesday 26 May 1943. They found themselves boarding train number 15 to Sobibór from Westerbork. The wagons were bare, with two buckets, one for water and the other to serve as a latrine. The trucks were just as they had been for cattle, no facilities for humans. The door slid closed, and the 62 people inside could not know what was going to happen.

Gemmeker was there on the platform. The Green Police were there, too. There was Dr Spannier, the medical superintendent, in a plain grey suit, and "Mayor Schlesinger," looking like Erich von Stroheim, the Hollywood director, in riding breeches and jackboots. His face was thought to be "nasty," and his hands were like shovels. Then there were the doctors ready to help if someone were to have a medical emergency. Gemmeker availed himself of the services of the camp doctor and camp dentist, Wolf. Gemmeker's face was impassive, and he never raised his voice but dished out punishments with a smile on his lips. He was seen as incorruptible, when it suited him. Gemmeker's trust in the camp doctor will be explained at a later point.

The train left at about 10 in the morning. The stench in the truck made them retch. The train trundled down the centre of the camp, along the "Boulevard de Misere," the main street of the camp. It passed through a few German cities, Wittenberg, Berlin and Breslau. After some time, the train halted. Everyone was ordered to keep back, or they would be shot. The doors opened, and the guards immediately began demanding anything of worth. The train then carried on to Sobibór, where again the doors were opened and men in blue striped uniforms whipped them out of the trucks, literally. Anything else of value was then taken from them. Younger men, including Jules, were put back onto the train, and it left for Lublin. Jules never saw his family again.

* * *

Tuesday 1 June 1943 – The Lvov Ghetto was liquidated.

* * *

The next train caused great sadness. It was train number 16 from Westerbork to Sobibór, leaving on 8 June 1943. It was Erev Shavuot, but it certainly was not the "Feast of Weeks" for those Jews in Westerbork. There were 3,017 deportees, and over one-third of them were children. Some 1,145 children were on this train. They were transferred from Vught over two days. First came the children aged from nought to four, and the next day, on the 7th of June, came those who were older than four and aged up to 17. Philip Mechanicus, a journalist who by this time was in Westerbork, described the train that arrived from Vught. Those children were brutally removed from one set of wagons and put into the cattle trucks. They were beaten and pummelled; yes, he used the word "pummelled." Who beats children? By this time, everyone felt sick when the wagons rolled into the camp and waited like a devourer of carrion on the boulevard. Philip asked why the train never got delayed, why it was never hit by a bomb, how was it that these trains always ran on time? This was known as the *Kindertransport*, the Children's Train. It was certainly not like Sir Nicholas Winton's Kindertransporte that took Jewish children to safety in England in 1938 and similar transports right up until the fall of the Netherlands. Philip recalled the debate about these transports travelling through the Netherlands as the country had closed its borders to refugees. A great deal of negotiation had taken place to allow the trains through to the channel ports so that the children could go to England.

Let me give you a name. I can give you a few. There was Schoontje Broekhuijsen-Ossendrijver and her adopted son, Salomon. Salomon would be nine on the 15th of November. His own mother had given him up to Schoontje and her husband, Jacobus, to look after in 1938. When the Germans started to round up Jews in July 1942, Salo was left in hiding with a family called de Jong. There he was called Jan. In March 1943, Salomon was returned to Amsterdam and to Jacobus and Schoontje. The reason is unknown why "Salo" was returned to a city full of Nazis. Salo wrote to the De Jongs a little note, hoping that they were well. In the letter, he remembered the happy time he had had playing with their children. He signed it "Jan" after many kisses. By 2 June 1943, Jacobus, Schoontje and Salo had been picked up just as the De Jongs received a letter from the family now in Vught. On Monday, 7 June, Philip watched as Salo arrived in Westerbork. Was Salo one of those beaten off the train?

Tuesday, the 8th, Salo and Schoontje were on the Sobibór train. They would be dead by the time the sun went down on Friday to mark the start of the Sabbath. Jacobus lived in torment for another half a year and died at the very end of January 1944 in Auschwitz. There were people who would remember that little family and look for them later.

On the same train was Harry Swaab from Tugelaweg 13. Harry and 13 others had been in hiding at the Alcazar Nightclub on

Thorbeckeplein 5 until they were discovered. To pass the time, Harry kept a diary, and they made cine films. He was the cameraman. The films and the diary survived, whereas Harry and the others did not. The Alcazar had many Jewish employees, and there had been riots there, as Jews continued to work there until 1941. The riots were instigated by Dutch Nazis. Clara Johanna Susanna de Vries, a well-known Jewish jazz trumpeter and 26 years old, had performed there on 9 February 1941. Her appearance resulted in broken windows and threats against the owners. The police did not intervene, even though Hendrik Koot, a member of the NSB, died five days later. Koot had been beaten on 11 February. Rauter wrote an article describing the action in the *Volk en Vaderland*, alluding to Jews as vampires. He wrote, "A Jew had ripped open the victim's artery with his teeth and sucked his blood out." *Het Parool*, the resistance party newsletter, described the event more accurately and recorded that Koot had been dealt a single but severe blow to the head with an axe or hammer. Koot's funeral was attended by thousands of waving Nazi flags. It was preceded by a horse-drawn hearse and a marching band. Retribution was swift. The area was sealed, and attempts were made to arrest Jewish *knokploeg* members, fighting members of the resistance, at an ice cream parlour. General unrest broke out with strikes. The police had been half-hearted in their attempts to enforce Nazi orders, and German troops were finally sent in.

According to Etty Hillesum, 8 June was a lovely warm day with a beautiful blue sky. She was sitting in the far corner of Camp Westerbork, writing a letter and enjoying the sunshine. She was sharing this little idyll with a German soldier, gun slung across his back, dangling as he bent down to pick lupins. She had heard the German soldiers singing as they marched along by the train. Dutch soldiers were also out that day. Etty knew the quota was short and had been made up of orphans. She had just seen the matron carrying a small lonely child to the train. People had also been taken from the hospital. The reason for the urgency and rough treatment of those from Vught might be explained as a result of important visitors being there from The Hague. Etty called them "big shots." Her description might make you nauseated, but she simply described it as an everyday event. She had been awake and working since four that morning, dealing with babies and carrying luggage. She was waiting for a job, and until she was allocated one, she would do what she felt was needed. She could wander about, observe, talk, sit and write.

The train shrieked and departed, blowing steam and smoke everywhere. Etty stood on a box for a better view. She counted the wagons, 35, and two carriages for Käsewieter and his men. She said that babies suffering from pneumonia were just lain on the floor of the wagons. She did not admit that she had put the babies in the wagon, but perhaps she had done so with as much care and love as she could show. Hands stuck out between the planks, waving like lost souls in a sea of depravity. Then Etty wrote something that made me realise she knew what was happening by this time, "and right before our eyes, mass murder." She was right – not something you can comprehend. And the soldier enjoying the sun? He wandered off, his arms full of lupins most likely for a courting expedition. That sweetheart, if Dutch, needed to be wary of accepting love tokens from the Germans.

Rachel Voorzanger watched members of her family leave that day and remembered many little children innocently waving goodbye.

A postcard was thrown from the train, dated the day the train left – indicating that they did not know where they were going, perhaps Poland or Riga. The writer knew how many were on the train, 3,000, mostly women and children. They described it as a misery and finished with the hope that they would meet again. It was signed by someone called Stella. No one could say who she was. There were 65 Stellas murdered at Sobibór who were from the Netherlands. On this train alone were four. Estella Bruinvelds from Amsterdam was only four years old, so she would not have written the card. Estella Marianna Monas Fransman was from Antwerp and was 40 years old. Two more were from Netherlands, Estella Zondervan Hertz, 50, from Sittard in the province of Limburg and Estella Duque Werkendam, 43, from Amsterdam.

The train reached Sobibór that Friday. Reichleitner saw that it was duly processed. He did not care about the children, no more than the man who had sent them on their way to him. Reichleitner never gave a thought about little Joseph Blok who died two days before his first birthday. He smiled from underneath his little hand-knitted woollen hat, made to match his little jacket. Gemmeker must have seen him pass as he stood by the train, before sending it on its way. Was there any pity for little Joseph from any Nazi or any who supported the regime, then or now?

The sad tale of this train does not end there. At Sobibór, Ursula Stern was sorting through little rucksacks that had obviously belonged to children, a lot of children. In the bags were pathetic notes, which she was able to read. These were the children from Vught. She was able to work out when the children had left Vught and passed through Westerbork, where she had recently come from. Ursula knew their fate. They had not gone to Riga as they had been told. She carried on sorting and kept her thoughts to herself, sorting through belongings, using the food she found to keep herself alive. Even in that sorting shed there was friction between the more liberal Dutch Jews and the more devoutly religious Polish Jews. Ursula kept quiet and bided her time. She did not wish to be betrayed for a careless word.

* * *

Monday, 21 June 1943 – Himmler ordered the liquidation of all ghettos in occupied Soviet territories. A year later, hardly any Jews were left in occupied Russia.

* * *

Monday, 21 June 1943 – Etty Hillesum's parents arrived at Westerbork from Vught. She asked friends for food parcels and gave her address:

Dr. E. Hillesum, Assistant, Jewish Council, Westerbork Camp, Post Hoog-Halen, 0, Drenthe. Top left: Barracks 34.

* * *

Monday, 28 June 1943 – All four new crematoria at Auschwitz were now operational, and with the gas chambers that could accommodate two thousand people at a time, 4,756 people could be reduced to ash in just one day.

* * *

Moshe Flinker was writing in his diary with a little more anxiety. "Things" seemed to have been going on for a long time. He reminded God that He had a covenant with them. Would God mind the impertinence of a teenager speaking honestly with Him?

* * *

Tuesday, 29 June 1943 – train number 17 left on time for Sobibór. Gemmeker saw it out of the gate. The smoke and steam dissipated as he went back to the camp office for a drink to settle him. He had just seen off 2,397 living corpses to a death camp in the East. The train guards had exchanged information with those at Westerbork along with booty pilfered from the hapless Jews. There were no survivors on this train.

Gerrit Kleerekoper, a diamond cutter, once a reserved occupation, giving protection from deportation, had gone to his death with his wife and their two children. He had been a coach for the Dutch Women's Gymnastics Team at the 1928 Olympics in Amsterdam, where they had won the gold medal. They had defeated Italy and Great Britain. Gerrit knew Lea Nordheim, who, aged 25, had been a member of that winning team. She was on the train to Sobibór as well. Maybe they sat and talked together – if they were inclined to do so in such degrading conditions.

Perhaps it was German cynicism or someone from the Jewish Council being perverse or naïve in sending Professor Ben Ali Libi

137

with the children. This was Michael Velleman. He was a 48-year-old magician. Perhaps he did entertain the children, who knows.

Etty said that 400 people from the hospital were included on this transport. With Philip she discussed what they wrote and saw. People from her mother's barracks got ready in a disciplined, dignified and calm way.

"On a list of artists, killed in the war, is a name that I have never heard of,
So, I looked at it with wonder: Ben Ali Libi. Magician."
(Willem Wilmink)

JULY 1943

THREE TRANSPORTS WITH 6,614 DEPORTEES

Friday, 2 July 1943. On this day, 1,367 people were transferred from Vught to Westerbork. Among them was the Drukker family. Willem Drukker, more commonly known as Wolf, was a talented musician and had been the conductor of the Cinetone Cinema. He got sacked when the Germans took over. There was also his wife, Marie, and his 19-year-old son, Sylvian (Syl). They had been in Vught since the 12th of February. A place was quickly found for Willem in the cabaret's orchestra. In Vught he had run his own shows. Marie would lose her husband and her son.

* * *

Monday, 5 July 1943: The German offensive at Kursk failed.

* * *

On Monday, 5 July 1943, Etty Hillesum, although already at Westerbork, learned that she was to be there permanently as an inmate. Etty Hillesum was a bright woman who had been working for the Jewish Council in Amsterdam. Her work had taken her into Westerbork on many occasions, mainly working in the hospital. A year previous she had volunteered for the Jewish Council for Deportation. She too found it to be a hell and thanked God for giving her the strength to accept things for what they were. She had not given in but had a quiet resolution to get on with life as it was. She had passed through hate, and she placed her complete trust in her God, the same God that had brought their people out of Egypt but had given them up to the Babylonians, saving them again, only to give them up to the Romans. I do not know whether Etty thought her God had this time given them up to the Nazis.

At first, she did not live in the camp but stayed with friends. She found strength in these friends and dreaded the day she would have to leave them. She feared having to be with the people she worked with because their attitudes were so very different from her own. She knew she was already working for the Germans without having to go to Germany, making coats for the Wehrmacht. Etty at this time had fallen for the lie that Jews were going east to work. She wondered why she had to go east when she was already working for the Germans here at Westerbork.

She did not have to, but she volunteered to go into Westerbork in September 1942. The love of her life, Julius Spier, had been due to go to Westerbork on Wednesday, 15 September 1942. Julius was a German Jew, a psychoanalyst and a follower of Jung. The Gestapo was due that day, but Julius died suddenly at home. Etty was bereft, as she was there, with him when he died. She had been given leave to be away from Westerbork, but a recurring illness prevented her return. She was permitted to come and go, but it was not until July 1943 that her status changed, and she could no longer escape the depression of the camp.

She often thought about the council she worked with. She found the members heartless but not without heart. Their actions were heartless, but she felt that there was good in them somewhere, if only they would give that goodness to her so that she could share it with everyone. Westerbork swallowed her up, yet there were times she managed to stay on the surface. She felt that if it were important to preserve their bodies, it was far more important to save their lives and vitally important as to how. Those who had been at the camp a long time became hardened towards others. She saw this in the Jewish Council and in the attitude of older inmates compared with that of the new ones. Sometimes she felt that there was contempt from the longer-term inmates towards the poor lost souls finding themselves in an entirely new situation they were totally unprepared for. How could one prepare oneself for Westerbork? Etty felt that how you responded to these new situations was the way in which you preserved your life. She was disappointed in those who switched off to what was around and became dulled to life.

She spent the whole of that Monday in July 1943 walking around the camp speaking with various officials. Philip Mechanicus had been chosen to be sent east. Etty tried her best to get Philip's name taken off the list, although she was not a skilful politician, at least according to her account. She did not know until the next morning that she had been successful. As she wandered around the hospital looking at the empty beds, she did not say she regretted that someone else had been put on the list instead of Philip. She accepted the way things were. But you can ask, was Philip's life more valuable than that of another?

* * *

Tuesday, 6 July 1943, 2,417 deportees, most of them arriving from Vught last Saturday, looked around at the wooden walls of their prison. Faces that were gaunt with fear stared back at them. Parents tried to smile confidently for their children to allay their fears. Pained expressions stared back into their parents loving eyes, eyes wide with fear. Etty had managed to keep her parents off the train. But Isidore Goudeket, once a competitor in the 1908 Summer Olympics in London, wished he were there again or at least in London. His muscular body was not so supple these days. His trade now was as a diamond cutter, and for selfish reasons, the Germans had kept people with this skill back from deportation. Now it was

clear they would not be needed, so they were being sent east. Isidore
had been ready for this. He had paid his guilder when he registered
as a Jew, back in March 1941. Jews even had to pay to register that
they were Jews, and even though he was exempt for a time, he still
had two suitcases packed and ready to go when they were required.
Another example of acquiescence? Someone prepared for the
inevitable. Etty Hillesum had noted a difference in how prepared
people were upon arrival at the camp. Those who had reported
arrived with luggage; those rounded up in raids arrived with little.
Isidore and his wife were arrested on Sunday, the 20th of June 1943,
and taken to a local park; from there they were put on a tram for
which the tram company was paid. They were taken to Muiderpoort
station and then by train to Westerbork. Salo Muller said his parents
even paid for their tram ticket – five guilders. Here he was now,
cramped into a filthy wagon, a number on a sheet of paper; his wife
was a number on a sheet of paper, too. Her name was Esther, named
after a heroine from the Tanakh who had saved the Hebrews when in
exile in Persia. Esther Goudeket was not in any such position today.
No one was about to save them. Isidore pulled Esther close to him,
and both promised each other that they would stay together whatever.
They were met at Sobibór with screams and shouted orders. They did
as they were told and as was expected. With a retained dignity, they
met their fate.

Isidore had heard Han Netherlandser many times on the radio.
Isidore still kept an interest in sport and listened avidly to Hartog
Hollander's commentary on the radio. It was a new thing and much
appreciated. Han was adept and skilful at making the listeners feel
that they were with him, watching the sporting event. And here was
Han, on the same train, wondering like everyone else what life was
all about. The majority of his 56 years had been well-spent, good
years, and it was ending like this?

Another man who liked sport was Mozes Jacobs, a physical
education teacher. He had listened to Han on the radio, and he knew
of Isidore, too, who also was a gymnast. He was 36 and still fit and
felt able to look after his wife and two children, aged 12 and 14.

Mozes felt strongly about what had happened to his country. Sitting in the wagon with the other prisoners, kept apart from the other deportees, he had been a member of the resistance and had been captured at Vierhouten and detained in Arnhem. He did not regret what had happened but was worried for his family.

Not one person survived from this train. All were gassed at Sobibór or died shortly afterwards from disease, malnutrition or murder.

* * *

On Friday, 9 July 1943, the service providers, *Dienstleiter,* were ordered to meet with Gemmeker, who was beaming and exuding pleasure. He informed them that they were invited to an event that evening, the likes of which had not been seen in Westerbork. He had brought cabaret to the camp. He told them they were to put on their best clothes for the first performance of the *Bunter Abend* (Colourful Evening) to be performed by Willy Rosen, Max Ehrlich and Chaja Goldstein. Max (Osias) Kormann was there at the first performance. He was incredulous. There was a simple programme printed for the audience and guests. Gemmeker sat in the middle of the front row with the Jewish Administration Heads and Professor Cohn, one-time chairman of the Amsterdam Jewish Council.

The *Bühne Lager Westerbork* presented Bunter Abend with music composed by Willy Rosen and Erich Ziegler, and lyrics by Willy Rosen starring: Chaja Goldstein, Camilla Spira, Josef Baar, Max Ehrlich, Willy Rosen and Erich Ziegler. If that line-up had appeared in Berlin in 1932, it would have been a sellout! Max Ehrlich had to make several last performances before leaving Berlin to join Willy Rosen in the Netherlands. So the audience was in for a very rare treat under surreal conditions, at 8 pm prompt:

Scene 1: A chat and rhyme with Josef Baar

Scene 2: Camilla Spira performs her repertoire

Scene 3: Max Ehrlich in his scene, "Theatre Visit"

Scene 4: "Words and Music by me" – Willy Rosen

Scene 5: Chaja Goldstein performs her repertoire

Interval

Scene 6: "Checkmate" a Sketch with Max Ehrlich, Josef Baar and Camilla Spira

Scene 7: "The Man without a name" with Max Ehrlich and Josef Baar

Scene 9: Willy Rosen and Erich Ziegler on two pianos

Scene 10: Camilla Spira Sings

Scene 11: "At the Racetrack" with The Company.

And that was it – just those six people on stage and a couple of others to help out. The council members sat there with mouths wide open, incredulity spread across their faces. How were they expected to respond? They just took their cue from Gemmeker. The other Nazis were already doing that. Josef Baar was warming up the audience. There were polite noises, but when Gemmeker started to roar with laughter, all knew that the evening was a hit. Camilla Spira was politely received, and then there were belly laughs for Max Ehrlich, who was nervous to begin with but then began to play his audience. No political jokes, Rosen saw to that. Max had directed the show, written by Willy Rosen. That had been Willy's appeal. His humour was observational. It offended none but all if they saw themselves in it. There were no jokes about Nazis, or Hitler or the Gestapo, Nothing that could get them into further trouble. Gemmeker had approved everything. He had acted as censor, but Willy had not given Gemmeker cause to use his blue pencil.

By Scene 4, the audience members were beyond warmed up. They roared with laughter. Some were crying, tears running down their cheeks. The tops of Gemmeker's legs must have been red from the slapping they received at every joke that hit home. Willy stepped out onto the stage and leaning on the piano, like some ghost from a second-hand shop, said the words that caused uproar – "Words and Music by me." The audience cheered at his catchphrase. Some had seen him in Berlin, in Amsterdam, in Scheveningen, the Dutch seaside resort, or in a dozen other places, and if they had not seen him, they had played his records, had sung his songs and hummed his tunes from the radio. With more than 600 compositions to his name, he was one of the most prolific writers of modern music and songs in the German-speaking world. Everyone knew Willy Rosen. I was never able to find out what he sang that night. Max Kormann did not say; he did not need to. That audience knew those songs. Willy sang his old songs, nothing new for this show. And when he shouted, "*Alle*," "Everyone," they all joined in as he banged his fingers down on the piano keys for everyone to hear. And if he played a wrong note, they were used to it. Willy, Max and the others were back in the Berlin theatres, responding to their adoring public. Scene 5 and Chaja Goldstein appeared as Yeshiva Boy to sing well-known songs. It was at a slower pace but much appreciated by the audience and by Gemmeker who would later invite Chaja and the others to his house, but I get ahead of myself. Scene 6 before the interval and a sketch with three stars. Again, the audience roared. What those outside the assembly hall thought is also known. Some thought it a disgrace, laughter in such a place, whereas others really wanted to be inside and were envious of those invited. The curtain swept across the small stage, and the audience had a break to go over what they had seen. The Jewish Council would have told Gemmeker it was exactly what was needed. If they thought it was collaboration, they kept that to themselves; they could see that Gemmeker had been amused.

The second half was filled with as many laughs as the first. The audience settled down, their thoughts forgotten, their heads cleared for a show that some called macabre and others superb. Max and Josef did a small sketch about a man with no name. Howls and shrieks of laughter filled the hall. Their circumstances were forgotten. It did not matter that this was not the *Ka-De-Ko* on the Kurfürstendamm in Berlin, or the *Lutine Palace* at Scheveningen, or the *Schouwburg* in Amsterdam, where they may have seen Ehrlich perform with Willy Rosen's *Prominenten*. It did not matter that there were no lights or that the curtain had holes in it. This was real theatre, and they laughed aloud their appreciation. Followed by another treat, Willy and Erich on two pianos, Gemmeker promised two upright pianos, in tune, which they got. Erich most likely played a "jazzed-up" version of the "Ode to Joy," his signature piece. It did not matter what Willy played; everyone sort of knew it. But the virtuosity of Erich Ziegler showed through despite that very few knew his name. Then Camilla Spira came out to sing. Camilla had sung on the Berlin stage with Max Hansen, the "Little Caruso," and Kurt Gerron, the entertainer and film director. She was the star of Ralph Benatsky's *Im weißen Rößl*, *The White Horse Inn*, and was there only a few metres in front of them, singing for this small audience. Her voice was deep and could have given the "basso" Wilhelm Strienz a run for his money in singing "*Im tiefen Keller sitz Ich hier.*" Shouts of "More!" sounded as Camilla completed her repertoire. Up next and last came Max and Josef as the newcomer and the expert in a skit about the races. If the cast was worn out by the end of the evening, the audience members were drained as they meandered their way across the camp to their barracks, especially the younger ones.

Gemmeker beckoned Willy over and said he wanted to see them in the morning, and then he left with his officers. As the Dienstleiter left, their faces still wore bemused expressions about what they had just taken part in, yet they managed gratifying smiles to Max and the troupe. Already Gemmeker's mind was set.

The following morning might have gone like this: Willy, Erich and Max reported to the Kommandant's office. They stood in the main office awaiting summons. They had already discussed what they thought he might say, that he had enjoyed the entertainment and that he was grateful. And that was it. The door to Gemmeker's office opened, and a *Feldwebel* ushered them into Gemmeker's presence. He did not offer them a seat, and his greeting was as usual and gave nothing away. He explained he was pleased with the way the evening had gone and that he had enjoyed himself and perhaps would invite

Miss Spira to his house sometime in the very near future. Gemmeker's mind was thinking along the lines of normality. He had worked it out. A person in authority could invite someone of fame to their house for drinks. Gemmeker knew the risk. If Himmler were to find out, it could be seen as fraternisation with Jews. Yet Camilla was only a half-Jew, through her father. She had appeared in at least 20 films or so and five of them while Goebbels was in charge of film production, so she was obviously acceptable in certain quarters. Besides, his excuse would be that it allayed fears and encouraged calm. The three men fidgeted while Gemmeker gave his critical review of the evening. These men had received critical acclaim from the great names in the German press, and here was someone obviously without a background in the theatre, least of all cabaret, complimenting and offering suggestions as to what could have been improved. Gemmeker knew exactly what he was doing. He would not reveal his heinous plan until they were about to leave. He drew the meeting to a close, indicating that they were to leave. As they turned, he then told them that there were to be more such evenings and perhaps on a grander scale; perhaps they could go away and think about how they could expand the show and make a list of anything that they needed. When Gemmeker said "anything," that is exactly what he meant. The three may have felt like falling to their knees to thank their Kommandant as if he had reprieved them from the firing squad, which is exactly what he had done. While they were involved in *Die Gruppe Bühne Lager Westerbork*, they were safe from deportation. Gemmeker would fix the performances for the night before the transports left, just before the audience would find out whether they were leaving or staying. It was as if he were sending them away with happy thoughts. The man was delusional. As soon as they heard their name for transportation, all thoughts and memory of the cabaret flew away with their hope. But three men ecstatic about what they had been told rushed off to spread the news and recruit others. That assembly hall would soon become unrecognisable from the grubby stage it was at that time.

I have heard people say that the cabaret only performed once a week before the departure of the train, but Etty spoke about Gemmeker enjoying one performance so much that he came three nights in a row and roared with laughter each time.

* * *

Sunday, 10 July 1943 – The Allies invaded Sicily.

* * *

If this entry is short, I apologise, these 1,988 people just disappeared. Gemmeker gave permission for train number 18 to Sobibór to depart. It left on Tuesday the 13th in July 1943, and none of those onboard were ever seen or heard from again. By Friday of that week, Kommandant Reichleitner at Sobibór had seen to it that they were all dead.

* * *

On Tuesday, 20 July 1943, train number 19 and the last from Westerbork to Sobibór departed. On board were 2,209 people, degraded and humiliated. Not one would survive, although they did not know it yet. Emanuel Querido may have had an inkling as to what might happen, but he kept it from his wife and to his own counsel. Emanuel had been a bookstore owner in Amsterdam who had then gone into publishing, and producing the first paperbacks, a year before Penguin did, so a forward-thinking man and entrepreneur. When German exiles came to the Netherlands and wanted books published, he founded another printing company to publish German works. He was therefore quite prominent on any Gestapo list. He was sacked from his own company and eventually went into hiding with his wife, but their hiding place was betrayed. They had been arrested and now found themselves sitting with other poor unfortunates. Their only solace was that they were together. What comfort was it though to be murdered with your soul mate?

Eva Dresden together with her mother, Anna, who had been Anna Polak, was on that train as well. Eva had been born on 26 June 1937 and was six years old. Her father was Barend and had married Anna the day before Eva was born. Eva died on Friday, 23 July 1943 together with her mother. Barend, also known as Ben, died on 30 November 1944 at Auschwitz. Grandfather Abraham also died at Sobibór. Eva's Uncle Izak was murdered in 1945. Grandmother Mietje on her mother's side had already died at Sobibór on 9 April. Aunts Klaartje, Leentje, Aaltje and Raatje Polak were all murdered, too.

In among the others on this last train to the death camp were Herman and Betty Snatager, still grieving for little Emanuel. They were killed along with the other 2,207 on board that train.

* * *

Sunday, 25 July 1943 – Mussolini was deposed.

* * *

You remember Jozef Wins from Naarden who had been betrayed? You probably do not; there have been so many names. He was sent to Sobibór back in June. Would it surprise you to learn he was still alive? Likely so, as not many survived. He had spent about six weeks there before being moved on. Jozef knew how the Nazis worked and how the SS always wanted things done at a reasonable cost. Why pay for printers when you have Jewish printers in a camp somewhere? Send around a circular asking for printers and get back a few positive answers. Send another order stating that they are to be sent to Lublin. From there, Jozef was sent to Radom, and that is where Jozef ended up – in Radom at an old printing works, about 100 km south of Warsaw, famous for the Łucznik Arms Factory. So you can see why the SS were there. The first job for Jozef and the others was to reassemble the printing machines. Once they were working, it was the Jozef's task to print items for *Ostindustrie, Osti,* an SS company.

The local Kommandant needed business cards. Jozef appreciated the irony; he was kept alive to print cards for some German who wanted to impress others when he presented them with his personal card. He knew his name; he had printed it often enough, SS-Obersturmführer Max Horn. Even Himmler did not have business card; everyone knew who he was. Imagine being handed a card when returning to the office to be told that some weaselly man in glasses had called by and left his card. Everyone knew Himmler; he did not need a business card. Business cards were for people who wanted others to know who they were when they were actually no one of note. Jozef also knew who was to be executed. He printed posters with their names on them, and he was to be there for a short while, watching names come off the press – names of those who shortly would no longer exist.

Young Moshe Flinker wrote in his diary that he would never give up hoping, for if he were to give up hope, then he would be lost and would cease to exist. How many in July 1943 were feeling lost?

AUGUST 1943

TWO TRANSPORTS WITH 2,005 DEPORTEES

Monday, 2 August 1943 – The uprising at Treblinka took place.

* * *

Sunday 8 August 1943 – Organised groups started to escape the Vilna Ghetto to join the partisans.

* * *

Sunday, 15 August 1943 – The Bialystok Ghetto was destroyed.

* * *

Monday, 16 August 1943 – The Soviets reach Treblinka. It has been razed to the ground and planted with lupins. All that remains of 870,000 victims are pieces of bone, hair and teeth in the ground. The last Kommandant was Kurt "Lalka" Franz. Why the nickname Lalka? His face was like that of a doll, innocent. He shot people, beat them to death, whipped them or let Barry, his Saint Bernard, rip them to pieces. Without Franz, the dog was like any other.

* * *

Wednesday, 8 August 1943 – The exhumation of bodies for burning at Babi Yar began.

* * *

Tuesday, 24 August 1943 was the day transports resumed to the main killing centre of the Nazi European Empire, Auschwitz-Birkenau.

Transports left Westerbork any day of the week but had something of a regular pattern to them. It could have been Tuesdays and Fridays or just Monday. You must have already realised that the days changed from week to week. Memories became blurred or, while someone was in Westerbork, it perhaps was that the trains left on a Tuesday, but it was not the same every week. It is similar to when the lists were read aloud. Some say it was an unearthly hour early in the morning or at 6 am or the night before. It changed; that is all. Although Gemmeker wanted normality, things changed over time. Personnel changed, and routines changed with them. Some say the lists were posted, as that was their experience. The times the trains left also varied. The size of the trains was hardly ever constant. You remember Etty Hillesum counting 35 wagons. Others liked to count as well. The number of people crammed into wagons changed too; it was not always 50 per wagon or truck. There is film showing 75 people per truck. Etty and Philip Mechanicus were observers, but even they did not always agree, although they did write things down, Etty in her diary and letters and Philip in his diary. They sometimes complemented each other as well. In a moment I will tell you about the first transport in August 1943. So if someone uses the word "always" when telling you about Westerbork, there is no need to correct them. It so happened it was always when they were there or that they remembered that it was always.

* * *

Since 6 April of this year, transports had *always* left on a Tuesday, so Tuesday, 24 August 1943 was no different. There were just over a thousand people on this train, among them 300 who were termed prisoners.

Etty wrote a little about the "gentleman" Gemmeker. That mild-mannered man who rode around the camp on his bicycle, or walked through the camp openly with his mistress, sometimes let slip his utterly mean streak. Some three of the prisoners tried to escape, and they were caught. Thus no real harm had been done to German order, but Gemmeker did not think like that. He ordered another 50 prisoners to be added to the transport. Philip remembered how the 300 "prisoners" were rounded up. They were taken out of the hospital and the punishment block. It was the Jewish camp police, the *Ordedienst*, that did it. They were not all put together in the trucks but spread throughout the train. Etty had been in the hospital the day before. Apparently the "prisoners" knew an extra 50 were going to be added to the 250 already indicated. News had gotten out of the office and rippled through the camp – 300 would be ordered to go, but no one knew whether they were going to be on the list. They were of course apprehensive, although some thought they would see family again if they did go. Poor souls. To make it worse, the train arrived that day and cut the camp in half, until it was due to leave at 11 am the next morning. There it stood, the potent symbol, that sword of Damocles, the monster that was ready to devour them and take them away. It was torture for everyone in the camp, wondering whether they were going to be on that train or not.

Gemmeker gave Ordedienst posts to Willy, Max and Erich. They would be the ones to assist people to the train, and this morning men from the service had staked out the paths to the train. When the train had first left from the camp, there were too many people milling about, so it had been ordered that anyone not travelling was to keep out of the way in their barracks.

Etty had an interest and had sneaked into one of the nearest barracks to get a good view. Her choice was commended, as someone said that this particular barrack provided the best view. As early as six o'clock the train started to gorge itself on human life. Etty's view was so good that she saw paper mattresses on the floor of some of the wagons, which were meant to ease the lot of the sick. She could watch the comings and the goings. At one point while watching the proceedings, she made a sound of disgust by huffing. She had seen something that made her feel uncomfortable, in a mocking sort of way. She had been watching the Flying Column, the men of the Ordedienst, clad in brown overalls, carrying bags, baggage and sick people, loading them into the wagons. She caught sight of one of Gemmeker's "favourites." It was Willy Rosen. She did not like what Willy was doing. In addition to loading people into the wagons, he was "entertaining" people with his cabaret revues. He was entertaining the Kommandant, more like. To Etty, this was a sort of collaboration, and she resented it. She resented the high profile of the Germans within the Bühne group. It reeked of German entertainers. The Dutch could only perform if their German were good enough. She did not really understand it was the Kommandant's "wish" that the whole of the proceedings were to be in German. As she watched Willy, she thought he looked like "death warmed over." Yes, he did not look his best, but then who did here? Willy had two jobs, and while he was useful, he lived. When no longer of any use, he would be sent east just like anyone else. There was resentment against the cabaret, yet others loved it. There was resentment against the Jewish Council, yet some could say how helpful they were. There was resentment about everything that one did not have any control over. The cabaret had now been going for a month more or less. In that time, it had become known that Willy was being considered for transportation. Willy played to the Kommandant. For several nights he had to sing his very, very best "I don't know why the Roses bloom." The Kommandant was pleased, and Willy was exempted from transport.

Around this time Gemmeker wanted to reorganise the camp. Mirjam Bolle was dismissive of his intentions concerning a café, a cinema and a dance teacher. She thought he lived in another world, which he did.

Those who survived and did not go east paint a different picture of Gemmeker than Etty does. No doubt there were some who like this picture of a more benign Kommandant, but I hope I am showing a perverse picture of this man. He sent extra people east as a collective punishment no different from the punishment thrown down on Lidice or Oradour-sur-Glane. Family members and communities were punished for the action of one. If anyone tried to escape Westerbork, terrifying repercussions occurred. Then Etty wrote that this man would have an all-male choir sing that Yiddish popular song *"Bei Mir Bist Du Shein,"* ביי מיר ביסטו שיין, *"To Me You're Beautiful."* Absolutley incongruous, although Etty said it sounded nice up on the heath. Gemmeker invited cabaret members up to his house, notably Camilla Spira whom on one instance he escorted back to the barracks, shaking hands with her before bidding her good night. Some said he loved the children and made sure they got a tomato each day, even in hospital, yet he sent orphans and whole families to their deaths. I could go on quite a bit longer about Kommandant Gemmeker who was giving more and more to the cabaret group. They got anything they wanted, even those brown overalls when there was not enough for others who needed to wear them in the camp. It was little things like that that vexed Etty. The fact that they left places in disarray after rehearsals also annoyed Etty. She found it vexing that their existence was almost flaunted to those about to go east.

From her vantage point in the barrack overlooking the train, in a soft breath, she uttered the word "Jester" with some contempt. Then another huffing sound as she spotted Max Ehrlich. Another jester, she noted. Max stood out. He was quite tall, but it still made him Gemmeker's court fool. Etty looked around for the third, Erich Ziegler. She could not spot him. He was only in the cabaret because he could play a jazz version of Beethoven's "Ode to Joy." And another thing that bothered Etty was Willy Rosen living in a bungalow in the camp, with checked curtains, with his peroxide-haired wife who worked at the mangle all day in the laundry. Etty had a certain dislike for the Rosens, although she might have known the Krauskopf girl from her days with the Jewish Council in Amsterdam, as they both had worked there. Willy and Olga Rosen, the nobility of the Westerbork cabaret, in their own private bungalow, even had typical German names. Then Etty spotted the third member of the triumvirate, Erich Ziegler, with his big round eyes even visible at this distance. The Kommandant's entertainment trio, his link to society in Berlin and his supposed membership in that society.

Etty's attention was caught by a group of men in green uniforms, the German guards. She did not like them as a group. When she had first visited Westerbork, she felt that the guards were approachable, like the one collecting lupins, but this latest group were oafish louts who jeered and laughed at misfortune. By this time, they may have been injured soldiers no longer fit for active service at the front lines. Etty let a snigger escape. The whole scene was bizarre. There were young women, dangling their legs out of the wagons and bouncing young babies on their laps, and there were the rough guards, scowling and, in between, the brown Flying Column rushing up and down with wheelbarrows and stretchers for the ill. It swirled around like an inferno, yet this was life, life in Westerbork. With Etty were some youngsters who had their noses pressed to the glass and expressed disgust at the behaviour of the guards in green. They wondered why they did not wear black, as black signified evil and that was what the guards are. The SS wore black; already at that young age, evil to these children was personified – the face of Nazi Germany, drunken louts, dragged from some cesspool where they were trained to be like this.

Etty saw a tall figure clutching a briefcase. This was the man you went to if you really did not want to go east and had a good reason for staying. This was the *Antragstelle* personified. Hans Ottenstein who worked in the camp's Appeals Department. If anyone could save you, it was him. He even snatched people from the moving train.

Gemmeker was there to see the train off. Philip Mechanicus saw him, along with Kurt Schlesinger. Many regarded Kurt as the criminal, doing the Germans' dirty work. Gemmeker was not happy. Not only had three "criminals" tried to escape, but also a little boy had. He had hidden in a tent, not a very original hiding place and therefore soon found. It was not much of a disturbance to routine but a disturbance and an affrontery to Gemmeker's authority. Everyone knew what the Gentleman Kommandant did. Etty knew. No Jew may run away. You could guess what Gemmeker did in retaliation for this one boy. Scores of others were to go to the East.

Gemmeker had arrived like the Queen of Sheba, sweeping with his entourage up the path to see his people off. A little old bent woman scurried away; her appeal to be spared has been declined by the despondent man from the Appeals Department. He would not be saving many today, least of all the boy who had absconded from the hospital in a desperate act of confusion. One of the others at the window saw Gemmeker. He muttered to himself and anyone who cared to listen that they used to have a Kommandant who saw them off with a boot, but their Kommandant now saw them off with a smile. Most saw through Gemmeker. But there were some who did not and adored him as if he were Willy Fritsch, Hans Albers, Louis Borel, Philip Dorn or Clark Gable. A group of "silly girls" would almost swoon for this debonair figure walking like any film star among them. I was told it was the grey hair on such a young head that did it for them. It may well have been these girls' sisters or even mothers who pined for a look from Oskar Karlweis when he had appeared in Willy Rosen's 1938 revue "Lutine Gold" or Siegfied Arno, Germany's Charlie Chaplin, appearing in revues from 1936 to 1938, such as "Vorhang Auf" and "Laatste Nieuws." Both men had long gone, having fled to safety.

Etty grunted in agreement with the man's remark about the smiling Kommandant. She could herself be very uncomplimentary about Gemmeker, the "hairdresser's assistant." He would walk bolt upright like a model officer. Some did not need to, but he had to. There was always that inferiority complex. He only got into the SS when they relaxed the entry requirements. So to show his importance, he perfected this bearing. It was all a game to him. As Etty said, he had life and death over everyone in that camp, and he knew that. He exercised that duty with a smile. This really was Death's Smile, unchanging and immeasurable. Etty never fathomed it. There were more expressions of disgust around her; it really was something to behold. They called it the "Transport Boulevard". Camp life was parading itself in front of them to be observed, commented on and reconstructed later.

The guards saw the Jews as they were portrayed in *Jud Süß*, Goebbels' film from two years earlier. It was the highlight of Ferdinand Haschkowetz's career, although he later regretted it. He had changed his name to be more Aryan and chose "Marian" to make himself more elite. That film finished Marian. To many Germans, the Joseph Süß Oppenheimer he portrayed was the typical Jew. They had seen the films taken in the various ghettos across Europe. They thought that Jews had big noses and that the structure of their head gave their lineage away. Was their perception of a Jew not challenged here at Westerbork though? The inmates did not all look like the pictures the Germans had seen. Etty and the others were looking out on a tapestry of people who happened to be Jews. It was no different from a busy railway station in Amsterdam or even Berlin except that this train was going to Auschwitz. Trains were leaving all over Nazi Europe that morning to one of many camps, where the deportees would be worked to death, be starved, die of hunger or disease or be shot or gassed. This was just one scene. Out of all the scenes, this was the most untypical with Gemmeker, upright smart, followed by Schlesinger. Etty described Schlesinger as an English squire, toasting everyone with whisky. To bring someone down to a lower level is to remind them of former positions. Etty did this with Schlesinger, for he had been a manual worker digging ditches just months ago. Even Gemmeker noted his huge shovel-like hands. Schlesinger was Gemmeker's "Bully Boy," the crowd parts.

The train was taking too long. It should have been ready, and Gemmeker was keen for it to be gone. A big friendly dog was playing with Schlesinger, yet he was a Jew, and the dog should have been snarling and straining against its leash, like the dogs at Auschwitz or "Barry" at Sobibór. In the camps, their roles were reversed: "Barry" was the man, and the Jew he was to bite was the dog. As many as 200,000 dogs served in Nazi units.

Hans Margules and others were closing the train's doors. It was ready to depart and awaited the signal from Gemmeker, who swung his leg over a bicycle frame and mounted. Like some insane Quixote, he rode the length of the train, right to the other end. An acolyte relieved him of his charger, then like Leo Slezak in some Wagnerian opera, he signalled that the train may depart. The train screamed, and another thousand "problems" left Westerbork.

Etty wondered where they were going. What was their fate? What would happen to the sick, for there was no nurse on the train. After a rest, Etty had to go track down her face flannel, which was lost in the laundry, such was life at Westerbork, as 121 children with other adults trundled their way to Auschwitz. Of these, 208 would not be gassed, and of those, only 28 would see the end of the war.

The train arrived on the third day, the 26th of August. It stood for an hour and waited. Everyone was locked in the wagons. Those looking out would have seen buildings, barbed wire and perhaps people in ill-fitting striped uniforms. Dr de Leeuw-Bernard was on the train. The doors were flung open on the early morning. The deportees were screamed at to get out with their luggage. At five in the morning, they were standing by the train. Although Etty thought there was not a nurse on the train, there were in fact five doctors and patients from the Nederlands Israëlitisch Ziekenhuis. Dr de Leeuw-Bernard saw her husband help get the sick off the train on stretchers. Lorries arrived to take the sick and elderly, who got onto them readily enough; they did not know it was a one-way route to the gas chambers. Then along came the chief SS camp physician, Dr Eduard Wirths. He selected 44 women for the experiments. A doctor in research sometimes make use of laboratory animals as subjects; the Nazis used people. The Japanese used "monkeys," Chinese prisoners. And then there was no one left by the train, just heaps of suitcases. A band of stooped men in blue striped uniforms descended to take them away to Kanada for sorting.

* * *

On Friday, 27 August 1943, Adolf Eichmann held a meeting at the SS Economic-Administrative Main Office in Berlin to discuss the fate of the 700 Jews who were at the Barneveld camp and the 2,400 Jews at Vught. A day later, Eichmann sent a cable to Harster instructing him to gradually deport all the Jews in Vught to Auschwitz. These were not to include the 80 Jews who worked for the Luftwaffe or those who worked in the diamond industry. On Monday, 20 September, Harster informed Eichmann that he had exempted two more groups, those who worked for Philips (the electrical firm) and others in the textile industry who were making uniforms.

* * *

It was Tuesday morning on 31 August 1943. The train waited. In spite of setbacks in the war, the transports from camp to camp continued. Eichmann wove his skills over the web of railway networks, and camps set up during Aktion Reinhard remained in operation.

The Nazis were good at subterfuge. They fabricated a wall of lies to mask what was really happening and offered hope as a competing lie. They kept going on about *Austauschjuden*. There were Germans who lived in other countries who could be exchanged for Jews living in the Nazi Reich. This latest ruse was to exchange some Jews for Germans who lived in Palestine at the outbreak of war and had been incarcerated by the British. Jews will quote from the Haggadah, לשנה הבאה בירושלים, Next year in Jeruslaem. To offer hope that you were headed to Palestine was particularly perverse. Jews offered themselves for this exchange. Westerbork had a group that was being

160

taught farming skills that would prove useful when they reached Palestine. They were exempt from transport.

Joint orders had been issued from Rauter and Harster who were the *Befehlshaber der Sicherheitspolizei und des Sicherheitsdienst, BdS,* "Commanders of the Security Police and Security Service," with new guidelines to facilitate the transportation of Jews. This was to follow Himmler's wish that as many Jews as possible are to be sent east. These orders were sent to the Central Office for Jewish Administration in Amsterdam. Why were there new orders? Himmler knew that the Soviets were moving towards German-occupied Poland. They had already overrun the site of Treblinka; others would soon follow. As the number of extermination camps dwindled, so would the number of Jews who could be disposed of. Therefore, time was of the essence and had to be used carefully. The matter had been fully discussed back in May and would be applied to services in the Netherlands. Eichmann's deputy sent out an order that all remaining Jews in the Reich were to go east or at least to Theresienstadt. Mixed-marriage Jews were still being exempted, and even Nazis were unsure what the actual policy was.

On the same day the last transport had left, 21 Jews were being transported from Groningen to Westerbork. One tried to escape but was shot. It was assumed he was dead, but the body was put back on the train for delivery so all 21 could be accounted for. Next came 350 who had been held at the Schouwburg Theatre, which was being used for detainment until there were enough for a transport. Many of the performers, including Willy Rosen, were detained in the theatre where they had once performed with the Nelsons, father Rudolf and his son, Herbert. Both survived Westerbork and the war. The theatre was devoid of much of its lights, curtains and other apparatus. Gemmeker had agreed to the request for proper lights for the cabaret theatre. It was the most modern of theatre lighting. No one had really complained about that, but when wood arrived for a new stage that had been looted from the synagogue at Assen, voices were raised in horror. To some Jews, it was as bad as building over the remains of a synagogue or a Jewish cemetery. You might be thinking of a road of Jewish gravestones. Oddly, this was never done by the Nazis, but the Communists? Now that is another matter.

* * *

The Jews were assembled at Westerbork for a large transport planned for Tuesday, 31 August 1943. It was Rosh Chodesh Elul, a time of repentance. I wonder what the Jews on this train needed to repent for. The Jewish Council offices prepared the list. Did those men repent? Some on the list had been in Westerbork a short time, others for ages. It did not matter. The ones compiling the list did not put their own names down. They did receive an order from Willy Lages, the commander of the Sicherheitsdienst, to take four names off the list. The original request had come from Abraham Asscher, one of the leaders of the Jewish Council in Amsterdam. He did not want his nephew to go east. It was only a short reprieve, the four went later.

There were 1,004 people on that train, including 160 children and 195 older people. Among them was Dr David Moffie. He counted the wagons, 30 of them with about 35 in each wagon. There was one wagon for the sick, lying on their paper mattresses. He said some of those patients were seriously ill. Gemmeker made no objection on humanitarian grounds. A sick person was a drain on the camp's resources. Dr Moffie also had a good look at what else was on the train. He found out that bread, margarine, sausages, beans and cabbage were purchased for the journey. There was so much white cabbage, it filled a cart. Those on the train were led to believe it was all for the journey. They were to find out it was not.

Philip Mechanicus also watched the train. He used an analogy that the train was like a shipwreck. The ship would sink below the waves, and all that was left of 1,000 or so people would be their belongings floating on the surface. People were not allowed to take much with them, only about 15 kilograms or 33 pounds. What they did not take was left behind. It floated around the barracks like flotsam and jetsam. Every trace of the owners had been swallowed up. At the

162

same time, Willy Rosen was watching the "Westerbork girls" rehearse on their new stage. Philip found it "loathsome."

The transport left. The people aboard may have been lucky enough to have seen the revue, had they been able to get a ticket. It was not that the tickets were expensive, but there were few of them. The assembly hall could not seat a huge audience. By the time that the front row was taken out for Gemmeker, in his large comfortable high-backed chair and his guests, not many seats were left. The Bunter Abend had been a success. Gemmeker had said so himself, and therefore more were put on. That month the new show had been called *"Humor und Melodie."* The next month would start with the second version. Each time a member of the cast or backstage went east, a new programme was printed to reflect accurately those contributing to the revue. The programmes were now printed on both sides of the sheet. Paper was available for the revue group; Gemmeker saw to that. The production had to be as professional, as in any theatre. The music was by Willy and Erich and the direction by Max Ehrlich. There were 18 scenes, starting with the whole cast on stage, Max Ehrlich addressing the audience and Camilla Spira dancing and singing. There were comedy sketches and new songs by Willy Rosen, some about life in the camp and how everyone looked forward to a little parcel arriving, especially if it had toilet paper inside. There were performances by Willy and Erich and a host of others and the group continued to grow. In this way, more people avoided transport. One visitor to the camp in August 1943 ensured that one member of the Bühne group would survive the war. In August 1943, after the success of the Bunter Abend, *Humor und Melodie* was put on, and some of the Westerbork girls persuaded Catharina Frank to dance. Catharina was not all that keen, but they persuaded her to put on a short skirt and kick her legs. She had taken dance lessons as a youngster and had recently given birth to her son, Clarence, on Saturday, 1 May 1943. Gemmeker sat in the front for the performance but next to him sat Adolf Eichmann. Gemmeker fawned. Everything had to be perfect. He roared with laughter, and Eichmann joined in, but during one of the dances, entitled "You

Should Always be Artistic. Behave Yourself," a particular woman with a pretty face and seemingly nice legs caught Eichmann's eye. He asked who she was and was told it was Catharina Frank. Not that Gemmeker knew, he had to ask. Catharina was brought to him. She said that her name was Catharina Frank but she was also known as "Dinnie." Eichmann complimented her on her dancing. She told him that it had not been too easy, as she had only given birth to her son, Clarence, a few months earlier. Eichmann must have been even more impressed. He made her a promise, quite out of the blue. He promised her that if she and Clarence were to go east they would go to Theresienstadt. Gemmeker nodded his approbation. He could not have done anything else, but notes were made that Catharina Frank was to go to Theresienstadt. Gemmeker instructed the Diensleiter of Catharina's special position. It was odd. Eichmann did not have to do that, yet he would do more. These Nazis often made gestures towards the camp inmates. They knew they had the power of life or death over people. It was like Hermann Göring and Joseph Goebbels repeating Karl Lueger's statement that he decided who was a Jew. Lueger had said this when he was Mayor of Vienna between 1897 and 1910. Goebbels was speaking with Fritz Lang, the famous film director about a project that Lang did not want to do and had excused himself as he had Jewish grandparents. Lang was told that he, Goebbels, decided who was a Jew, and whenever Himmler visited Ravensbrück, he would release a few of the women. They behaved like feudal lords.

A few more of the women in Westerbork wished they had "beautiful" legs. Catharina and Jacques had entered the camp last May as a newly married couple. She had been six months pregnant, and Jacques Frank from Amsterdam, 31 years old, the proud father, had been deported on Tuesday, 15 May 1943. By the following Friday, he was dead.

In August 1943, when Eichmann discussed deportation with Catharina, did she mention her husband and that she hoped to meet up again with him, as he had already gone to Sobibór? Did Gemmeker and Eichmann feel a twinge of guilt knowing that Jaques had been dead for nearly three months? If Gemmeker had asked Eichmann about Jacques, he would have been told that the chances of their meeting again were nil, as had he gone to Sobibór, he was almost certainly dead. Did Eichmann make enquiries back at the office about the transport on the 25th of May? If he did, he most likely got a short telegram back from Reichleitner stating they were all dead. I am sure that Gemmeker would then have asked Eichmann how he knew Jacques was dead and then would be told exactly what kind of place Sobibór was. No doubt Eichmann visited for the day or longer, as he was in the camp for the evening. And not once did Eichmann and Gemmeker discuss what happened to Jews in the East? It may have been that this was the time that Eichmann told Gemmeker how pleased he was with the "smooth running" of the trains from Westerbork and that it was a pleasure to see. Did Gemmeker later check the records for Jacques? I doubt it. That would have shown an interest. Jacques, the proud father of a few weeks, had gone to the East.

I digressed – that revue group again. Dr David Moffie was able to tell about the journey, leaving Westerbork on 31 August. The train stopped a few times so those aboard could get water. He was also called upon to another car, where people had fallen ill. As appointed train doctor, he was allowed to wear an armband indicating his position. Nevertheless, the train arrived as expected on Thursday, 2 September 1943. Some 259 men and 247 women were taken into the camp. The rest were gassed.

Alexander Roodveldt said that they had had no idea what was about to happen. They had all been singing when they had arrived. That soon stopped when the screaming started. They were forced off the train with their luggage, ready to carry on walking, but they were told to leave their belongings. Alexander ran to catch his wife and children and helped them onto the lorries. They were some of the first up on the lorry and got seats. Unwittingly, he had helped them to their deaths. The children were excited, and off they went. Alexander asked a guard when he would see them and was told "Sunday." He soon found out that he would never see them again. Can you imagine the pain you'd experience when told they had been murdered? Do you cry, scream, collapse or become silent and stare at the ground? The last was probably the best. Eye contact was a bad thing. Expression of any sort was punished, so any grief was better kept hidden from the guards, or one was dead. Alexander, David and three others from that train lived to see freedom.

* * *

On Tuesday, 31 August 1943, Ernst Kaltenbrunner, head of the Reich Main Security Office, *Reichssicherheitshauptamt*, issued directives about transportation of Jews to Bergen-Belsen. Harster in The Hague has to comply and aus der Fünten issued orders that certain Jews were to be deported. These were to include Jews with dual citizenship; Jews with South American passports; Jews destined for exchange in Palestine; Jews with ties to foreign countries; Jews who had fought in the war – they were to go to Theresienstadt, unless there was no capacity and then it would be to Auschwitz; Portuguese Jews and Jews whose papers were stamped "120000."

I wonder whether Gemmeker remembered he had sent two British Jews, Leon and Mrs Greenman, to the East. I doubt it. Oh and the Jews with 120000 on their papers? These were Jews who worked in the diamond industry and those who worked for the Joodse Raad.

It was not Zöpf who had sent out this little list but Gertrud Slottke, his right-hand woman. Anyone who did not bump into her should have been happy. She was a manipulative and confirmed Nazi. It would not be surprising if she had put people on lists whom she did not like. There were also Jews from Barneveld Camp, the privileged Jews. It was Slottke's idea to utilise normal passenger trains to send smaller groups to various destinations. They would of course be guarded by the Security Police. This idea came to fruition. The instructions also allowed these Jews to be deemed "inmates," and they could wear their own clothes. They were not prisoners. They wrote letters and were under the administration of the older Jews. Slottke thought that sending 5,000 Jews in these transports in a removal process from the Netherlands was much better in the scheme of things. It ended with words that spelt doom for many. Bergen-Belsen was due a speedy expansion and would be able to accommodate more transports than it had previously.

* * *

Tuesday, 31 August 1943 – The children's playground was opened by "Uncle" Gemmeker. There are four seesaws, two horizontal bars and a sandbox. Philip was there to see it being used by the children of the camp.

SEPTEMBER 1943

FOUR TRANSPORTS WITH 3,276 DEPORTEES

Friday, 3 September 1943 – This day marked the start of the deportation of Belgian Jews, and Himmler was made minister of the Interior.

* * *

Monday, 6 September 1943 – Marga Himmler had 50th birthday blues, as she had "nothing" to look forward to.

* * *

Tuesday, 7 September 1943, was a notable day for the Germans, the day the 75th transport was due to leave Westerbork. The train had 27 wagons, and there would be 987 deportees when fully loaded. The youngest deportee was not even one month old.

Philip watched the train fill with its human cargo. He had been at the camp for nearly a whole year, but it would not be an anniversary he would note with any celebration. He had watched the deportees pack the previous evening. He did not think they were doing it with any sense of courage or resilience but more out of resignation and

168

acceptance. You notice here that these people were packing the previous evening, not from the early hours or from sunrise. Since the previous day they had known they were to travel to the East. You see these people's reactions manifest by animals at the zoo, Philip said, where they have sort of given up and simply go through the motions of existence or life.

Mischa (Michael) Hillesum, the gifted pianist and composer, was getting aboard the train. You know the name? Yes, it was Etty's brother. He would turn 23 this month, if he were to reach his birthday. Mischa was under the protection of a Dutch orchestra conductor, Willem Mengelberg, who was sort of pro-Nazi and in the position to call in a few favours. He asked Rauter for a favour, which was to keep this aspiring musician and composer in the Netherlands. Rauter agreed to the request and offered Mischa a place at Barneveld, a camp for "special" Jews. It had been opened the previous December and was in Gelderland. About 700 privileged Jews were in a castle known as "De Schaffelaar." The inmates there paid for their own keep, and the guards were all Dutch. Knowing Etty as we do, it came as no surprise that Mischa turned down Rauter's offer. He wanted to stay and look after his parents. He might have used the word "protect," which would not have gone down well with Rauter but allowed Mischa to score a point against the Nazis. Mengelberg was disappointed, and Rauter was furious. He vowed that he would never help the family again. You know how mothers want the best for their children? It might have been best if Mother Hillesum had kept quiet and not written to Rauter asking for Mischa to be exempt. Red rag to a bull was putting it mildly. Rauter gave orders that the whole family were to be transported that day or at least as soon as possible. And so it was not only Mischa on the train but also his three family members. Etty was there too. She had been offered escapes but like her brother, she wanted to be with her parents. This was very noble of them both, but it meant they turned their backs on survival. This was the sort of person Etty was. She grieved for those who suffered and willingly took on their suffering, not to ease the pain of others but to share in it in some vicarious way.

Her friends tried to get Etty's name off from the list, it seems with Etty's approval, but the order had come from high up in the Netherlands Occupation Forces, and there was no way for the Jewish Council to have it revoked. They had all been surprised by the speed at which an order had been changed. They had been expecting to go later, but suddenly it was *tomorrow*, Tuesday, 7 September. This was Rauter's doing. They did not know it, nor did they ever find out that "Mother H," as she was known, had poked the hornets' nest and that they were all going to be stung. Orders from The Hague usually ended up with someone getting stung.

One of the Dienstleiter sought out Etty before the train was to leave. He told her that he had tried everything, but there would be no last-minute reprieve. Etty and her family were resigned, calm and reticent. As was typical of Etty, she had to go talk to someone in one of the wagons farther down and lost her space. She ended up alone in wagon 12 while the others were in wagon number one.

In the other wagons were many orphans, all alone. They only had each other for company or to keep safe. Gertha Bonewit-Kaufman and her husband, who held the title of "Wagon Leader", sat and waited.

Gemmeker went through his little charade and waved the train off. Hands are waving out of the small openings high up on the wagons. Etty wrote a short postcard to a friend back in Westerbork, Jopie Vleeschhouwer and told her that she hopes to meet again. She threw the card out of the train, and it fluttered down by the tracks.

Jopie Vleeschhouwer received the postcard from Etty, dated 7 September with a post mark for the 15th of September. It was found by a farmer who did not know Etty but posted it just the same. A simple act of kindness.

Gertha Bonewit-Kaufman gave a brief description of the journey. As soon as the train reached Germany, it stopped to change engines, and the Jews were asked for any gold items. There were two tons of cabbage on this train, bread and sausage, enough for the thousand hungry souls who got none of it. We can guess what might have happened to the food meant for the Jews. It could have exchanged hands on the black market, a dangerous operation, as the SS did not like theft from the state, or it might have been given to German citizens along the route. The train arrived at Auschwitz on ninth of the month. Some 187 men and 105 women were selected. The Hillesum parents, Rebecca and Louis, went straight to the gas chambers along with 693 others. Only eight people from this transport saw the end of the war. Etty and Mischa were not among them. The selection had been rather rushed and not terribly efficient, so some younger people went to the gas chambers rather than to a work detail.

Later that month Jacob (Jaap) Hillesum arrived in Westerbork.

* * *

Thursday, 9 September 1943 – Catharina Frank was issued a special pass. This might not have seemed of much importance to someone always in the camp. She received the special pass because of her involvement in Willy Rosen's revue, and while the revue was on, she would be allowed out after curfew, as long as she was on her way to or from her "apartment" and work. Every member of the revue group would have had such a pass.

Philip Mechanicus noted that two more horizontal bars and three high swings had been added to the children's play area. He also noticed that little Kurt Ikenberg was playing there. Kurt's parents, Klara and Ludwig, had come to the camp before the German takeover. Kurt was born in the camp on Sunday, 6 July 1941. He was now just over two. He knew no life but the camp. He called for his mama on Friday, 13 March 1942, took his first steps around his birthday in 1942, and on Thursday, 10 September 1942, he could walk unaided. By Thursday, 12 November 1942, he could call for his grandparents, *Oma* and *Opa,* although they were never in the camp. Kurt's parents were German and, as members of the "old elite," they were interned by the Dutch. They were part of the alte Kampinsassen. So unlike Jewish Dutch babies, he had some time to grow up in the camp. Had he not been German, he would have gone to Auschwitz early on, but Gemmeker used the German Jews to run the camp. Their deportation was delayed, but they would go.

* * *

Saturday, 11 September 1943 – The first families were deported from Theresienstadt, the ghetto in the Protectorate of Bohemia and Moravia, to Auschwitz.

* * *

It was Monday, 13 September 1943, and Philip Mechanicus was quite upset. A 65-year-old woman had just committed suicide. She did it for her daughter. Tomorrow she was due to be deported to Theresienstadt via Bergen-Belsen. Her daughter had volunteered to go with her. The daughter did not go, because her mother had killed herself. In one of the most miserable places on earth, one can find the most selfless acts of humanity. Admiration for such courage and love is endless, yet none came from any German in that camp.

* * *

On Tuesday, 14 September 1943, another train was standing impatiently awaiting Gemmeker's signal. Did he ride his bicycle down the asphalt path? Did he wish the 1,310 deportees well? Would the deportees all meet next year in Jerusalem?

In Amsterdam, the Jewish Council had little left to do. The Security Police last May had demanded it be given access to the 7,000 people the council employed. Plans were in hand to agree to the demand.

Someone had a special interest in this train. Untersturmführer Alfons Werner, SS number 212674, located in The Hague, was responsible for seven of the wagons. He represented the department of Wilhelm Zöpf. Inside the seven wagons was a prized cargo of 305 "*bevorzugte Juden.*" These were Jews the Germans want to use as bargaining chips in any game of poker that they could get others to sit down to. The threat was always the same. If no one wanted to show their hand, these Jews would be killed.

I can tell you when the train left because Werner noted it. At 10:42 precisely, the train started its journey. Gemmeker could get the trains out before or after 11 o'clock. It only meant that the train had to wait somewhere else for the tracks to be clear. Gemmeker did not like it to wait in Westerbork. If the deportees started to grow thirsty on a hot day elsewhere, it was someone else's problem and not his. Almost nine and a half hours later, at 19:15, the train stopped at Soltau. The seven wagons were uncoupled and later went on to Bergen-Belsen. Twelve hours or more in a wagon. Can you imagine what it was like? Eleven days later, they were transferred to Theresienstadt. Actually, not all of them; they would be 24 short. No one can recall what happened to them. Did anyone care? They were lost, swallowed up by the monster that was Bergen-Belsen.

On the list were 43 employees of the Joodse Raad, 100 of the *alte Lagerinsassen*, 300 from Vught and 40 boys from the *Hachsharah* programme, a Zionist youth programme that prepared boys going to Palestine. Here were 40 who would not be in Jerusalem, next year or any other year. Then there were 500 others from the camp, including two doctors who volunteered to go with the sick. They were doing what they had thought was right and honoured their Hippocratic Oath.

Dr Elie Aron Cohen found himself a place and settled as best as he could in one of the wagons. Elie, at that time 34 years old, was quite open when he spoke about Westerbork. He thought it was a friendly place where you could visit, make a date, visit a prostitute, flirt and drink. He said that the crazy train came once a week. Here he was sitting with the others in the "Crazy Train." When it happened to him, Elie accepted it. He had no faith in exemptions. Elie watched as one man from his wagon went off. He came back after a short moment, having met with Gemmeker. He told everyone in the wagon that he had been appointed *Wagonführer*. It was his job to see that no one would escape. Why? Because if anyone did, he would be the first to be shot. The mood was gloomy – if it had not been gloomy before. Another instance of Gemmeker's system of retribution, but in this instance, the threat was not deportation but instantaneous death. But then what was the difference? If anyone escaped the camp, ten others from that barrack were sent east.

Somewhere on the train was also Marianne de Hond, the wife of Maurice. Marianne would survive but would be kept for some time in Barracks 10 at Auschwitz, where the experiments were conducted. There were 250 women who were sterilised, but Marianne and a few others would go on to have children. No other members of her family survived.

Rozette Lezer was born Rozette Lopes-Dias in Amsterdam on 19 September. On Sunday, she would be 22 years old. She was there with her mother. Most of the family, including her husband, Moses, had already left and were already dead. When Rozette arrived in Auschwitz, she would be number 62511. There she would come to know Dr Carl Clauberg as one of his "patients." She was one of his medical experiments concerning sterilisation.

In another wagon sat Ruth Wertheim-Zielenziger. There seemed to be disagreement about time. It was 10:42, and Ruth noted that the train had not left. They were a resourceful group in the wagon and immediately started to share what they had. The wagon was not full, so all their packs were hung along the sides of the wagon. Remember how someone said you could not hang up your packs? Ruth's group could. They had their suitcases in the middle, and Ruth got out a tablecloth and covered the cases.

Do we not owe it to these people to remember them? These poor Dutch and other souls whom the Nazis wanted to have disappear forever. How often do we hear that it should never happen again? And yet it keeps happening around the world to other groups that are despised by others.

The train was ready to leave at 10:42 or 11:00 – as Ruth thought. Are 18 minutes important? Well it can mean life or death in the scheme of fate. As the train started to move out of the camp, Gemmeker did not see that Ruth's group had opened all their shutters, which were obviously not nailed shut. Behind a curtain in their wagon was a barrel. This was the toilet. It was emptied twice, but it still was overflowing when they reached Auschwitz.

You know what happened when the train reached the German border. The engine was changed, and the guards took the opportunity to filch the belongings of the deportees. Ruth's group said they did not have anything, probably blaming other soldiers. But they did. They tied them all up in a bundle and then threw it out of the wagon into a river. It was another point scored against the Germans, but this little act of defiance went unnoticed. Upon arrival when an 80-year-old woman refused to let go of her purse, she was hit over the head by the Kommandant with such force that blood spattered from the wound. This was Ruth's welcome to Auschwitz.

To the relief of the wagon leaders, there were no escapes from the train, and all 1,005 arrived at Auschwitz. Remember that the other 300 had left, heading towards Bergen-Belsen. Of the men, 233 were admitted to Auschwitz and numbered, and of the women, 194. The other 578 went to the gas chambers. Ruth described how 100 unmarried women were separated from the married ones. They were shaved by men, including pubic and underarm hair. To complete the humiliation, they were given dirty, ill-fitting clothes and marched to Block 10. They saw women who were no longer of any use going to the gas chambers. If you have a delicate disposition, I would not read this next part – skip the next paragraph. These women had been subjected to experiments. Their reproductive organs had been operated on. They had been inseminated by various artificial methods, and they had been injected in the chest. Blood and urine had been extracted for tests.

It was the "Beast" who conducted these "laboratory tests." That Dr Carl Clauberg's nickname. He called himself a gynaecologist. This man had treated an officer's wife from Himmler's entourage. Clauberg felt he could ask Himmler whether he could be transferred from Dachau to Auschwitz to conduct experiments in mass sterilisation. Now why did he specifically ask to go to Auschwitz? He knew from someone that he could experiment on humans at Auschwitz; that was the reason. How common was this knowledge? I do not know how many women he abused as a doctor, but I have heard that whatever the number, 700 of them survived to recount their stories. But then would you want to admit you had been violated in such a way? The number was probably far greater than the brave 700 who came forward. He later moved on to Ravensbrück to escape the Soviets.

The survivors of that train count 21 men and 52 women, including Ruth and Elie and three of the boys, aged 15 or 16 when they had left Westerbork. What sorts of lives did the people have since those days in Westerbork? Elie went on wrote medical papers on the effects of having been in such camps.

It might surprise you how people then were expected to get on with their lives and that it was expected that what these people had experienced would have little effect upon their lives. There was a period in which what had occurred was not spoken about. The war was over, and who wanted to relive it – men who had experienced breakdowns after combat like D-Day or their experiences in Japanese POW camps or the thousands who'd been released from extermination and concentration camps? Racked and wrecked mental capacities to deal with life or twisted perceptions were left untreated. Some hid their tattooed numbers, and others wore them like a badge. Many wanted to pick up their lives where they had been left off. They did not have time for disabilities that could not be seen. Mental scars were still misunderstood.

I mentioned the 300 who went to Bergen-Belsen. Their story has a few more twists and turns. They were the first to be assigned to go to Theresienstadt as well as the German Jews who had fought in the Great War. Willy Rosen had been wounded on the Eastern Front and was a recipient of the Iron Cross 2nd Class. Germans Jews could be sent straight from Germany to Theresienstadt. Willy's mother had been sent there on Wednesday 2 September 1942, directly from Magdeburg Station. She was murdered there on Saturday, 21 March 1943. Willy probably did not even know she was dead.

Up until now, everyone had gone from Westerbork to Auschwitz or Sobibór. Sturmbannführer Wilhelm Zöpf had risen quickly in the ranks of the SS and was an old friend of Harster. In a discussion with Eichmann, he asked about the status of exempted Jews. There were some in the Netherlands, and he wanted to know whether they too could go to Theresienstadt, or could they be sent to Bergen-Belsen? It was agreed that perhaps it should be Theresienstadt. The Nazis were a bit touchy about murdering the Germans in Westerbork, even if they were Jews. Permission had to be given by Berlin for execution of Germans, unless of course they were Jews sent to a camp without any status. On Friday, 6 August 1943, Alfons Werner in The Hague had contacted SS-Hauptsturmführer Franz Novak in Eichmann's Berlin office, enquiring as to whether Theresienstadt had the capacity to accept a group of 200 Jews of status, or were they to go to Bergen-Belsen?

At 30 years old, Novak from Wolfsberg was Eichmann's timetable wizard. Novak worked closely with Otto Stange of the *Deutsche Reichsbahn*. He considered the matter, and the answer was in the affirmative that Jews from the Netherlands could be sent to the ghetto in Theresienstadt rather than to Bergen-Belsen. Thirteen days later, a letter was sent from *Gruppenführer* Wilhelm Harster, the head of security, to Reich Commissioner Arthur Seyss-Inquart. He was asking for permission for the attached list of Jews to be transported to Theresienstadt. This tells us that down the line, they were all seeking permission to deport this group of Jews with special status. No one wanted to be blamed if there were a complaint; such was the workings of the SS. If it had gone against Himmler's wishes, there would be hell to pay. Reich Commissioner Seyss-Inquart was suitably high enough to make a decision and get away with it if it was the wrong one. Harster pointed out that some of those on the list had decorations from the Great War, or they had contributed something to the Reich. Some had families that were already in Theresienstadt. Some discussion had taken place about those listed: Julius Magnus, for instance, had been a lawyer to the last Kaiser, and some Jews were even members of the NSB, the Dutch Nazi Party. Seyss-Inquart gave his permission, and the list was prepared to include up to 305 people. This transport was so important that Untersturmführer Werner travelled with it to Bergen-Belsen.[1] Obviously, he travelled in the carriage with the guards who were on their best behaviour. There must have been two sets of guards for this train, as it split from the other wagons destined for Auschwitz.

Joseph Fritz, a survivor, did not say whether the train stopped for the usual fleecing of the deportees. This train probably left at 10:42, as Werner was indeed aboard, and not 11:00, as Ruth Wertheim-Zielenziger had said. Werner wrote in his report that the train arrived at Bergen-Belsen at 23:15 on 15 September. He waited with the guards, the *Begleitkommando*, until 6:30 the following morning until Siegfried Seidl, responsible for the foreign nationals at the camp, arrived. Seidl was from Austria and had already served a term at Theresienstadt before moving to Belsen. Werner complained about Seidl in his report, and Joseph said that while they were waiting in the train at Belsen, the doctors asked for assistance, as ill people were aboard the train. The guards answered coarsely with profanities. The women went first to the camp in trucks and the men followed.

With his duty carried out, Untersturmführer Werner then headed off to Berlin to meet with Novak and to discuss the continued deportation of Jews from the Netherlands. Novak said Belsen was at full capacity and was seeking extra provision. He was given instructions for future deportations and returned to The Hague. Zöpf's right-hand "man" was Gertrud Slottke, a woman of formidable reputation from West Prussia. She added her thoughts that within the Jewish Solution, the removal of all Jews from the Netherlands was the preferred result. She told Rauter to speak to Oswald Pohl from Himmler's office who had the Ostindustrie as part of his brief. He was also responsible for the distribution of prisoners throughout the camp system.

There is some thought that this transport was initiated by Slottke to begin the process in Seyss-Inquart's plans. She was out to impress her bosses.

* * *

Wednesday, 15 September 1943 – This day marked the start of the deportation of Jews from Italy.

* * *

Monday, 20 September 1943 – The actor and film director Kurt Gerron arrived in Westerbork. Gerron was famous for starring in the film *Der Blaue Engel*, The Blue Angel, which most people remember for the part Marlene Dietrich played.

Ten men were executed nearby Westerbork camp by firing squad. They were cremated and then buried behind the crematorium. Their names were:

Jans Diemer, 21.
Andries Diepenbrug, 41.
Wessel Jan Knot, 28.
Pieter van Laarhoven, 26.
Rendert de Poel, 35.
Geert Por, 25.
Anne Rutgers, 22.
Jan Toet, 25.
Roelof Tuin, 37.
Johannes Vis, 30.

They had carried out robberies and set fire to Exloo Town Hall where the census was stored. The census survived in the fireproof safe. They were also responsible for the murder of Willem Reilingh, a collaborator and high-ranking member of the Dutch Nazi Party. Reilingh had been riding his bicycle between Zuidlaren and Midalren but met up with Johannes Vis and did not make it to where he was cycling. Reilingh's son was a member of the Dutch Waffen-SS and was killed in the Soviet Union. Reilingh had been a consul for the Netherlands in Sweden in Monrovia. The Dutch resistance was afraid he would turn too many people over to the Nazis, and he was therefore assassinated.

The next day, Werner Stertzenbach was working at the crematorium. He had been ordered to burn the bodies of ten resistance fighters. He saw that four others involved in covering up the activity, perhaps bringing the bodies from the forest, were being taken to the train in the camp and were bound for Poland. A few days later he disappeared from the camp and submerged himself into Amsterdam, not wishing to be sent east having been witness to the executions.

* * *

On Tuesday, 21 September 1943, another train bound for Auschwitz cut the camp in half like a lazy python whose prey enters without any stalking action on the python's part, for Gemmeker kept Auschwitz well fed. Swirling and circling around Westerbork were other trains, trams and trucks that delivered Jews to Westerbork. The 979 deportees were ready. Everyone had managed to have at least some food, oatmeal and coffee.

Martha van Gelder de Lange, 26, was there with her husband, Bernhard. They had been in the camp since 3 July. They had arrived with 1,598 others from Vught. Now if you ask some about the sympathy displayed by Gemmeker, they will relate the story of Machiel Prins. He had arrived with his mother and had been born premature on 31 May 1943. You remember the Children's Train? Machiel should have been on that but he was very frail, so the poor little baby had been left behind. Up stepped Gemmeker. He found an incubator and a paediatrician and nurses to look after the poor little soul, one of whom was nurse Trudel van Reemst. She said that Gemmeker came every day to enquire after the infant's well-being. The baby made good progress and was measured every day. Reports were given to Gemmeker. He got to a weight of three kilogram. Now this was good of Gemmeker, right? He had a heart. There was a good side after all to Gemmeker, that "Gentleman Kommandant." Well, ask me where Machiel was at this point? He was on that train together with his mother.

Joseph de Jong was on the train, too. He was 22 and had been arrested with his family just over two weeks ago. They went to the Joodse Schouwburg and waited. Joseph and his girlfriend, Celina, were married there. Food was taken into the theatre to be shared with the "guests." Joseph said that they could have slipped away easily enough but were fearful what would happen to their parents. It would not just have been his parents. People did escape from the theatre, especially children. Some died there. They were all transferred from a freight depot in Burneokade. A couple of youngsters jumped from the train: The boy escaped, but the girl was shot dead.

You could get picked for some unpleasant duties at Westerbork. It was wise not to get picked like the four chosen to go collect ten bodies from the forest to take them to the crematoria. Ten people were murdered by the Nazis, and they did not want any witnesses, so those four were on the train, isolated from everyone else.

Elisabeth Feldman was 27. She was arrested in Harlem and ended up at the theatre. She had just learned that Max, her husband, was one of those four picked. She met him before getting on the train. He was sobbing to her about what he had done the night before.

Theresia van Praag Sigaar Soetendorp, 22, was on the train as well. She and her husband had been hiding. They had aborted their baby to stand a better chance of survival, but someone had turned them in. They went to the theatre and had been there ten days before being sent to Westerbork. They looked a little bulky because they were wearing several layers of clothing.

The formal macabre charade took place, and the train left.

It would take two days to reach Auschwitz. In each wagon were again two barrels. One of the barrels was emptied a few times on the journey but remember there could be 50 to 70 people in each wagon, all of whom could see the private actions of everyone else. If they were lucky, they could get a sheet to be shielded from view. You get told different things by different people on different transports. Some are adamant that they were given three days of food in a package. There was jam, butter, cheese and ten cucumbers to share in the wagon. Who wanted to eat? The conditions were hardly conducive to satisfying hunger. It was grim to say the least. Someone had the foresight to suggest that they might be separated, so men and women packed their bags accordingly. Joseph was able to say that they went through Hamburg, Berlin and Breslau.

A total of 979 men women and children left Westerbork, and 979 arrived at Auschwitz. There were 60 children, including baby Machiel. They left the train with their luggage but were to leave it on the platform, as it would be sent to them later. It was their first sight of men in blue striped suits, dogs and SS men with whips. The message got through quickly. A lone voice of a woman started the *Kol Nidre* prayer:

"May all the people of Israel be forgiven, including all the strangers who live in their midst, for all the people are in fault."

Of those standing there, 531 were selected to live some sort of life, and so they entered the camp. The rest went to the gas chambers, 388 adults, 59 children and little Machiel. A member of the Sonderkommando, those selected to do various jobs in the crematoria, related a story about how they had waited for the gas chamber to become quiet and then opened the large doors. There was a pyramid of people around the metal frames from floor to ceiling where the gas pellets of Zyklon B rattled when dropped through the hatch in the ceiling. The pellets gave off cyanide gas, and the people clambered over each other to try to reach the air, and in that pyramid they died. The men of the Sonderkommando entered, but they could hear crying. Atop of the pyramid was a baby. They informed the SS guard. He went into the chamber, they heard the crack of a pistol, and the crying stopped. Baby Machiel may have been that baby. Nothing touched the brutal hearts of those guards. Baby Machiel was treated the same as everyone else was.

Joseph described how the horror began for those selected to live. Guards asked them if they would like to take off their watches. They complied with the request, but did not hand them to the guards, but dashed them to the floor. These were watches given by father to sons or to wives as tokens of love. Boys already at the camp, came up asking the new arrivals for valuables, as newcomers would not be able to keep them. Joseph said hardly anyone believed the boys but threw them cigarettes. When they reached the barracks, they had to turn out their pockets, and Joseph had to hand over a photograph of his wife. We all know how sometimes you cannot remember a passed loved one, and we get pictures out to look at them and recall that this was them on that day. They were in Monowitz-Buna, a sub-camp of Auschwitz, where an Italian-commissioned factory-made synthetic rubber. They found out that 300 Dutch had been there before them. Monowitz-Buna would be known as Auschwitz III from November 1943.

Some one hundred of the women were unlucky. They were selected and taken to Block 10. Do you recall what happened in Block 10? This was where the Doctors Clauberg and Mengele were based. In the weeks from 24 August 1943 to that day, 244 married Dutch women were selected for Block 10. Less than half survived to see the end of the war. Theresia van Praag caught a glimpse of her husband in the camp, just two months before he died.

Fourteen men and 44 women struggled through hell and survived. I say survived. They were physically alive at the end of the war.

Thursday, 23 September 1943 – The Vina Ghetto ceased to exist.

* * *

Monday, 27 September 1943. Gemmeker was presented with a book on his 36th birthday from everyone in the cabaret group. It was a book about the revues they had performed in the camp that Gemmeker so much enjoyed. Even Frau Hassel, sitting at his side in the front row, seemed to enjoy them. Gemmeker was presented with the book from his grateful Bühne Lager Westerbork. It was entitled *Humor und Melodie* with a title page stating the shows were directed by Max Ehrlich, the revues were by Willy Rosen, music was by Willy Rosen and Erich Ziegler, with between-scene links by Max Ehrlich. The album had been put together by Lange with photographs by Rudolf Werner Breslauer, cartoons by Leo Kok and Hans Margules and text by Max Ehrlich. Most of the references were to the show *Humor und Melodie* performed in September 1943.

The book is rather sycophantic in an eerie way. Why give your persecutor a present? The only reason is that you want to keep him happy and stay on his good side. Anything to not have to go east. Some in the camp had useful skills and were exempt or spared. This group had a skill for keeping Gemmeker amused and exploited it. No matter whether it made them unpopular, and after all they were doing something they enjoyed. There were 41 pages to see. No doubt Gemmeker showed it to people. It was not everyone who gets a present from such stars as he had under his thrall. There are humorous little scenes that poke a bit of fun at Gemmeker, not too much, such as further demands for 70 metres of material. Most of the stars appeared in it, and it contained a photo of the Westerbork Girls with Catharina Frank. To me they were all just as lovely. What went through Gemmeker's mind, we will never know.

* * *

Wednesday, 29 September 1943 – The Barneveld Camp for privileged Jews was closed and all were transferred to Westerbork, including the family of Alfred Drukker.

On the same day following raids and the closing of the Joodse Raad, Amsterdam was declared "Jew Free" apart from all of those hiding in safe houses.

* * *

The Sicherheitspolizei were angling for the 7,000 Jews employed as part of the Joodse Raad to be handed over. On Wednesday, 29 September1943, the eve of Rosh Hashana, the New Year, about 2,000 Jews, including members and leaders of the council, were arrested and sent to Westerbork. That really was the end of the Jewish Council in Amsterdam.

OCTOBER 1943

ONE TRANSPORT WITH 1007 DEPORTEES

Friday, 1 October 1943 – A great many Danish Jews escaped to Sweden and elsewhere.

* * *

Monday, 4 October 1943 – Himmler was in Posen at a conference. He made the first of two speeches to a patient audience of 33 Obergruppenführer, 51 Gruppenführer and eight Brigadeführer. This first speech lasted three hours. It was recorded and then transcribed by SS-Untersturmführer Werner Alfred Wenn. Two copies of the recorded speech survived from Nazi archives. Part of the speech was to justify past actions such as mass shootings, ghetto liquidations and the extermination camps as part of their higher purpose. Himmler stated, "... *wir hatten die Pflicht unserem Volk gegenüber das zu tun, dieses Volk, das uns umbringen wollte, umzubringen.*"

This translates as "... we had the duty to our people to do that, to kill this people who wanted to kill us." The speech was supposedly not for circulation.

* * *

Tuesday, 5 October 1943 – Reichskommissar Arthur Seyss-Inquart informed the General Kommisar that all *Volljuden* could be deported but not "Mischlings," children of mixed marriages or Jews who have an Aryan spouse and those who are exempt for other reasons, including Volljuden who had "protectors." Westerbork had a few of these Jews who paid for protection. If Willy Rosen's first wife had not divorced him, he would be one of these "spared" Jews. Elsbeth may well have been coerced into divorcing Willy by the Gestapo in Berlin.

* * *

Wednesday, 6 October 1943 – Himmler gave another speech about the difficult decisions he had to make concerning Jewish women and children. At first Jewish children had been left out. Himmler then gave orders that the children were also to "disappear from the earth." Albert Speer gets a mention, as he was at the conference. He claimed later he had had left before the speech was made, but then why did Himmler mention him? Speer wrote about his attendance in a letter to Mrs Jeanty: "There is no doubt – I was present as Himmler announced on 6 October 1943 that all Jews would be killed." Speer made many claims. As Hitler's favourite architect and minister for Armaments, he made use of Jewish slave labour. He made use of any slave labour from whatever source. He claimed he just asked for a labour force from Fritz Sauckel and that he did not know that the labour force was coming from concentration camps. Each man was as guilty as the other, yet the final decision to spare a life went in Speer's favour, not to his subordinate, Sauckel.

* * *

On Thursday, 7 October 1943, Gabriel Italie was writing in his diary about another inspection by SS officers. These happened every so often, and everyone in the camp realised that nothing good for the Jews came from them. These inspections were usually followed by new orders. A tour of the hospital usually meant that many would be discharged or transported to fill quotas. Germans were not a common sight in the camp, as there were so few of them. Gemmeker and the other officers were more than happy to work outside the camp wires. The odd German soldier walked through the camp. One could be evil one day and sweetness and light the next, if officers were around. Mirjam Bolle stated that work in the fields suddenly became much harder when the Untersturmführer appeared. Buckets are a lot heavier when filled to the top.

* * *

It was Wednesday, 13 October 1943, and Kommandant Gemmeker issued Camp Order 52. Hartog van de Goen from Barrack 64 had escaped. Gemmeker decided that his sister and mother, Vrouwtje and Rosine from Barrack 64, would be transferred to Barrack 67 as "S Cases," punishment cases, and would be transported east. He was explicit that this was a warning against any future escapes.

* * *

Thursday, 14 October 1943 – Reichleitner took a day off from duties at Sobibór.

Do you remember Ursula Stern? She was deported from Westerbork to Sobibór and was sorting belongings when she found all the little rucksacks from the Kindertransport. She was still alive in Sobibór. She sometimes worked as a member of the *Waldkommando*, the forest detail. There she cut down trees and sawed them into smaller parts. They needed the wood for burning the bodies. They had also dug wells and built barracks to store captured ammunition.

In Sobibór, plans had been made in utmost secrecy. One could not really trust anyone else in a camp. It was not that the Germans planted spies as they did within POW camps, but life was so precious that some would do anything to hang on to it, even if that meant betraying other Jews. Ursula or Ulla was one of the few in on the plans. She knew what but not when. In a one-hour period, they were to lure as many SS into the barracks and kill them. Soviets dressed as Germans would march Jews to the gate as if going to work outside. Ursula told no one of this, not even Selma Wijnberg, her friend. The only person you could trust was yourself, and who knew whether you would crack under torture? Poor Selma was ill with typhoid and might have said something in a fever. Yet Selma did know and said nothing. Things went awry at roll call. The Jews did not behave as they should have. First, roll call was early – confusion. Some did not know whether to line up, as the usual guards were not there – already dead. Second, a Ukrainian guard ran over. Many guards were Ukrainian. They supported the Germans, as they had pushed Stalin out of their lands. This guard tried to restore a bit of order, but then someone shouted that the war was over. The prisoners turned on the guard, and he was killed. The SS came on the scene, and a firefight broke out between armed prisoners and SS. Jews started to run everywhere. Ukrainian guards emptied their rifles into the backs of fleeing prisoners. The largest group, including Ursula, ran towards the main gate. Some climbed the fences and were blown up in the mine field. Ursula climbed a fence and knew about the mines. They all ran across the minefield, some fell from a bullet in the back, others stepped onto a mine. No one looked around; they ran. They ran for the forest, ran for their lives, ran without a thought. Ran. Ran. Ran.

Kathy Gokkes was running too. She ran too close to *Oberscharführer* Frenzel who shot her in the leg with his pistol. That did not stop Kathy, and she carried on running with Eda Lichtman. Both joined the partisans; one's price for freedom would be death.

Ursula stopped running. She fell in with a young Polish woman. They wandered around as if looking for something. A man appeared in front of them. A partisan. What would he do? The Polish woman ran forward and threw her arms around her husband's neck. This plan was wide and encompassed many who did not share their little piece of the plan. Obviously the partisans were involved. In some way, communication had been kept with the partisans as well as the Soviet POWs. Ursula joined the partisans. She had little choice. Her

189

chances of survival in the camp were slim; her chances outside the camp were a little less slim. The only difference was that she was at liberty and at least able to move around within the confines of a war area. In some respects, it was as bad as the camp, she thought. The group that she found herself with had been sent ahead of the main army. They did not just wander around and kill Germans wherever they saw them. They were highly organised and trained and had a chain of command. Ursula slept in the rain, in the snow and on the ice. But she lived. She could not afford to fall sick, and she could not afford to be wounded or injured. There was one other deportee who survived with Ursula, Saartie Wijnberg, Ursula's friend Selma. Selma had a good friend in Chaim Engel. He carried her backwards and forwards from the latrines when she was ill and saw to it that she got food. They had met in the sorting barracks. She had given him a knife, and he had helped her live by killing the SS guard. And then they ran together out of the main gate. They escaped and found refuge with a Polish couple. They paid for their shelter. They hid in a hay loft for nine months and came out when the Germans had retreated. But even then, their hardship was not over. They lost their baby while trying to get back to the Netherlands after the war and ultimately did not get back to the Netherlands either, because the Dutch police decided Selma was no longer Dutch because she had married a Pole. Can you imagine how she felt? After all that she had been through, Dutch bureaucracy turned its back on her. She was so upset with the action of her country, she no longer wanted to live in the Netherlands.

* * *

Monday, 18 October 1943 – The Jews in Rome were deported. Many Italians tried to aid them.

* * *

There had not been any deportations from Westerbork for a while. Sometimes this happened if there were disease in a camp or if

Westerbork was not included in transportations, as it was not a priority because actions may have been occurring elsewhere and the killing centres were at full capacity.

Tuesday, 19 October 1943. The train that had arrived yesterday from Vught bound for Auschwitz was ready to leave. The Berlin office of SS-Hauptsturmführer Franz Novak arranged for this train. On it were 1,007 transportees. Among them were 27 children, three offenders and five classified as sick. Klara Weenen-Goudeketting had her husband, Gerrit, fussing over her. She was in her fifth month of pregnancy. Gerrit and Klara had been married just over a year, and this was their first child. I know that none of these people should have been on the train, but some really should not have. You remember Eichmann's instruction that those working for the Reich were exempt? Well someone ignored that. Arthur Pop and Izak de Lange were on that train, and they worked for the Luftwaffe. Originally, they had been in Vught with their families, gone away to work and then were sent back to Vught to find that their families had gone east.

Philip Mechanicus was watching from a safe vantage point, away from the train but with a good view. Also watching was Dr Gabriel Italie. Philip saw the Jews from Vught arrive, no winter clothes and no exemption stamp in their documents, so they were going straight away, most likely on the train that they arrived on from Vught. Many had special permits. This meant that they were on what is called "Calmeyer's List." These were half-Jews on a list kept by the German Hans Calmeyer of the *Reichskommisariat*. He looked the other way where the authenticity of documents was concerned and passed people through as half-Jewish with a nod. Some say this came to about 3,700 Jews. He could not save all of them but was doing his best. Sometimes it was good to be on a list.

Gabriel saw about 30 wagons, which were not alike because they were from various countries across Europe. The French ones had "40 men – 8 horses" written on the side. Gabriel was told the wagons smelled, and he saw that they were given some sort of cleaning before the deportees boarded. As usual there were no goodbyes at the train. Others had to be in their barracks. Gemmeker knew how quickly a riot could be sparked, and he did not have the troops necessary for that sort of control.

Both Philip and Gabriel saw Georg Hermann Borchardt and Joseph Gompers. At the last minute there was a flurry of activity, and both were being taken off the train. It seemed they were on someone's list, but it was a temporary stay for both.

Georg Hermann would disappear in many ways. Willy Rosen would have known Georg, who had written a novel in 1908 called *Jettchen Gebert*. In 1918, it was made into a film by the famous Richard Oswald, with whom Willy had worked. Then the book was turned into the operetta *Wenn der weiße Flieder wieder blüht*, and the title song rose through the German record charts of that time. Willy knew that song. It was a hit and was sung by Willy's friend Austin Egen with the Marek Weber Orchestra. Unfortunately, Georg Hermann Borchardt's part was forgotten. He never got a mention. This was the lot of many Jewish composers and writers – their compositions were falsely attributed or even called folk songs.

Philip had sympathy for one man on the train. He did not know his name, but he knew he was a dentist. He shared something in common with Philip. They were both on a list; well, everyone was on one list or another, but they were on "Puttkammer's List." The Nazis liked Erich August Paul Puttkammer so much that he was called "Puttkammer Our Lord" by the Dutch Gestapo.

Puttkammer had been born in Luppisch in Poland in 1891 but was granted Dutch citizenship in June 1939. He worked at the *Rotterdamsche Bankvereeniging*, known in short as ROBAVER Bank. He was set up by the bank in a separate office with secretarial help to assist Jews. He used influence and money to get that "*Sperre*" stamp on documents. Jews then approached him to seek safety and, for a price, he was able to secure them that special stamp. He charged about 30,000 guilders per person. They would then be safe from deportation. Puttkammer was paying off Germans to leave the

Jews alone for a time. It cost each person over $11,000 or nearly £3,000. In the United States, you could buy at least three average size houses for that money, and in England, that was over five houses. It was a good deal of money. He accumulated about ten million dollars. If the Jews did not have the cash, he took gold, jewellery and anything that had value, even paintings. Puttkammer also allowed his bank account to be used by the Nazis to collect ransom monies. One family ransomed was the Salomon Mayer family. It was arranged by Margarethe Frielingsdorf in Zöpf's department on behalf of Berlin. Salomon paid 120,000 Swiss francs and an extra 50,000, and Frielingsdorf noted the transaction as complete through Basel on Wednesday, 21 October 1942; 170,000 Swiss francs was equal to $30,261 or the equivalent of a person in Sweden working for more than 33 years. It was a vast sum of money, nearly £10,000 or 13 large houses in Britain at that time. And still there was no guarantee to not have to go east. On the train sat one dentist who was proof of that. Philip Mechanicus himself as well as Paul Rehfisch and his family had also been duped by Puttkammer. Philip was waiting for his own day to come.

Philip had a memory of the wagons being sealed, as there had been outbreaks of polio, diphtheria and hepatitis at the camp. No one else confirmed it. Philip did not mention the British aircraft that flew over the camp. It caused quite a stir and some, unsuccessfully, had tried to slip away. Arthur Pop said there had been some excitement at this but that the overwhelming mood was one of gloom. If they were gloomy now, what were they when they arrived at Auschwitz? Arthur lived to say what it was like when they arrived at Auschwitz. It took until the fourth day, and they arrived on a Friday. An SS man told them to leave their luggage, as they would get it back later. Then there was the usual selection with 490 entering the camp and 506 going off the gas chambers. They were then put into quarantine because the camp commanders were worried about an epidemic that had been reported at Westerbork. So perhaps Philip was right about the wagons being sealed. This strikes me as odd. There were transports coming into Auschwitz all the time, yet the camp chose to accept nearly 500 from this train and put them into quarantine for a month when there were other transports for which that would not have been necessary. It was lucky for the 11 people who survived to the end of the war, ten men and a boy. When asked what he did for an occupation, Arthur lied and said he was a boxer. This meant he was fit enough to labour in the Jawischowitz coal mines.

These were the people involved in that transport: Ferdinand aus der Fünten, Adolf Eichmann, Albert Gemmeker, Will Lages, Franz Novak, Hans Albin Rauter, Gertrud Slottke, Otto Stange and Wilhelm Zöpf. They represented the following departments: The Central Office for Jewish Emigration in Amsterdam, *Reichstransportministerium* - *Judenangelegenheiten*, *Räumungsangelegenheiten* and *Schutzpolizei* along with the Marechaussee and the Rijksinspectie van de Bevolkingsregisters. It would typically be these people and organisations involved in all transports from Westerbork. The train was operated by the Deutsche Reichsbahn and Nederlandse Spoorwegen. It took the following route: Vught Camp, Westerbork Camp, Beilen, Drenthe, Nieuwe Schans, Groningen, Bremen, Hansa, Liegnitz – Silesia, Auschwitz-Birkenau in Nazi-occupied Poland.

That was Sukkot 1943. The gathering of the harvest and the miraculous protection of God should have been remembered. I am sure that difficult questions were asked of God in private prayer.

* * *

Thursday, 21 October 1943 – The Minsk Ghetto no longer existed.

* * *

Monday, 25 October 1943 – The Soviet Army liberated Dnepropetrovsk in Ukraine. Only 15 Jews were left from a population that had once numbered 80,000.

NOVEMBER 1943

ONE TRANSPORT WITH 995 DEPORTEES

Wednesday, 3 November 1943 – The Germans started *Operation Erntefest*. Around 43,000 Polish Jews were killed at the Lublin Reservation and Majdanek Concentration Camp. This concluded Operation Reinhard. It was undertaken to stem further Jewish revolts.

* * *

Thursday, 4 November 1943 – Julius Streicher wrote in the Nazi newspaper, *Der Stürmer*, about the disappearance of Jews from Europe and that the "Jewish Reservoir" in the East had also ceased to exist.

* * *

Monday, 8 November 1943 – Jozef Wins from Naarden was still alive in Radom. The ghetto was going to be closed, so the SS shot children and the elderly. The rest were to be transferred to a weapons factory at Szkolha. As the Soviets were advancing, it was decided to move the workforce to Tomaszow-Mazowiezki, 110 km away. The Soviets advanced farther, and the Germans retreated. There was constant movement, and Jozef ended up near Heilbronn, at Kochendorf, in the salt mines.

* * *

Wednesday, 10 November 1943, Eichmann convened a meeting in Amsterdam and had invited Wilhelm Zöpf, Erich Naumann and Gemmeker. I say "invited," as it was not a request but rather an order. Gemmeker was moving in the upper echelons. They were there to talk about 3,000 Jews who had been intended to be exchanged for Germans in Palestine who wished to return to Germany. There were 40 lists, all but two of them were torn up, and with that, all those Jews were therefore condemned. They discussed 2,500 Jews going to Bergen-Belsen, to the Star Camp, *Sternlager*. If ever Gemmeker denied being at this meeting, he only needed to be shown the minutes that included his name as being present. And you know they must have discussed the fate of Jews on any list that was torn up. This may well have involved discussion about the fate of certain groups as to which were to be kept alive.

* * *

Thursday, 11 November 1943 – Auschwitz Commander Höß became the new inspector for concentration camps. The new Kommandant at Auschwitz divided the camp into three sections. It was agreed that 400 Jews intended for Palestine along with 600 criminals, Jews who had broken some antisemitic law, were to be sent to Auschwitz. Now tell me that at that meeting the extermination of Jews was not discussed. How can you discuss Auschwitz and not know what it was?

Earlier that year, on 1 January 1943, Machiel van Oosten was murdered in Auschwitz. He had been separated from his wife and his two youngest sons. They were in Westerbork. He was in Auschwitz with his oldest son, Jonas, who had been named after Machiel's own father. Machiel's brother, Maurits, was also in Auschwitz. They were all from Assen. Jonas, at age 16, was murdered five days later on 16 January 1943. Maurits was murdered the following month on Sunday, 28 February. Let me list Jonas's immediate family so you can see the impact of the Nazi ideal on just a part of this family:

Grandfather Jonas died Thursday, 8 October 1942, aged 77.

Grandmother Gonda (Godschalk) died Thursday, 8 October 1942, aged 71.

Father Machiel died Monday, 1 January 1943, aged 43.

Mother Johanna (Jakobs) died Friday, 24 September 1943, aged 41.

Uncle Maurits van Oosten died Sunday, 28 February 1943, aged 41.

Brother Maurits Henk died Friday, 24 September 1943, aged ten.

Brother Israel Berty died Friday, 24 September 1943, aged 15.

Cousin Johanna Esther died Friday, 19 February 1943, aged 12.

Cousin Leo died Wednesday, 30 September 1942, aged 16.

Aunt Heintje died Friday, 29 February 1943.

All died? Rather they were murdered at Auschwitz. This was only a small part of the family. There were many others. Some families murdered by the Nazis did not have one surviving member to carry on their name or family.

* * *

In Westerbork, the polio epidemic had worsened since August, and transports had been suspended for nearly a month. On Monday, 15 November 1943, the quarantine was lifted. On Tuesday, 16 November, 995 people stood ready to leave Westerbork for Auschwitz. The epidemic would continue until December, but Eichmann was keen to see transports resume. Monday evening, the list was read aloud, and here they were, ready to travel. There were 281 men, 291 women, 257 elderly and 166 children. No longer exempt, there were also Jews from the Jewish Council. Philip Mechanicus saw many young men along with sick from the hospital and hospital workers. Gabriel Italie was there as well; his heart was touched by the plight of the orphans from the camp, leaving so early.

On the train, Ilse Ledermann-Citroen was busy writing a note. She would throw it from the train. She was expecting to go to Palestine, as were the others. There were 43 in her truck. She felt they were decent people, and they were. It was the others who were not, the Nazis who had put them into those wagons. She felt that the journey was going well. Ilse and her husband, Franz, had been holidaying in the Netherlands when their cousin told them not to go back to Berlin where Franz was a lawyer. He felt he had to go but returned when he was denied non-Jewish clients. Then the Nazis invaded the Netherlands. A good friend got them false papers, but Franz thought hiding was too dangerous, so they complied with the German orders. And now they sat on the train, Franz and Ilse Ledermann, holding hands, smiling at each other and those around them. She cared for him, who was 15 years older and not doing as well as she was. They had been in the camp since 20 June. By Friday they would both be dead.

Lex (Samson) van Weren, the trumpet player, sat in another wagon and looked around at his travelling companions, musing as to why he had come to be there. He felt a little comforted, as Rabbi Dasberg from Utrecht was there too. The rabbi would sing and pray through the journey. Lex was a bit aggrieved because most of their valuables had been taken from them by Lippmann. Rosenthal & Co. at Westerbork. The train stopped, and the doors opened. The green-uniformed police demanded money, watches, and pens – anything of value that they had left. It happened every time the train stopped, five or six times. The green police beat them. For ten hours, they sat in a goods yard in Bremen where there had been an Allied bombardment. Then the train arrived at Auschwitz. At dawn the doors opened.Another survivor told what happened next. Jacob de Vries said they had to leave their luggage, the men had to line up and the women and children had to step forward. They were then loaded into lorries, more than there was room for, and driven away. Franz and Ilse went with them. There were 220 men left, or so Jacob thought. Among those men was Georg Hermann Borchardt, the German writer; he would live for another month.

The camp recorded 275 men as entering the camp, with 189 women. There were no children. They had gone with the 531 others to the gas chambers. Those who entered the camp were quarantined for a month. Lex, Jacob and 14 other men survived.

* * *

Friday, 19 November 1943, a rumour was going around Westerbork camp that the next train was going to Bergen-Belsen. This is what happens when you put thousands of people together. Information is power, and one needs be the first to know. Sometimes rumours prove to be true; sometimes they prove to be false. In this instance, it was announced that there would be a transport on the 23rd of November. Volunteers were sought, but no one came forward.

* * *

Sunday, 21 November 1943. Fräulein Slottke visited Westerbork. She was interested in the people with American or British passports. She wanted to send a transport to an exchange camp near Celle in Hannover called "Bilsenbergen." It was actually Bergen-Belsen. She wanted 1,000 people, but there were not enough, only 400. They added the veterans and those destined for Palestine, and the numbers only reached 600. She indicated that the third and fourth lists were now valid again. Those people would also be exchanged. Irvin van Gelder observed the goings on and thought it quite a party, in an amusing way. Henry with his wife, Hetje, and their two children, Irvin and Sonja, had been hidden by the family of Klaus van der Veer. But they were arrested in December 1942 and sent to Westerbork.

* * *

Monday, 22 November 1943. Philip Mechanicus was not very happy, nor were a number of other people happy about what they have just heard. Any parcels sent to the camp were now to be opened before they reached the barracks. There was a strong suspicion that cigarettes, tobacco and other esteemed comestibles were to go missing.

* * *

Tuesday, 23 November 1943. The train was standing waiting. It was a proper passenger train with carriages. Still not enough had come forward to travel, so the day before, Slottke forced all those who were eligible to register for the train. There were a thousand of them. Philip Mechanicus said it looked as if they were off on a pleasure trip. Then it was announced that a freeze has been ordered on all trains out of Westerbork. The transport would not be leaving. Everyone was ordered back to work.

The train left later that evening – empty. Siegfried Seidl at Bergen-Belsen was informed that his "Foreign Jews" would not be arriving, but they might be coming in the new year on the 11th of January.

* * *

Sunday, 28 November 1943 – The conference held in Teheran between Churchill, Roosevelt and Stalin vowed to bring those responsible for the atrocities to justice by returning them to the countries where the crimes had been committed for judgement.

* * *

Thursday, 30 November 1943 – Etty Hillesum died in Auschwitz, but she is still remembered.

200

DECEMBER 1943
ZERO TRANSPORTS WITH 0 DEPORTEES

Epidemic

Thursday, 2 December 1943 – The first Jews from Vienna started to arrive at Auschwitz.

* * *

On Sunday, 5 December 1943, *Sinterklaas* visited every barrack in the camp. Philp Mechanicus told how Sinterklaas made jokes in many of the barracks. Gemmeker was either in a good mood or away in Düsseldorf.

* * *

Sunday, 12 December 1943 – Himmler's house had been bombed. Marga was glad that Himmler was home to sort out the mess caused by the bombing. It was sorted very quickly – of course. She had donated to others who had been bombed out and lost everything. Marga had people staying with her on a semi-permanent basis: Mrs

Hofemeister (her husband was Oberst, later General Major, Georg Hofmeister, who was very ill), Mrs Albers (who was destitute), Mrs Rausch, Mrs Ney and the Rogozinskis.

* * *

Thursday, 16 December 1943 – The senior surgeon at Auschwitz reported 106 castrations.

* * *

Friday, 17 December 1943 – Himmler celebrated an early Christmas with his family. Gudrun got a "thousand" presents from her father.

* * *

Willy Rosen's revues had been running since July. There have been various programmes, allowing for new cast members and cast who had left. By this time, the group had run three versions of *Bunter Abend*, three versions of *Bravo da Capo* and various versions of *Humor und Melodie*. They had an enlarged stage built from the wood salvaged from a synagogue, lights, curtains and anything that a professional theatre might have. Members of the group were allowed out of the camp to source material for costumes and scenery. Willy was able to liaise with publishers to claim royalties for new and old songs that had not been properly licenced. Members of the group had special passes which allowed them to be out after curfew, so long as it entailed walking back to their barracks from a rehearsal. Gemmeker bent every rule and convention for his revue group. For anyone who had been a follower of cinema or theatre, it must have been quite something to have had these people performing for you in your camp. Tickets were still rationed though, as the hall was still the same size. Gemmeker funded the cost of everything, that is, if it could not be requisitioned. By now the group had grown. There was a proper front of house, hairdressers, costume makers, choreographers, and a large orchestra made up of well-known musicians, especially artists such as Martin Roman, Maurits van Kleef and Jacques Barendse. Hans Krieg, a composer, was the rehearsal pianist with Ludwig Belitzer as conductor. Theatres in the Weimar Republic would have fallen over themselves trying to book these people to appear.

On Saturday, 16 October 1943, *Bravo da Capo* version three had opened. At least 23 people were working backstage, which did not include the seamstresses or costume makers known as Gruppe Hertzberg. There was an orchestra of 11 musicians and a chorus line of eight women. Seventeen performed on stage. The front of house was run by Eugen Frankenstein.

You can easily see that here was a group of well over 50 people that was exempt from transport, for the moment, while Gemmeker was content. Even the great Kurt Gerron appeared in *Bravo da Capo* to perform a one-man scene *Eifersucht,* "Jealousy." This was not his first show; he had appeared in *Humor und Melodie II* with Camilla Spira but as guest and had not been included on the programme. It had also been Camilla's last performance. Kurt Gerron, originally called Gerson, had lived the high life. His house had been in the most fashionable part of Berlin and he had premiered the role of Tiger Brown in the original production of *Die Dreigroschenoper,* "*The Threepenny Opera,*" by Brecht and Weil and had sung with the *Dreigroschenband,* conducted by Lewis Ruth (Ludwig Rüth), one of the premier band leaders of the Weimar Republic. Gerron had appeared in and directed 55 films. His rotund physique and moonlike face were recognisable across Europe. He was another whom people had begged to get out, but he had stayed and left it to too late. With the rise of the Nazis, he had gone to Paris and then Amsterdam appearing at Amsterdam's premier theatre, the Stadsschouwburg. Here he reprised *The Threepenny Opera* and is famous for his recording of Mack the Knife's "Shark Song." Like Rosen and the others, he was caught by the sudden invasion of the Netherlands by the Germans with their theories on race. Kurt found himself interned in Westerbork, with his wife and a host of others from film and theatre. They were all in this mess together. They swapped old stories and reminisced about days past, congratulated each other on past productions and thought of others who had left, like Dietrich, Sig Arno and Curt Bois, a good friend of Kurt's. They were more like *Dick und Doof,* Laurel and Hardy, but Curt with a "C" was even smaller than Laurel, and Kurt with a "K" was bigger than Hardy. If Kurt had gone to America, he would have done as well as other film directors like Wilder, Ernst Lubitsch or Fritz Lang had. There were times in Westerbork when they laughed at having "got one over" on the Nazis with the Jewish involvement in the dubbing of *Snow White.* They laughed at the thought of German audiences watching Disney's film not realising they were listening to Jewish Voices.

Camilla Spira had been dropped from the programme and had left that autumn. She had been arrested as a half-Jew. Her father was Jewish Fritz Spira. He was an actor from Austria, born 1877, but he had settled in Berlin and appeared in early films. He was arrested in 1941 in Vienna and sent to a concentration camp. He was already dead by this time. Camilla's mother, Lotte, also a theatre star, died shortly after. Somehow Camilla met with *SS-Oberführer* Walter Schellenberg, who was head of the Foreign Intelligence Service. He gave her a name to contact, which was Hans Calmeyer. She found about "Calmeyer's List" and dutifully reported to him that her mother had told her in 1933 that she was illegitimate and that her father was Victor Palfy, a Hungarian. Calmeyer issued Camilla with a pass that allowed her to leave Westerbork. She was collected by a large black limousine. Later, evidence from an anthropological report completed by Hans Weinert, an investigation by the Gestapo and various photographs of the Hungarian, Camilla was pronounced a full Aryan and avoided the fate that awaited so many. By doing this, she also ensured her Jewish husband, Hermann Eisner, and her children were safe from deportation. I suppose one cannot criticise her for denying any Jewish ancestry that she might have had in these circumstances. She saved the lives of her family, who were Jewish. I imagine that there was some talk in Westerbork about what she had done.

* * *

On Tuesday, 21 December1943, the first candle of Chanukah was lit. People gathered and spoke of hope. It is not the "Jewish Christmas." If ever they needed to remember the triumph of light over darkness, these were the times. The first candle of the menorah, sending out its light into the dark corners, glowed on the faces of those assembled. Westerbork was allowed a proper menorah and proper candles. If you left Westerbork and walked east non-stop for 50 hours and knew your route, you could reach Bergen-Belsen. There too they were celebrating Chanukah. They had saved fat from scraps of food and pulled threads from clothes and twisted them to make a wick. Their menorah was an old potato. The twelve children in the camp were given dreidels carved from their wooden shoes. Twelve children. Is there not hope there, one for each tribe? Under pain of death, people made their way to Barrack 10. They waited for the *Bluzhever Rebbe*, the oldest rabbi in the camp, who would say the Chanukah prayers. Choking back his tears, for he had lost his family, the rabbi in a soft voice chanted the three blessings:

"Blessed are you, Lord, our God, sovereign of the universe, who has kept us alive, sustained us, and enabled us to reach this season."

בָּרוּךְ אַתָּה אֲדֹנָי אֱלֹהֵינוּ מֶלֶךְ הָעוֹלָם שֶׁהֶחֱיָנוּ וְקִיְּמָנוּ וְהִגִּיעָנוּ לִזְּמַן הַזֶּה

They all wept. Not one was without loss. Can you imagine a more moving moment in such pitiful circumstances? The rabbi reminded them that they were joining with Jews everywhere, they were one with the Jews in Westerbork and they were one with the Jews all over the world. The rabbi starkly told them that whatever would befall them, the Jewish nation would survive. God would see to that.

By Tuesday of next week, it would be day eight of Chanukah.

* * *

Friday, 24 December 1943. Christmas and Chanukah were banned in Westerbork on the orders of Gemmeker. The Ordedienst went to Barracks 73 to see that the Catholic converts from Judaism were not celebrating. They were not allowed one twig of green or a candle. They were not even allowed to keep Sundays. Gemmeker had just come back from Düsseldorf and his wife. Perhaps this had put him in a bad mood. There was speculation around the camp to explain his irritable mood; perhaps Germany was losing the war? Yet Gemmeker put on a great display in the hall for invited guests from Amsterdam. Rudolf Breslauer was told to take photographs, and Jews had to dress as waiters to serve the guests. There was greenery everywhere for Gemmeker and his celebrants.

JANUARY 1944

THREE TRANSPORTS WITH 2,855 DEPORTEES

Monday, January 1944 – The Soviets pushed the Germans back to the original Polish border with Soviet. The Red Army had rid the Soviet Union of the Wehrmacht.

* * *

Monday, 3 January 1944 – Reichleitner, previously Kommandant at Sobibór, was killed by Italian partisans. Unfortunately, hardly any of the inmates remained there to cheer the news.

* * *

Things at Westerbork had been quiet. There had been a few comings, of course, but there had not been any goings. The epidemic was over, and there had not been any transports for eight weeks. Now it was Tuesday, 11 January 1944, and the trains had returned. It seemed, especially to Dutch Jews, that it was mostly they who had been sent east. They were right. There were not many Jews left in the Netherlands. There would be another 1,037 going east today, headed to Bergen-Belsen. Bergen-Belsen was a residential camp, *Aufenthaltslager*, a camp where one stayed. It had opened in late autumn in 1943 and was now becoming a concentration camp. It held certain groups of Jews that were valued for exchange, as per Kaltenbrunner's instructions of last 31 August. Out of those destined for exchange, only about 350 ever reached the foreign country they had been destined to go to.

Fred Schwarz was an old hand. He had been at Westerbork since 1940 and had watched the trains leaving, but this one he remembered. He noted that everyone was paranoid about their papers. The papers had to be right, or they would not be going to Palestine but to Auschwitz, which was not an exchange camp. Everyone knew that much. The papers were checked, re-checked and checked again. While the deportees boarded the train, near-audible sighs of relief could be heard. Philip Mechanicus noted this train as it left in the middle of the day. It was due to leave at one o'clock. They could take as much as they could carry, and there was no weight limit. Many watched the departure. Many others carried on playing cards or chess, as they had seen it all before. Philip then noted that the train did not leave until the early evening. There were 1,037 on board: 436 for Palestine, 385 for a German-British exchange and others for foreign exchange, along with some sick and even some Soviet citizens and diamond workers.

Perhaps Gemmeker chatted with Alfred Käsewieter, if he were commanding this train to Bergen-Belsen. Käsewieter and the Begleitkommando would accompany the train all the way to Bergen-Belsen.

Sitting in one of the carriages was Mirjam Bolle. She worked for the Joodse Raad and was accompanied by her family. They were cramped because of their own luggage; she and her sister sat on top of the rucksacks on the seats. Then the Flying Column arrived and started to put more suitcases in each compartment. The train was cold, but they thought it would warm up when the engine started. The train left the camp at half past five. As soon as it was outside of the camp, it stopped again. Mirjam did not say why, but it was most likely for the formal handover from the camp to the Wehrmacht guards. At a quarter-past six, the train moved off again. It also stopped to pick up more guards for the journey. Mirjam found out about the provisions. They had not been loaded, and the train remained unheated. Mirjam Bolle was deported from Westerbork to Bergen-Belsen on 11 January 1944. In Bergen-Belsen, she and others on the train saw the people who would be going to Theresienstadt, but they had not been allowed to speak with them. Eventually, they would be sent to Theresienstadt, although some would not reach the ghetto. Mirjam herself would actually get on a train on Monday, 26 June 1944 and reach Palestine.

In another part of the train sat the van Gelder family, Henry, Jetje, Irvin and Sonja. They eventually made it to Slottke's train, which she had difficulty putting together last November when she had visited the camp. The family would first go to Bergen-Belsen.

Mischa Gelber was five years old when the Nazis invaded the Netherlands. He was now nine years old and on the train with his family. His father had been told by friendly police that the Jews were going to be rounded up. They believed that they did not have to worry, as they had Red Cross certificates that would take them to Palestine. So they did not hide and were indeed rounded up. The certificates would save them, for a time. They had been at Westerbork for five months but were now bound for Bergen-Belsen. They were placed in the Star Camp. The family spent the day together but were separated at night. Both Mischa and his father would contract typhus, and they would all see the piles of dead around the camp. Yet there was further suffering to endure.

Israel Taubes was one of those fortunate few who actually reached Palestine.

Later he remembered that night, how the Germans claimed that postcards had been thrown out of the windows, and as punishment everyone had to hand over their pens and anything else of value. The train stopped at Nieuweschans to exchange locomotives. It stopped farther for several hours at the Soltau freight yard. Mirjam reckoned the train travelled for 14 hours at a slow speed. At 10:00 am on the

Wednesday, the train stopped at the Bergen freight ramp. They saw Waffen-SS soldiers who were in a fighting unit and who stood at 30-metre intervals with rifles unslung and dogs. The compartments were opened, and everyone was ordered out. The luggage, the sick and the old were put into trucks and then had to march to the camp six kilometres away. They saw Kommandant Obersturmbannführer Adolf Haas, 50 years old, square features and a Hitler-like moustache. He had been in the post for less than a month. In rows of five, they marched across Lüneberg Heath for two hours. Upon reaching the camp, there was a roll call, registration, theft of any surviving money, and they were segregated by sex and allocated barracks.

Some 248 children had been on that train. Of all the trains leaving Westerbork, this had one of the highest survival rates – 385.

* * *

Philip said that the word on the street was that the next train was going to Theresienstadt. Someone from the camp office had told someone, who told someone else, and within an hour, it was throughout the whole camp. It was Tuesday, 18 January 1944, and the train was due to depart at 10:42 precisely. Zöpf had told the Gestapo in Prague that this was so. There were a great many people involved in this transport, not just the Jews. Many were interested in what was going to happen, even someone from the *Reichskanzlei*. Philip knew many people were involved in arranging this transport. He seemed to know a great deal and had good sources. Gemmeker was preparing for Theresienstadt, as were Slottke and Zöpf. Zöpf sent a detailed "manifest" of the train a week later, which Gemmeker had prepared. Included in the manifest to Obersturmführer Anton Burger, Kommandant of Theresienstadt, was an instruction to disregard any worthless passport from Honduras or Paraguay. The countries had only paid lip service to Jewish requests for assistance and would not honour them. Every category of "inmate" had been discussed with Eichmann, who decided personally whether the

210

category would be included. War veterans could now take their families; of these, there were 385. Nearly a year ago, Gemmeker had started his "one thousand list" as it was known in the camp. On it were 1,807 names, all German Jews. Gemmeker had added Dutch names to "keep the peace" in the camp and to avoid shouts that it was biased towards the Germans. He needed a quiet, model camp.

Dr Fritz Spanier from Düsseldorf served as the chief medical officer. I said I would let you know why Gemmeker regarded this doctor favourably – Fritz had been Gemmeker's general practitioner before the war. There were some who had worked for years to run the camp in an orderly way. First, there were the 12 administrators, the hospital staff, the Jewish police and of course the actors and others from the Bühne group. The last category was Gemmeker's pet group, his favourites who provided him with a great deal of pleasure. Some in the camp referred to their activity as "A Dance on the Grave" – *Ein Tanz auf dem Grab*. Philip was probably unaware that four members of the cabaret group were on the train. Ruth Pagener, dancer, number 526 and the large figure of Isidor Herman Feiner, number 187. Feiner had sung in the Halle revues in the Weimar Republic and recorded many popular songs, notably *"Großmama Lass Dir Die Haare Schneiden,"* "Grandma, Get Your Hair Cut!" He had sung with the top bands in Germany. Among the crowd was also Arthur Joseph Durlacher, the opera singer, stagehand and singer for *De Gruppe Bühne Lager Westerbork*, the cabaret group, destined for Theresienstadt, then Auschwitz and then on to Bergen-Belsen. He sat looking at the card in his hand, reducing him to a number, 166. With him was his son, Gerhard, whose hands were sore from working the camp forges. He followed his father on to Auschwitz. His mother died in Stutthof, in northern occupied Poland – not a death camp but where more than 60,000 people died or were murdered, by shooting, lethal injections, hypothermia, beatings or disease. Somewhere on the train was another member of the group, Fritz Bernhard, number 46, towards the front. Not all from the group were exempt. The cabaret stars were not his only favoured people. There were some who impressed Gemmeker with their enthusiasm, their prominence and their money also. None were immune though. Gemmeker could use them to fill up the train if spaces needed filling. Philip reported that members of the 1,000 list had found themselves on the list for deportation again this time. They thought they would only go on the last train and then only to Theresienstadt. More than half were leaving, and this included some of the most prominent. For some reason, it was felt around the camp that Theresienstadt was a friendly alternative in former Czechoslovakia, and the Germans were using passenger trains. Some volunteered for Theresienstadt rather than Auschwitz. Philip was a little scornful of those who thought somewhere else would be better than where they were now. They were, in fact, all worse.

Hilde Bischoff was sitting in the train. She had volunteered. She felt it was an "elite" transport. It left on time at 10:42 am. There were cattle carts for the food, 1,000 loaves of bread, 100 kilograms of jam, 30 kilograms of butter and 42 kilograms of sausage for the deportees and 25 kilos for the guards. The train stopped just at the camp gate, where the German forces boarded and counted the deportees. It was at this point that the German Army accepted control of this train. Hilde was allowed to step out of her carriage at every stop and even had her photo taken. The ride lasted 24 hours, the doors opened and coffee was put inside by Jews wearing slightly different yellow stars from hers. The doors were then locked, and the deportees spent the next 24 hours sitting and waiting. That must have been a stressful time wondering what was going to happen.

There were two special people on that train who were being well cared for. In other words, nothing was to happen to them: Hartog Cohen and Lion Morpurgo. They were fine art restorers. They were restoring pictures for the *Gemäldegalerie Dresden* at Westerbork, but Gemmeker caused a bit of a panic by putting them on the transport. They had been restoring four works of art that were destined for the art gallery in Linz. You might know who regarded Linz as his hometown. It was in Linz that Hitler had decided he would build a huge art gallery, designed by Albert Speer, to house his art collection and that of the state. We know that the Nazis looted a great deal of art, but at the same time, across Europe, works of art were being selected by teams of "buyers" for Linz and for Hitler's own collection. Many works of arts, typically belonging to Jews, were on the market at considerably reduced prices. Hitler, you know, did pay for all his paintings, but these experts were art collectors who also slipped more than the odd few away for themselves. Hartog and Lion were working for Hitler in restoring these works of art. The order for the safe treatment for these two Jews came from the highest authority, and if that meant the relaxation of the "cleansing" of the Netherlands, that was how it was to be. Seyss-Inquart had ordered a workshop to be built for the two men at Westerbork. But time ran out, and they were to be deported.

Dr. Erhard Göpel was responsible for "special cases," and he agreed that the paintings could go with them to Theresienstadt. Hans Albin Rauter sent an order to Gemmeker at Westerbork to that effect on 14 January. One of the art experts wanted some materials he had left at his home, so he was escorted to collect them. There was a problem in that there was not a workshop at Theresienstadt. Eichmann's liaison officer, Hauptsturmführer Moes, would ensure there was a workshop at the ghetto. It was at this point that someone got cold feet, most likely Eichmann himself. It had to be someone with some authority in Berlin to stop this project, which was sanctioned by high-ranking officers in the Netherlands. These paintings had most likely been obtained by means that could not be called legitimate, forced purchase. Eichmann did not want these paintings to be stolen. It would seem few people could be trusted in the Reich. An agreement was reached. The paintings would be stored in the Jewish Affairs safe in Prague. Lion and Hartog, together with their families, would be sent back to Westerbork. This went on through the rest of January, all of February and into March. At that point, Seyss-Inquart intervened and said that he would take personal responsibility for the paintings. That meant everyone was off the hook if anything went wrong and Hitler needed to find someone to blame. These paintings must have had a considerable value and even more so after restoration by two of the world's best restorers. Lion and Hartog were sent back in February to Theresienstadt, and the paintings also followed. They arrived Saturday, 26 February 1944. Both were able to attend to the paintings while in Theresienstadt. They were supposed to return to the Netherlands when they had finished, but someone spotted the opportunity for another enterprise. Camp Kommandant Karl Rahm, newly appointed and recently promoted to Sturmbannführer, kept the two and made them paint pictures that he sold. I do not know for certain what happened to the two of them, but I guess Rahm did not want witnesses. Lion may have died in May 1944, but Hartog was kept on and died in September 1944 in Auschwitz, having left Theresienstadt on the 28th of September.

From that train, 132 survived the war.

It was Tuesday, 25 January 1944, and, in the scene Philip described, rain was lashing down. There were 26 wagons to carry 1,000 deportees. It was 948, but 1,000 is not a bad estimate on Philip's part. There were 168 children among those headed for Auschwitz. The youngest is only a month old. Gemmeker had made up most of the numbers with those being punished for misdemeanours. They were mostly likely people caught in hiding. There are 590 of them. There are many young men from Aliyah, the Diaspora heading for Palestine, as well. There are elderly men from hospital and 31 children who do not even have names. They were orphans, who no German can spare a thought for. To Gemmeker, they were Jews no one wanted in the Netherlands. One ten-year-old had held his breath and raised his temperature by 0.1 degree so he would not have to travel, as if someone could not have misread the thermometer, said it was 40 degrees and that he was unfit for travel. Gabriel also saw that the transport was for the old, the "criminal," the sick and the young. All these to Gemmeker were eating into his budget.

Esther Presburg was cursing her luck in one of the wagons. She had been in hiding for 18 months before being arrested. She thought about Cornelis Johannes (Kees) Kaptein, the head of the Dutch detectives, a fervent Jew Hater and very violent. He had already arrested hundreds of Jews. He was 28 years old and already a rich man, having relieved many of his prisoners of their belongings. He would beat you rather than look at you.

Little Charles Salomon Viskoop was in one of the wagons too. No mother or father; they were both dead. Charles was ten months old. His father had died 11 days after Charles's birth on 17 February 1943, and Sem Viskoop had died on Sunday, 28 February without ever seeing his son. The mother of Charles, Veronica, had hidden Charles in a safe house. Veronica was arrested and sent to Westerbork in September 1943. She was then sent on to Auschwitz and died there on Tuesday, 30 November. She went to her death still thinking her son was safe. On Friday, 24 December, almost a month after her death, Charles was betrayed and brought into Westerbork. Who would betray a baby? Gemmeker was sending a ten-month-old orphan to Auschwitz. You know without asking what happened to baby Charles. He was one of the 229 who went straight to the gas chamber. I hope that someone held him tight as they died together, two lost souls bound together. That would be the best that we could hope for Charles.

Josephina Kesner found herself in another truck with her sister, Florence, and friends. There was not even enough room to sit down, as they were packed in like inanimate goods for transportation She held some food for her parents, hoping that at Auschwitz they would be reunited when working on the farms. The others told her to eat the food, but she refused with a teenager's determination. When the train arrived, they were greeted by Mengele with his shiny boots. They were so innocent. Germans and dogs to the left and right; old people and young children on the lorries. They watched the flames coming from the chimneys. When they asked, they were told that that was the *Himmelkommando*, heaven's detail. Their parents, Salomon and Maria, had already joined that group just two months' previous.

Esther was able to talk about the journey. It followed the usual route. The train stopped to empty the barrels, and just before they got to Auschwitz, they were given bread and sausage. Upon arrival on the following Thursday, they left their luggage by the train and went through the selection. Roosie Corper-Blik and Esther were two who survived. Roosie had been destined for Palestine. Of those arriving, 259 were selected, and 689 were murdered immediately. There would be 28 others with Roosie and Esther who would see the end of the war, including Josephina and Florence.

* * *

Tuesday, 25 January 1944 – Hans Frank, the Gauleiter of Poland, noted that out of 2,500,000 Jews who were in the general government, there are now only 100,000 left. While shaving that morning, he would have admired "The Lady with the Pearl Earring" by Vermeer. Riches untold were at his disposal.

* * *

Tuesday, 25 January 1944 – You might recall that 23 of the 305 deportees aboard the transport in September bound for Theresienstadt were kept behind in Bergen-Belsen. Frank Onno-Levita claimed that several Dutch Jews had already died in Bergen-Belsen. Others were murdered elsewhere. Esther de Rosa, who was pregnant, had been deported together with her husband, Louis, had given birth to Anton on 6 December 1943. Without warning, parents and child were sent to Theresienstadt with 279 others on Tuesday, 25 January 1944. Louis was later sent to Auschwitz in September and died there. Esther and Anton followed in October and were murdered upon arrival. From that original transport on Tuesday, 14 September 14 1943, only 51 survived.

* * *

Thursday, 27 January 1944 – Moscow announced the siege of Leningrad which had started in September 1941 was now over.

FEBRUARY 1944

SIX TRANSPORTS WITH 4,562 DEPORTEES

If you are thinking again that by now there really could not be many Jews left in the Netherlands, you are right. Otto Bene informed Reich Commissioner Arthur Seyss-Inquart that 100,000 Jews had "left" the country. They both knew what that meant. Gemmeker had played his part in this.

At Camp Westerbork, the original inmates were no longer the majority as they had been before these transports. Their deportation had been blocked for various reasons depending on which list they sat. Those lists continue to lose their exemptions. Jewish spouses in mixed marriages could now be deported (45), as could Jews who had spouses in neutral countries (70). There were the "T-Kinder," children destined for Theresienstadt to join their parents. Someone in the camp office was trying to pull the wool over other administrators' eyes. These children were supposedly going to join their parents in Theresienstadt, but their parents were still in Westerbork. There were some who had helped maintain the camp and were part of the camp organisation (141). There were the elderly soldiers who had been decorated or were disabled (118), and then there were some adjudged as contributing to the war effort (53). A total of 427 were at Gemmeker's disposal.

Harster had received agreement that Jews from some ten foreign countries could be deported. Jews from Hungary, Romania, Spain, and Turkey could be repatriated, but there was a restricted window during which these countries would be allowed to take back these people.

Tuesday, 1 February 1944. A transport from Westerbork left for Buchenwald. It seems to be common knowledge that Jews who went to Buchenwald were murdered. Nothing was ever heard of about the first group from the Netherlands that went to Buchenwald in February 1941. Now transports were leaving from Westerbork to Buchenwald; mostly foreign nationals had been sent to Buchenwald. Buchenwald was one of the first camps on German soil and opened in 1937. The first prisoners held there were mainly communists. Over the gates were the words *Jedem das Seine,* "To each his own." The Kommandant at this time was SS-Obersturmbannführer Hermann Pister, who had been in Himmler's motor pool and was "old," at 58, compared with many in the SS. The prisoners were mainly Jews, Poles and Slavs, the mentally ill and physically disabled, political prisoners, Romani people, Freemasons, criminals, homosexuals and POWs. Homosexuals were on the bottom rung of life and were subject to more beatings and torture than were other groups. The POWs were primarily flyers. Many of these had been apprehended out of uniform in occupied France and were there as "spies." Buchenwald was mainly a work camp where inmates were worked to death. This was known as *Vernichtung durch Arbeit.* Buchenwald was also a site for experimentation, especially with vaccines. The death rate overall was one in four. The many sub-camps supported German industries. Little wonder that if anyone knew anything about Buchenwald, it was somewhere where they did not wish to go.

Jews who were due for repatriation were not to be sent to occupied Poland, but Gemmeker could send them to Theresienstadt, Buchenwald and Ravensbrück; women and children in particular went to Ravensbrück.

The transport on the first of the month was of Hungarian Jews to Buchenwald, travelling in the first part of the train. Most of them had been at Westerbork since September 1942. They went without their wives or children and were part of "Operation Repatriation". They were not to be treated as prisoners. Their wives would be sent to Ravensbrück the following Saturday.

When the train arrived at the ramp at Bergen-Belsen, the wagon with the Hungarian Jews was uncoupled and proceeded to Buchenwald. In the carriage was Samuel Kallus Arijowicz. He and his wife, Sarah, had been duped by Friederich Weinreb who had a deferment list that was no more than a list of names. You know the pattern: Take money from the Jews, write their names down for them to see and tell them they will be exempt. Weinreb was a respected Jewish scholar, the last person you would think could do such a thing. He fabricated a story about a train going to Lisbon. He even had a German general who had approved the list but who did not exist. Weinreb had been arrested and sent to Westerbork in January 1943. Some German's brain went tickety-tock and came up with a further ruse. There were some on Weinreb's list who were in hiding. If Weinreb were released, he could go back and draw these Jews out of hiding. Weinreb was allowed home to entice these Jews out of hiding with his lies. The tale this time was that Jews were going to be exchanged for Germans who were in Brazil. In February, the plug was pulled on this scheme, and Weinreb went into hiding with his family. He survived the war.

Samuel Arijowicz knew of five Jews who died within two months of getting to Buchenwald. Sarah was sent to Ravensbrück. Binyamin Zeev, also known as Ignaz Wilhelm Laufer, survived. He had been forced to work at Rehmsdorf manufacturing gasoline from coal. They were always in fear of being bombed. Of these 27 sent to Buchenwald, 11 survived.

* * *

On board of the part of the train destined for Bergen-Belsen were 908 Jews. Originally 921 were supposed to go, but some had been discarded, and some had gone into hiding. Gemmeker still applied the rule that if someone escaped from a barrack, ten people from that barrack would be transported. The chances of evading capture were slim. Even if the escape attempt failed and you did not make it, ten people were still sent east with you. Gemmeker was such a gentleman.

On this train were also 570 people who had associations with a foreign country. Of those, 247 thought they should be going to Palestine, although only 42 had approval. Thirty-five held Dutch and British passports, but we know how Gemmeker felt about those, even though 18 had been approved to go via Switzerland. Twenty-eight had siblings abroad, 18 on South American passports and ten children who were regarded as British or American. Two hundred children were on the train, 141 Germans and 98 classified as sick.

Two of the people on the train were Kurt and Lily Zielenziger. They had passports for Ecuador but fell afoul of the order to ignore passports from Ecuador. Kurt died in Bergen-Belsen on 19 July 1944. Lily wrote to her sister in Geneva informing her she was a widow. The aunt told Erich, her nephew, that his father was dead. Erich's mother died on what was called "The Lost Train" to Theresienstadt. She died of typhoid and was buried in the mass grave at Tröbitz with the dentist Paul Rehfisch.

One family on this train had travelled all over. Walter Blumenthal and his family were from a little town called Hoya near Hannover. Walter had already lost most of his siblings through tragic accidents and illnesses before the war. Life was therefore precious to this family. In 1938, things for the family changed radically. Walter's parents had a shop in Hoya and were well respected. They had found it difficult when the Nazis ordered the boycott of Jewish shops and businesses. The grandparents were old and had not wanted to move, but they both died within months of each other. There was then no reason to stay in Hoya. The shop was sold at a knock-down price along with stock and furniture, and the family moved to Hannover. Things in Hannover were not much better; they were there following the Reichskristallnacht, the night that resulted from the expulsion of all Polish Jews in Germany.

These Polish Jews were given one night to pack, a suitcase and then they were all put on trains for Poland. Poland only accepted half of them, and 4,000 were left at the border, isolated between the two countries, threatened with death if attempting to enter Poland and death if trying to get back into Germany. British citizens who had gone to help reported that some were shot by the Germans. Sendel Grynszpan says they were left, told by the Nazis to get out of Germany and to go to Palestine. He wrote a letter to his son in Paris about what had happened, which was received on Thursday 3 November 1938. They had no money whatsoever and needed help. Herschel Sendel Grynszpan was living with an uncle in Paris at that time. Over the weekend Herschel bought a pistol and six bullets and on the following Monday, 7 November and went to the German embassy. It has been widely suggested that Herschel was having an affair with Ernst vom Rath, both having met in a well-known homosexual meeting place *Le Boeuf sur le Toit*. It is possible that Herschel tackled Ernst over the weekend about what had happened to his father. Ernst came out with some Nazi ideology about purging the country and argued with Herschel, who was incensed and said some cutting things about Ernst. Herschel had brooded over these and decided on a course of action. When Ernst was informed that Herschel was downstairs at the embassy, he may have thought Herschel had come to make up and thus said it was all right for him to be admitted up to the office. Herschel was shown to the office where he then fired five shots at the diplomat. Two hit their target. Herschel escaped, but when arrested by the French police, he admitted what he had done and gave them a postcard written to his father, claiming that he had to protest in some way and that the world should hear. Herschel supposedly denied later that he had murdered the German in a jealous rage, which would question this suggested account. On the basis on this and his denial that it was motivated out of jealousy, there is an argument to recognise Herschel as a resistance fighter. Vom Rath died two days later, and Hitler was informed at Munich, celebrating the anniversary of the Putsch. The next day, Jewish children were thrown out of state schools, all Jewish cultural events were cancelled and all Jewish publications were closed. Any Jew owning a weapon would receive 20 years of imprisonment. Goebbels told the *Gauleiter* that if the people wanted to vent their anger against Jews, then there was to be no interference. In other words, pogroms were to be organised. Hence, the *Reichskristallnacht* of 9 and 10 November 1938.

Walter and his family were lucky, but Walter was arrested and sent to Buchenwald. He was there for 11 days but was released when his wife presented papers to prove they were waiting for visas from the United States. The family fled to Rotterdam to wait for the visas. Like many Jews in the Netherlands, they were trapped by a slow-moving bureaucracy and were still there when the Germans invaded. They had been put into Westerbork in one of the small dwellings, the small bungalows built in rows. That had been on Monday 9 October 1939, with 19 other families, including Werner Bloch. So they were there when on 1 July 1942 when the Germans took over the running of the camp. Hopes of going to the United States were dashed when the Germans bombed Rotterdam, even though they had paid for their tickets. They all made the best of life in the camp, but then Walter had the idea of applying to be part of the Palestine exchange. The Red Cross made the arrangements and was successful. The family would be going to Celle and then to Palestine. They walked down to the train on the Boulevard of Misery on 1 February 1944 on the first part of their journey to Palestine. When they looked at the train, they could see that there was nothing special about this journey, and it was not to Celle but somewhere close called Bergen-Belsen. Walter and Ruth had heard stories about some of the camps. The British public had read about the mass murders of thousands upon thousands of Polish Jews and felt it too outrageous to believe. Walter and Ruth both felt it best to ignore it and not tell their children, Albert and Marion. Marion and her family were in a carriage with bench seats and very little privacy. Marion remembered the train stopping to be checked by the Germans.

Let me tell you about Paul Siegel, aged 19, from Germany. He knew of Gemmeker's rule and did not wish to escape. He thought that jumping from moving trains was something you only saw at the cinema. He had been in Westerbork since his capture in November 1942. What he did do was liaise with the Dutch resistance and get himself issued fake papers. He actually got onto the train as Paul Siegel and then, hiding out of sight at the back of the wagon, took off the top set of clothes to reveal clothes befitting a member of the camp staff who was about their business loading the train. He had papers to this effect. He then walked over to and hid in the hospital, which by this time in the camp's story was very large and easy to hide in. The next morning, he walked out of the camp gates together with Martin Uffenheimer and disappeared. At Bergen-Belsen, the man in charge of foreigners was bemused that Paul Siegel had not arrived and that his remains could not be accounted for. This was an instance of the workings of the Nazi organisation. One man from thousands could not be accounted for, and it was reported to Zöpf back in Amsterdam.

Do not doubt that the Germans were indeed able to account for each name and number of those in their system. Never doubt their ability to do this. The poor souls murdered in *Einsatz* operations on the Eastern Front became just one number among two million.

Paul saw the end of the war and got to Palestine, and he saw his Israel that he had dreamed of.

Jean Freund from the cabaret group was part of the group destined for Palestine, too. Jean was going to Bergen-Belsen. Before the war, he had had his own band but was content to play in the orchestra for the revues.

Hetty E. Verolme was on that train as a child. She was quite sure that the train left about ten o'clock. It travelled all day and all night. Outside was darkness, and they could not see anything. The train stopped at a large station for 90 minutes. She could not sleep because she was so nervous and worried. Hetty said that when they arrived, about 30 SS men with dogs were there; she did not like being screamed at by the SS. They were told to leave the large luggage and to line up. Mothers and children clung to each other. Hetty's dad and some other men were loaded onto the trucks with the large suitcases. The long line of people started to move off. Hetty saw a bridge over the railway line with people watching them.

Marion Blumenthal added that it was pitch black and raining. She recalled seeing African children in the camp. One of those children wanted Hetty's doll, and Marion's brother stopped the child from taking it. She was small, and the snarling jaws of the dogs were at eyeline. Her brother, Albert, was her protector. Marion and her mother were in one part of the Sternlager. Do not assume it was anything to do with being special; it was just because of the star they wore on their clothes. Marion simply said that Bergen-Belsen was hell.

Also on the train were the Boas family consisting of Philip, 37; Suze, 32; Boy, who was just eight; and Eddy, who was three years and eight months old. They were arrested and had been sent to Westerbork on 28 September 1943. Eddy remembered their treatment in Bergen-Belsen where his father would push a cart around collecting the dead.

Mirjam Bolle, who had arrived previously, was disappointed that the new inmates could not offer much news. She recalled seeing the train move off with the Hungarians to Buchenwald. She was able to write letters to Leo, who was back in Westerbork.

* * *

Philip Mechanicus walked about the camp the day after the train had left, complaining how thin the number of people was starting to look. There were not the crowds there once were. With regularity the trains had been leaving bound for Bergen-Belsen, Theresienstadt or Auschwitz.

Of those deported to Bergen-Belsen, 80 would survive.

* * *

Saturday, 5 February 1944, a group set out from Westerbork to Ravensbrück. Ravensbrück was a concentration camp for women. It was run by men in senior positions but also had some women officers. It was a fearful camp, just as bad as any other and in some respects worse. The guards at concentration camps were usually those who could not succeed in life and had come to the camps with a huge dislike for others whom they could lord over. The Germans had been told that they were far superior to other nationalities. Their history had been traced far back – according to what they read in books and newspapers and to what they saw and heard at the cinema. Himmler had sent expeditions across the world, even to Mongolia, looking for the progenitors of the Aryan race to which Germans belonged. To them, Jews were vermin. In films, Jews were shown spreading like a plague of rats, and they had to be eradicated. The female guards had no sympathy for the women prisoners, and these guards certainly behaved just like their male counterparts. No distinction was made between men and women; all were expected to work and were sent out of the camp to work at various industrial installations. There were 70 sub-camps for slave labour. Conditions were horrific and made ghastlier by the fact that children were there. Some were born there, and some perished there, just like at any other camp. It had gas chambers, operated by male prisoners from a small camp not far away, although many executions took place behind the crematoria by shooting. Himmler was a regular visitor and gave out freedom like largesse. His mistress lived not too far from the camp. Of all the camps, Ravensbrück was more than likely the most multinational. Poles made up the largest majority, but it was the children from almost every conquered nation in Europe who made it so multinational. There were children from Lidice, and there were Roma and Sinti children. There were British secret agents, a member of the Rothschild family – Elisabeth, a Polish countess and Gemma, the sister of Mayor Fiorello LaGuardia of New York. All these people were held as bargaining chips like in poker until the Germans had played out their last hand. The most horrific aspect of Ravensbrück was some of the experiments conducted on the women there. Women were infected with gangrene and then various things in attempt to cure it. Legs from two women would be amputated and then attached to the other donor. Women were given wounds akin to those suffered by soldiers on the front and were treated – all in the name of advancing medicine. Think of any word you can, such as "brutal," and it does not even come close to what women suffered in Ravensbrück or anyone in any other camp.

The group being sent to Ravensbrück consisted of 63 Hungarians, 30 children with 33 women. Their men had gone to Buchenwald. Neomi Friedman was on that train and was only seven years old. She sat in a carriage with her mother, Frieda, and her 11-year-old brother, Uriel. Their mother was holding her youngest child, Chaya, who was 16 months old. Uriel was lost to them in a year's time, as he was too old to stay at the camp. The father, Cantor Ben-Zion Moskovic, was in Buchenwald. They had all hoped to go to England. He had been told to go by the *Viznitzher Rebbe* – Yisroel Hager and waited for news in Antwerp. As a stop gap, he applied for a post as cantor in Amsterdam but left before the successful candidate was announced. The whole family were at Antwerp Station. They were going to England where Ben-Zion had been offered a post, but he happened to come across a friend who told him he had been successful in Amsterdam. So Ben-Zion took the family to Amsterdam. Then the Nazis invaded, and the cantor and his family found themselves in Westerbork for the next four years. Oddly, the Nazis liked the Jews to sing. The cantor was made to sing, and as a goldsmith he might prove useful. What sort of ending are you expecting for them? Did they ever meet again? In this instance, all of them survived, but Ben-Zion's voice was of little value from working in asbestos mines. Ben-Zion thought about what he had been told by the Viznitzher Rebbe and often wondered whether perhaps he should have done what the Rabbi said and gone to England.

This was one of the few transports where everyone on that train survived to see the end of the war.

* * *

Philip Mechanicus was disgusted. He was watching the Flying Column carrying the sick from the hospital to the train. It was Tuesday, 8 February 1944, and 1,015 people were due to leave the camp. They had been dressing the patients since two o'clock this morning. Beds with occupants were pushed onto carts and then hauled by horse to the train. Snow fluttered down from the sky and covered everything in a wet, white dusting. It was a cattle train, and they stood out in the open. The children were the most pitiful. They had scarlet fever and diphtheria and were weeping as they were carried to the train. Someone died while being pushed toward the tracks. Thoughtfully, there was an empty wagon for anyone who died on the way. Philip saw Jews with exemption stamps who were no longer honoured, Jews from the detention barrack, orphaned children, Calmeyer-listed people and those fooled by Weinreb. Children were treated just as harshly as were adults. When children were upset for periods of time, they wet their bed in their sleep. Such children were forbidden to drink anything after noon and then given a spoonful of salt before they went to bed. Those poor things must have had a raging thirst. And the harsh treatment sometimes came from other Jews. They objected to the noise, or boisterous activity or even the space the children took for looking at the stamps they had collected. Gemmeker ensured the children were healthy enough to travel. They were examined weekly by the doctor, they went to the dentist, they had a hot meal every day and they were given clothes and shoes if they had none.

Their hair was cut and abrasions dressed – all so that they were able to travel.

Out of one of the wagons came a small girl's voice asking her mother where they were going.

Food was mentioned a great deal by those who passed through Westerbork. When you have food, it is a pleasure and not constantly on your mind, but when you do not have enough and hunger gnaws at your stomach, then food's importance is greatly increased in your consciousness. Abraham Wittenburg said that they were given bread on the journey several times. He had been put with the detainees. Those back in Westerbork had noted peas, groats and carrots as well. Cabbage was not mentioned this time. They were not for use on the train, for there were not any cooking facilities. So where did this food go?

The train arrived in Auschwitz on Thursday, 10 February, and 800 were murdered immediately. A total of 185 entered the camp; of these, 155 would later die. The children with scarlet fever and diptheria, if they had not died on the journey, went to the gas chambers. Eichmann visited the camp this February.

* * *

Friday, 11 February 1944 – Catharina Frank was issued with another special pass which entitled her to go to her place of work, hospital service area 4, during the hours of curfew. It was called an Alarm Pass. Pass? It was a scrap of paper, only big enough to hold the 11 lines of type. It was signed by Arthur Pisk, head of the camp police. Pisk forced young boys and girls to work as messengers. He was feared by the other prisoners; he represented the "Jewish SS," of which there were just over more than 180.

* * *

228

Do you remember Leo Kok? He had something to do with Gemmeker's cabaret group. He could often be seen walking around the camp, with drawing pencils and water colours. This month he would do a portrait of Mischa Breslauer. Max Michael, to give him his proper name, was the son of Rudolf Breslauer from Leipzig, the photographer. Rudolf and his wife, Bella, had been in Westerbork for two years with their sons Mischa and Stefan and their daughter, Ursula. Gemmeker had used Breslauer to take photographs of the camp. Mischa was eight years old and sat very still as Leo sketched him and then coloured the portrait. He was a handsome little boy. Leo painted quite a bit when he was not making the backdrops for the Bühne. Breslauer took photos of life in the camp, but Leo made drawings from life, two men cutting up aeroplanes engrossed in their work. There was Liesel Reichstaler Heynemann staring from the page, also drawn in February. A train was drawn sitting at the station, waiting in the snow. There was a sketch of Hans Krieg, his big round head from the side, cap on head. Later in the year in August, Leo would sketch the women exercising in the camp with a display of kinesthetics; 38 girls and women dressed in blue, spelling out the letters "L.H." for Lotte Heider Lehmann. Three letters may have been a bit too much. There was the lovely sketch cum cartoon of Camilla Spira, which was in the book given to Gemmeker. Leo also did self-portraits. It was a privilege and honour if he asked you to pose. Leo was a popular chap.

* * *

Tuesday, 15 February 1944 – Jewish Orphans from Hungary were on their way back from Transnistria, the newly acquired area by Romania. These areas had been described as "killing fields." There were two camps, but people were placed in this part of Romania without any form of subsistence and left to die by the hundreds every day. Possibly 100,000 Jews died here. The Hungarian orphans aged up to 15 were sent back to Hungary and an unknown existence. Hungary was doubtful about Germany's winning the war and had thought about its policy towards Jews after contact with the Allies. Those over 15 were left to die.

* * *

The same Tuesday in Camp Westerbork, there was a train destined for Bergen-Belsen; 773 would travel east, and 700 of those would be murdered upon arrival. Slottke had a direct hand in this transport and recorded it in some detail. Gemmeker's personal stamp was all over this one too. The Netherlands – van Gogh was not popular with Hitler. Diamonds, however, were extremely popular. They were so sought after that it was proposed to establish an industrialised area for diamonds. Sometimes this project was on, sometimes off. Diamonds were literally hard currency in any country in the world. "sought after" was putting it mildly. People experienced in cutting diamonds or with knowledge about diamonds were spared from deportation. They were safe on a list, until it was decided that an industrial area for diamonds was not needed. There were many fanciful ideas from the Germans for when they had won the war, but as it progressed, these ideas were quietly dropped. One could not say why, as that would be defeatist talk, and no one wanted to appear in front of Judge Roland Freisler, famous for show trials and a participant at the Wannsee Conference, on a charge of sedition. Therefore, the diamond experts were no longer needed and could be deported. There were nine on this train. Most of the others had already gone to Buchenwald, where there was no need for diamond experts. And there were more on this train with South American passports. Gabriel Italie said that Honduras seemed to be the flavour of the day. There had been hundreds, but no one seems to know how many today. Slottke had eight lists, and four of those lists covered Jews who held such passports. Hauptsturmführer Ernst Mös from Eichmann's office had given the authorisation. He was Eichmann's liaison officer with Theresienstadt and Bergen-Belsen. Mös was in Belsen on 26 April 1944, 10 November 1944, and 26 March 1945.

Jacob Joshua and Salomon de Wolff were somewhere on the train. They had been duped by Weinreb into parting with their money and thought they were exempt. But they were not. Many others on that list had already left back in January, but these two had Paraguayan passports. Netty Hirsch could tell you about these passports. Her father had some sent to him from Zurich. Netty, her father and her sister, Hetty, were all to be deported.

How about Gemmeker the gentleman? Thirty-six ill deportees were on this train. There had been sick deportees on trains before, and we all know they did not last long at the other end of the journey, but 11 days earlier, Gemmeker had decided that there would not be any more *Transportunfähige*. This meant in effect that no one was considered too ill to travel, apart from those who were going to die within three to eight hours. He thought that one big transport would ensure the swift recovery of many ill patients, who would no longer be seeking asylum in the hospital. This had taken place on 25 January. Two had received surgery and were on this train: Rachel Pik and Jozeph Melkmann. Jozeph was sure that going to Bergen-Belsen saved his life. Like the Blumenthals, he was a *Palästinajude*, a Jew for the Palestine exchange. He went when he saw it was a passenger train; he could have stayed and convalesced. Instead he convalesced at Bergen-Belsen, as everyone was put into quarantine following a fear of polio coming from Westerbork. Salomon de Wolff and Jozeph Melkmann worked in the shoe department where they tore apart old shoes to reuse the leather. Ruth Blumenthal worked in the canteen, so she was able to hide odd scraps of food to share with her family and barracks. Walter and Albert, in another part of the camp, were able to deal for a time in cigarettes. The family met up for a short time after roll call before returning to their own parts of the camp.

Another family on this train was the family Hess, consisting of the father, Charles, the mother, Ilse, and their twins, Steven and Marion. Charles and Ilse had left Germany in 1936 and settled in the Netherlands where the twins had been born. Charles worked away from home and came home from a trip to find his wife and children had been seized and were in Westerbork. He then marched down to the police station and stated that the Germans had taken his family and that he needed to be with them. He had apparently arrived in a first-class carriage. All of them had with them their ready packed suitcase which had stood by the door of their house. Steven had not liked Westerbork because it was either hot or cold. It was Charles and Ilse's wedding anniversary. Charles had tried to get them sent to Bergen-Belsen, as he knew it was in Germany and the family spoke German. Steven would be grateful one day that it was not Auschwitz, as Bergen-Belsen did not have gas chambers. He remembered children from the hospital being sent to Auschwitz on 8 February the week before. When the train arrived near Bergen-Belsen, they all got out at Celle. Steven made a dash to pet one of the dogs. His father ran after him and was shouted at by a guard that he would shoot. Charles told him he could shoot, but he wanted his son. Instead of shooting, the guard told him he had "guts" and to get his son back into line. At the camp, there was not much for the children to do. They picked lice off each other, popped the lice bodies and then lined them up. They also learned to count, using the human bodies piled up outside the barracks. Part of the game was to work out which arm belonged to which body. It was what children did.

* * *

Philip Mechanicus walked around the camp feeling ill at ease. He was popular, and the day before, he had shaken many hands of people going to Bergen-Belsen. He felt that his soul had almost joined with theirs and that it would never let go. This was what he saw the day before:

People going on the transport lined up at the door of their barracks. Philip thought they were like a caravan, travelling to some far, distant land, almost on a pilgrimage. At the windows were many faces looking out and shouting final farewells. There were arms reaching out the windows, and people left the "caravan" to rush over, shake a hand and then rush back into the line. Philip saw the Ordedienst trying to keep order. Gemmeker's order was that

232

everyone stay in their barracks who was not travelling, but relatives find this difficult. The train left and stopped at the gate for the formal handover to the Wehrmacht when everyone was counted. The train of 12 passenger cars disappeared into the future. Time at the camp stood still, only interrupted on Tuesdays – usually, or other days of the week – usually.

Philip had watched 773 people go east. Of these, only 73 would survive.

* * *

Sunday 20 February 1944. Gemmeker may well have been on edge. Zöpf was in the camp to measure skulls and noses. This was to be done by an expert on cranial measurements and the relationship of these to racial characteristics. The Nazis put great store in these and the work by geneticists in eugenics started by Sir Francis Galton, a cousin of Darwin and supported by Ernst Rüdin, who propounded the "Master Race" to Hitler. Worthy men such as the archaeologist Flinders Petrie found that their work was vandalised by Nazi eugenics to support their hypothesis that a Jew's characteristics were personified in their skull structure. The "expert" had measurements and photos, recordings and diagrams to show what Jews looked like. Zöpf was in the camp together with SS-Sturmbannführer Herbert Aust from the Race and Settlement Office to measure some heads and to identify some Jews in a camp where everyone was supposedly Jewish. Those not involved found the proceedings amusing. It was not amusing for those who were to be measured. They were struggling to prove they were not Jews in the Nazi sense and could therefore return to Spain and Portugal. They were Sephardi Jews. The camp watched as the Sephardi were measured and recorded. If you looked around the camp, everyone you saw was a Jew, and no one looked alike. Even those who were related did not look alike; they did not share similar features. There were so many different-shaped heads, lengths of noses, position and types of ears. The camp was a complete melting pot. Aust completed his measurements and took his findings away with him. He forwarded them to Naumann. The Sephardi waited for the findings.

* * *

On Tuesday, 22 February 1944, Aust's findings were communicated back to the camp. The Sephardi Jews were declared to be *Rassisches Untermenschentum*, racially subhuman. There was no need for them to be returned to Portugal or Spain. Franco, the Spanish dictator, had given Hitler a list of 6,000 Jews in Spain, but they were not deported to Germany. Portugal, on the other hand, had accepted thousands of Hungarian Jews who were safe until the war ended. The Sephardi, according to the Nazi, Aust, provided a "political menace" and could be treated like all other Jews. They could go to Theresienstadt immediately. Kaltenbrunner, Zöpf and Naumann felt themselves right to have treated them as Jews. Aust had been responsible for the *Lebensborn Program*, the breeding of suitable non-German women as mothers to Aryan children, fathered by pure-blooded German men. There were hundreds of children who were bitterly resented and treated with contempt, even in civilised countries like Norway.

* * *

It was Friday, 25 February 1944, Rosh Chodesh Adar, and 811 souls were ready to leave the camp to Theresienstadt. There may have been a couple of reasons for Westerbork Jews being sent to Theresienstadt. The first had to do with quotas and it was Theresienstadt's turn, or someone was still trying to negotiate with Portugal over the Sephardi Jews. The Jews were happier to travel in carriages rather than cattle wagons, yet as the Blumenthal family found out it was no guarantee that the destination was better than any other, which included Auschwitz. Slottke made a report that the Jews were in an uplifted mood when they travelled in passenger carriages. How did she know? Had she left her office and visited Westerbork to see first-hand? Perhaps she had, or she just surmised and reported it as fact to Zöpf. But we know Slottke visited Westerbork. Many Jews made requests to go to Theresienstadt.

Philip also gave a reason for this as well. He watched the crowds making their way to the train. This time it was not a slow caravan but almost a rush. He felt that there was almost a panic that anyone who turned down the opportunity to go to Theresienstadt was destined for Auschwitz. Those leaving on this train were therefore happy and relieved not to be going to Auschwitz. He noted that even that morning people were asking at the camp office to have their names put down for Theresienstadt.

Max Mannheimer was quite happy to be going on the train. When he found out what the destination was, he was not frightened. He said he knew it to be a model camp. How he knew that I do not know. The Theresienstadt film had not been released yet. Perhaps Max got his timings a little mixed up. It would be a "model camp" but not quite yet. Even sick people who could hardly move after operations had put their names down. Max thought it a good sign that it was a proper train, albeit third class. Freight cars were added to the train to carry 800 loaves of bread, 80 kilograms of jam, 24 kilograms of butter and 35 kilograms of sausage for the Jews, and 25 kilograms of sausage for the guards.

On Tuesday, 7 March, Zöpf sent a telegram to Obersturmführer Burger, the commander of the Theresienstadt ghetto. Eight separate groups were on the transport, 23 disabled war veterans; 45 Jews and their families who were members of the *Verdienstjuden*, Jews who had been of service to the Reich; 36 Jewish spouses whose mixed marriages had been invalidated and who had half-Aryan children; 88 Jewish spouses from valid intermarriages and Jews who had relatives in neutral countries; 308 Sephardi Jews from Portugal; 79 Jews who fitted profiles from the Central Bureau for Jewish Immigration; 35 parents and children of Jews who had helped run Westerbork from the start; and 197 Jews who had been promised deportation to Theresienstadt by Eichmann, mainly construction workers. Eichmann had told them personally they would be looked after, and here again he was keeping his promise. For all the horror attached to Eichmann, he seemed to have kept his personal promises, yet have no doubt: He was one of the largest and most active "cogs" in the Holocaust Machine.

One person on this train had also been personally promised by Eichmann a place at Theresienstadt when she and Eichmann had met the previous August. This was Catharina Frank (Brucker) and her son, Clarence. No doubt she was nervous, but did she feel at least some ease that Eichmann was "looking after" her too? Remind me about her later.

Sitting quietly talking to his wife was the large figure of Kurt Gerron, the film star and director. He would direct his last film in Theresienstadt, the "model camp." But he did not know that this notoriety would then overshadow his pervious achievements and cloud the end of his life. Here he was waiting as number 247 on Transport XXIV/4, which would arrive in Theresienstadt on 26 February 1944.

Margaretha Kahlenberg, number 338, was also bound for Theresienstadt. One of the dancers from the cabaret, she did not feel like dancing today. She had been one of those Philip Mechanicus had written about with disgust who were dancing as the trains were leaving.

On the same list as Kurt were Herman Italiaander and Fritz Siesel, but they did not get to Theresienstadt. They had volunteered to join this transport. They went dutifully to the train, and once in one of the wagons, they put on armbands that identified them as members of the *Gepäckdienst*, porters. They meandered back through the crowds and then just slipped away from the throng and left the camp. As simple as that. They were picked up by friends the next day.

Felix Gustav Flatow was another Olympian to be transported, but this time, not Dutch. He was German. He had competed in the 1896 and 1900 Olympics in Athens and Paris, excelling on the parallel bars and the horizontal bar. He won two golds in the team events and had competed alongside his cousin, Alfred. His reward was also to flee Germany in 1933 to The Netherlands and then to be arrested New Year's Eve 1943. His cousin had already gone to Theresienstadt, so perhaps Felix hoped to meet up with him; however, he did not know that his cousin was already dead and that he too would starve to death at age 70. He sat there on the train thinking who knows what.

On Saturday, the train arrived at Theresienstadt to be met by the SS and Czech police.

MARCH 1944

FOUR TRANSPORTS WITH 1,544 DEPORTEES

It was Friday, 3 March 1944. A list of names and numbers was now a mass of people, and 732 waited for the train to depart. There were children, of course, 94 of them all under the age of 18.

Gemmeker was a father. How did he feel about sending off children? Perhaps he did not have the same feelings for children as other fathers did. Yet there were plenty of camp Kommandanten with children. Some of them had their families with them. Many guards had children, but it seemingly did not affect how they related to Jewish children. Perhaps they were even more of the monsters than they were labelled. It is often thought that camp personnel were not family men or women, because there was the perception that these men and women were incapable of love. Of course, this was far from the truth. Himmler had children by his wife and his mistress, and he came across as a doting father. Rudolf Höß of Auschwitz had five children. What must it be like for their children to find out that the father who dangled them on his knee was responsible for so many deaths? Hans Frank was very much a family man, with five children also, as well as being a mass murderer. What do you do? Change the family name? Hide? Ignore what they did? Distance yourself from the man you did not know while still loving the man who was your father? Worse – perhaps agree with what happened. Many children sorted that out for themselves. Most Jewish children across Europe did not get that choice. They perished with their parents. Some were separated and died alone, not knowing a mother or father's love at their tragic end. Some survived, parentless. How do you deal with that, knowing that for some reason you did not die with your parents? What do you do with that knot that gnaws away at you? Yet these parents were shown as loving, often making sacrifices so that their children could survive – giving their children to non-Jewish friends to hide and care for or sending them away with false loving promises of seeing them soon. There can be no hate for these parents, just a long-lost love that pours out of the soul with nowhere to go. It perhaps becomes a love of life and other family, for siblings or their own children.

Besides the children there are the young men and women. Some were members of a group called the *Vereeniging tot Vakopleiding van Palestina Pioniers,* pioneers headed for Palestine. They were there training for a life in Palestine, but now they were on this train. They were also training in resistance activities, but it was not for those activities they were on the train. Gentleman Gemmeker insisted that they too should go east, and this time the train went to Auschwitz. Now why was this? They were not harming anyone in the camp, except that six of them had escaped, so Gemmeker ordered that the whole group be sent off to Auschwitz. Another group of people was sent to be murdered as a result of a fit of pique. In this way Gemmeker was no different from Deppner or Dischner. One of those who escaped detailed her modus operandi. It was similar to how others had. It was a wonder that the Germans had not yet worked it out. Lotti Siesel handed in her papers at the barracks and then walked to the train, allowing one of the *Hulp aan vertrekkenden*, "Aid to Deportees" to carry her bag. She then slipped one of their armbands on her arm and walked to the school where she hid. Two others were there. Then with false papers, they walked out of the camp. Now you might think that papers could not be forged inside the camp. Some documents were professionally printed, but many others became scraps of paper with type on them, easy to forge and copy. Permission to leave the camp looking as though it were signed was enough.

There were 132 so-called half-Jews. How odd does that sound? But it was what the Nazis called people who had only two grandparents that were Jewish or "full Jews." Can you see how easy it was to slip into using classifications devised by the Nazis? It was utter nonsense. In this group were non-Jews caught helping Jews. This was Nazi logic. People caught helping the Jews deserved the same fate as Jews, even if they were not Jewish.

Those travelling had to be ready by 4:00 am early morning. Dina Snabel Maas described how they were loaded into the crowded train. They had luggage and a blanket. It was March, and it could be cold in the Netherlands. There were the usual barrels in the wagons. The wagon was already dirty, and with each knock of the train, effluent spilt out of the waste barrel. During the night, they had to change trains and found that the floor of the new wagon was covered in tar which clung to their blanket and clothes. The SS confiscated anything of value during the journey. When they arrived in Auschwitz, Dina saw what she thought was a frozen plain. Scurrying about were men in prisoner clothes and many SS guards. Emile Franken remembered he was told by two Dutch prisoners not to get on the lorries. Emile was selected for labour with another 178 men. Dina was selected with another 75 women to enter the camp, and they were all tattooed. The trucks drove away 477 women, children and elderly to be gassed. Besides Emile and Dina, another 23 people survived.

* * *

Tuesday, 7 March 1944, and Bühne Lager Westerbork presented Bunter Abend 4, starring Otto Aurich, Jetty Cantor, Max Ehrlich, Franz Engel, Liesel Frank, Johnny and Jones, Esther Philipse, Mara Rosen, Willy Rosen and Erich Ziegler under the direction of Max Ehrlich. The music was by Willy Rosen and Erich Ziegler. There were 16 scenes, starting with the first scene, an Usherette showing people to their seats and ending with the entire "bastion" performing in a sketch. There was singing, jokes and laughter. Willy and Erich played at two grand pianos on stage. This performance is notable for the inclusion of Johnny and Jones who were Nol (Arnold Siméon) van Wesel as Johnny and Max (Salomon Meyer) Kannewasser as Jones. They were big radio stars in the Netherlands, and their greatest hit had been *Mijnheer Dinges weet niet wat swing is* or "Mr Dinges doesn't know what swing is." They sang with American accents. The lyrics were often funny, and they were famous for parodies. One of these parodies was hits by Willy Rosen, which they performed in Westerbork. They were actually able to sneak off from a work detail in Amsterdam to a recording studio where they recorded this tribute to Willy Rosen. The two of them were in Westerbork with their wives. Their job was to dismantle aluminium aircraft parts. Gemmeker was not pleased with the performance of Johnny and Jones, and they were banned from the Bühne. Gemmeker did not appreciate the sound of their Americanized accents. They were relegated to singing in the camp café where real coffee was not served. Their performances there were very well received, and they were out of earshot there as far as Gemmeker was concerned.

* * *

Friday, 10 March 1944 – Himmler received communication from higher SS and police leader, Hanns Albin Rauter, which estimated that between 9,000 and 10,000 Jews were in hiding in the Netherlands. But he reported that they were capturing between 600 and 700 a month. Dutch collaborators had been paid four guilders for information and seven and a half guilders for each arrest. This had now been increased to 40 guilders per person, which was a little over $21 or £5 at that time.

* * *

Wednesday, 15 March 1944, a transport to Bergen-Belsen left with 210 deportees. It should not surprise you to know that 14 sick people were to leave in this train along with 44 children. Of these, 47 were destined for exchange with Germans in Palestine, which the Red Cross would arrange. These Jews had had their exchange confirmed but not their passports stamped with visas, although they had certificates issued to that effect. They would have to wait until July for further information.

Sitting on this train and realising that his time had now come was Philip Mechanicus. He would no longer be watching any more trains arrive and leave from Westerbork. He was going to find out what the journey was like, a journey that he had seen so many others start before him.

Renata Laquer remembered the journey vividly. The way she described it, you could almost feel as if you were there with her, but then what words can describe that horror or adjure the hearer to partake in it? The train left at 8:00 am and took until 2:00 pm the next day to travel 350 kilometres. They sat among their luggage and clothing. Renata felt that it was all stop and start, with lots of shunting and hours when they did not move at all. The green-uniformed SS gave them bread at Bentheim. Just before the border, she had thrown some postcards out of the window. She watched them flutter down to be picked up by a railroad worker who somehow communicated visually that they would be posted. She noted the empty street in Germany devoid of women or children and longed for an end to the madness, as she called it. Finally, after passing through a heath, they saw an empty station and concluded that they have arrived, especially as there were guards with shepherd dogs as there were in Vught. They were treated correctly at the station, and luggage was offloaded. They would have to walk. Renata smelled disinfectant and cabbage soup when they arrived at the camp. They were put into quarantine. Renata was unhappy her blanket was wet.

Louis Tas, 24 years old, also spoke of the drizzle and rain under the grey clouds at their arrival. The barracks looked frightening, and there were watchtowers everywhere. Their isolation in quarantine proved to be a good precaution, as Susanne Birnbaum, her sister, Regina, and brother, Zwi, came down with polio almost immediately.

Mirjam Bolle had watched the transport arrive, and she described some of the people she recognised: Izak de Vries, Elie Dasberg, Mrs Van Tijn and two children of Karel and Gien Hartog, who all looked thin and starving without proper clothes and with violent diarrhoea. They all had a craving for food which they would not lose. Their faces exuded hunger. Of the 44 children who arrived at Bergen-Belsen, at least four would be murdered.

* * *

Thursday, 16 March 1944 – Gemmeker received a telex from Zöpf, ordering the deportation of 24 Jews who no longer had Turkish citizenship. Gemmeker sent them off straightaway on 23 March. Most were murdered upon arrival.

* * *

On the weekend of 18 and 19 March 1944, German troops marched into Hungary, as the Hungarian government's support for the Axis was somewhat flagging. Admiral Horthy, the Hungarian regent, refused to sign a document calling for German intervention in the country. The Jewish population of 725,000 was under immediate threat, especially when Eichmmann arrived along with Sonderkommandos. I wonder what promises he made to Himmler.

* * *

Although the inmates of Westerbork did not know it, the end of the war was in sight. Inmates got news, clandestine radios and hearsay. The war was not going well for the Germans in the East against the

Soviets. The Americans and British were coming north through Italy. Surely, it would only be a matter of time before this madness ended. The Germans sensed it too and became angrier and more impatient. Talk of defeat was now a crime. Loose ends needed tidying up, and Gemmeker had this in mind as transports were put together according to guidelines from above. Small groups that were no longer protected could be sent east. This would make room in the camp for new inmates. The Jews arriving now were mostly classed as criminals, for they were ones caught in hiding and had disobeyed the "call up" instructions.

A group of Jews had been sent from Vught to Westerbork, including Dr Arthur Lehmann who was head of the Jewish administration at the camp. All Jews had to leave the camp. Then it was realised that certain operations could not continue without them. One such company was Philips, the electrical manufacturer. The factory was closed and emptied of its workforce. Along with Jews were all the non-Jews. Gemmeker had told Laman Trip, a Philips executive, that he would not guarantee the safety of those workers while at Westerbork. If needed, they would go east with everyone else at the camp. Rather oddly, they were soon ordered back to Vught, where their reception was rather perfunctory. No one was to meet them, and a shouted instruction from the office told them to go back into the camp. Rutger E. Laman Trip had phoned the Philips' head office and was instrumental in saving those people's lives. The head office had phoned some high-tanking Nazi and then he had phoned Gemmeker. The Kommandant at Vught was Hans Hüttig, and he had been thwarted again in deporting the Jews who work for Philips.

Previously in and out of protection were the diamond workers no longer needed; they were placed on this transport. Plans for a diamond industry had been shelved yet again, for the moment.

Louis de Wijze, a member of the Bühne group, knew the transport on Thursday, 23 March 1944, well. On board were 599 men, women and children. Louis also saw what happened along the way and at arrival because he was being transported east that day too. Jewish mental patients had been taken from Woensel by the SS. One was missed. There were 23 of them for the train. Some could not get out of bed. One of the wagons was for these patients, completely left alone for the whole journey. They had no idea where they were. They did not know what Westerbork was. Gemmeker knew about them and saw that they were loaded onto the train even though they were confused and frightened. Three days they travelled without food or water or any attention. When the noise of the train ceased, when it stopped, they could be heard screaming and crying. Their cries for help and love rang emptily around Spandau Station in Berlin. There was no one there who cared. People from Berlin who claimed not to know anything about the ill treatment of Jews were silent.

Louis could always see these poor tortured souls in his mind, tumbling from the cattle wagon at Auschwitz, covered in their own filth. He had not been transported before because he was a member of the Bühne group but also because he was a member of Bauer's Palestinian pioneers. So doubly protected you would have thought. But a member of the group had escaped, and Gemmeker ordered that all remaining 50 members were to go east. Louis said they had clean barrels in their wagon. The others did not, and they were crammed in the wagons. Louis thought this a privilege. Do not for a moment think that Gemmeker arranged for the clean barrels.

Another group sent so that the camp was "tidier" were the Jews from mixed marriages, half-Jews or Jews thought to be special. These too had also been in an out-of-protection status. These were the *Schutzhäftlinge*. Their fate was now sealed, no more in doubt. When they reached Auschwitz, they were admitted into the camp.

Westerbork Camp was a cosmopolitan town, with many nationalities and with people from all over the world. The one uniting factor was that they were all Jews. Although some felt that they were no longer Jewish, having been baptised into the Christian Church, in the eyes of the Gemmeker, they were all Jews.

There was one group of 49 people from Turkey. Most had passports which had expired and were therefore considered stateless. There was Dora Bedak-Petenbaum, from Poland, who lived in The Hague with her family, Rebecca her daughter and husband, Herman. The Turkish authorities had turned their backs on them, and they were no longer considered to be Turkish. They all went east on 23 March 1944 and then no farther.

Max Freidman was the head chef at a Turkish restaurant at Boschstraat 216, Bezuidenhout. The fact that he and his family were Turkish was ignored. Max and his wife, Helene, had a daughter called Ruth. Max did not survive.

There are many others forgotten by a country they had thought of as their own. Forgotten by the world, they were even given up to the Germans for them to do with as they wished.

* * *

Now you might have thought that all resistance fighters were shot out of hand, like those who had been buried or cremated clandestinely. But 29-year-old Alida (Letty) Henriette van Gelder was a teacher at the Talmud Jewish School in Amsterdam and was a member of the resistance. She had worked with others setting up a safe house for those escaping the Nazis. They were betrayed, most likely for money or for some "grace and favour" from the Nazis. All eight Jews at the house died in Auschwitz. The Germans had another purpose for Letty, as they did not think she was Jewish. They felt she could be tricked into giving away more members of the resistance. Letty had been arrested with "Willy" Westerweel, Wilhelmina Dora (Willy) Westerweel-Bosdries, wife of Joop who was a resistance fighter. They had set up the safe house in Rotterdam. They were both taken to The Hague and questioned by the Gestapo. But then they were released on some pretext, at different times. They did not know they were being watched. Letty returned to Rotterdam and was looked after by Willy and Chiel Salomé. Chiel was also a resistance member. But another member of the Westerweel group was Karel Kaufmann, who had been turned by the Nazis. He handed them over, and they were arrested, ending up in Vught or Westerbork where they were transported to various camps. Letty sat in the cattle car with professors, artists and some of the half-Jews. There were 39 "privileged" people. Letty had been classified as one of these Schutzhäftlinge, owing to her British citizenship because her mother was from England. Letty saw the journey as a preparation for what was to come. She, Duifje Bouscholte-Wijman and five other women were among the Schutzhäftlinge.

D.A.A. Mossel remembered being questioned by the doctor at Auschwitz at about 8 am when they arrived on the third day. He wanted to know about the conditions in Vught, whether there were any diseases. He was not concerned for those in Vught; he just wanted to be aware of what diseases they may have been bringing into the camp. Mossel had been appointed "doctor" for the transport, as he had been an orderly in the hospital.

As the doors were opened at Auschwitz, there was an icy blast that entered each wagon. Looking out, they could see a sea of white snow. The trucks were waiting, and 239 climbed up and were driven off to the gas chambers. The remaining 304 men and 56 women entered the camp. Of those, only 74 survived to the war's end, including Louis.

* * *

Friday, 24 March 1994 – Roosevelt warned Hungary that it should cease anti-Jewish measures. He also condemned Nazi and Japanese atrocities and the countries' despicable crimes.

* * *

If you look at a map, you can see that camps were strewn across occupied Europe. The vast majority were to the east of Germany. Camps were in Germany itself though. Some were well known, such as Sachsenhausen, close to Berlin. Nearly everyone in Berlin knew about it or of it. Perhaps they even knew someone who was in there or had been but had been moved elsewhere. It was not a death camp as such, although people died there. There were public hangings in front of the camp for attempted escapes. In the isolation facility called *Zellenbau* were 180 cells where some were kept for long periods. It was here that British commandos were kept before execution at the war's end. There were many political prisoners, such as Ernst Busch, a communist and performer famous for appearing as the street singer in the *Dreigroschenoper* by Berthold Brecht and in the film by Pabst. He had fled the Nazis; he was not popular with them, as he had recorded a few anti-Nazi songs, but they caught up with him when they invaded Belgium, and he was then incarcerated in Sachsenhausen. Another performer had been Paul O'Montis, Pavel Wendel from Hungary and a huge cabaret star and recording artist in Berlin. He was imprisoned there for being a homosexual. He died after enduring six weeks of continual torture and beatings, and his body was sent to Hartheim to be cremated. Sachsenhausen was not a death camp, yet 30,000 people died there from disease, malnutrition, beatings and executions.

Just 90 kilometres from Berlin was a women's camp. If a camp could be worse than any other, this one certainly was. I was going to tell you that they were not single camps. You might know the name of the main camp, but each of these had numerous sub-camps. Ravensbrück had 34 sub-camps, each with inhuman conditions. Dutch Jews laboured for the aircraft industry in one of these smaller camps, Neustadt-Glewe. People in Ravensbrück were in protective custody, indefinitely.

On Wednesday, 29 March 1944, three women were sent from Westerbork to Ravensbrück. This was Slottke's idea – to send small numbers of Westerbork inmates off to the East on regular trains under escort. There would not have been a train leaving from Westerbork for just three women, as this was too costly to consider. The three were two Hungarian Jews and one Spanish national. You would have thought that the Spanish nationals would have been sent back to Spain. Franco and Hitler had met way back on Wednesday, 23 October 1940 at Hendaye on the border between France and Spain. The meeting had lasted 12 hours by which time Hitler had had enough of Franco and vowed never to meet him again because he was so boring. Relations continued, but not in a warm manner. It is possible that this Spanish woman was just to insignificant for the SS or anyone else to concern themselves with.

According to Rauter, the transport of these three women should have happened a day later, on Thursday, 30 March. Perhaps Slottke had found an earlier train.

* * *

Thursday, 30 March 1944 – The Soviet Army liberated the area known as Transnistria. The Jewish committee in Bucharest was able to repatriate about 2,500 Jews. The rest were murdered by the German and Romanian armies.

* * *

Friday, 31 March 1944 – Etty Hillesum's brother, Mischa, died at Auschwitz, although some believe he died in the Warsaw ghetto, having been worked to death as forced labour. Like so many, Mischa's full story will never be known.

Günther Witepski was also in Auschwitz. Before the war, he had been in an entertainment group called Ping Pong. Then he had appeared in the cabaret programmes *Humor und Melodie* and *Bravo da Capo* at Westerbork Camp. It was his day to die as well.

APRIL 1944

ONE TRANSPORT TO VARIOUS DESTINATIONS

2,265 Deportees

You could almost say that for Gemmeker, there were now very few restrictions as to whom he could send east, but there were still restrictions as to where they could go. On Wednesday, 5 April 1944, one train left Westerbork, but it had five transport destinations: Auschwitz, Bergen-Belsen, Theresienstadt, Ravensbrück and Buchenwald. In addition, 625 Jews from Belgium connected to the train at Assen. They were destined for Auschwitz.

Slottke had a hand in arranging much of this train's transport with the help of Margarethe Frielingsdorf. She was the keeper of another list – one of *Angebotsjuden*, wealthy Jews who could pay for their lives, known as the *Frielingsdorf Liste*. Added to this list were Jews from the list held by Jan Jacob Weissman, who had an arrangement allowing wealthy Jews to have deportation deferred. Have you built up a picture of all those lists circulating around Zöpf's office?

Saloman Mayer reportedly paid 120,000 Swiss francs to Weissman. A further 20,000 francs had been demanded along the way. This was the equivalent to nearly £10,000 at that time or about £446,000 today.

Slottke wrote to Eichmann's department in Berlin on the day of the transport about the Romanian Jews in the Netherlands. All the Jews from mixed marriages and those left after the *Heimkehraktion*, "Operation Repatriation," were now in Westerbork. She reported that 21 Romanian Jews, one Spaniard and one Hungarian had gone to Buchenwald and 37 Jewish mothers with children to Ravensbrück. The Romanian Jews had asked to go back to Romania, of which there was a slim chance. A month earlier, Rauter recorded that 133 Jews had been returned to their "homelands," but that did not include one Romanian. At Bergen-Belsen, the wagons were uncoupled, and the train carried on towards Auschwitz.

* * *

Ravensbrück: There were five headed for Ravensbrück. One of these was the wife of Paul Katz, who went on to Auschwitz.

* * *

Theresienstadt: There were 289 indicated for Theresienstadt. This group was composed of German war veterans, construction workers in Westerbork and camp administration, *Stammliste*. Eichmann had personally told the members of this group that he would take care of them. There were 26 Jews being sent as a request from the Bureau for Jewish Emigration in Amsterdam and four Portuguese Jews who were awaiting classification, just as 308 had been before them. There were 39 Jews whose classification the Nazis felt needed to be addressed. These were *Geltungsjuden*. They were deemed to be Jews but may have held Swedish or American citizenship. It is often thought that Sweden had a comfortable relationship with the Germans at this time but, whatever it might have been, the Nazis did not extend it to Jews. It also appears Sweden had a more comfortable relationship with the Allies.

At this time there seemed to be a shortage of trains for transportation. The Allies were gaining the upper hand in the air, and trains were the favourite targets of some pilots. There was also the shortage of steel. As in Britain, the Germans had also developed a train specifically for the war years. This was the Deutsche Reichsbahn's Class 52. It was one of the main three, the other two being the DRB 50 and DRB 42. There were others, but these were produced in greater numbers. The DRB 52 used less steel and had been designed by Richard Wagner, the chief engineer. Seventeen manufacturers were producing the trains across the Reich with 6,719 DRB 52s being built. Five of these manufacturers used forced labour, and these included Henschel in Kassel, Borsig in Poland using labour from Auschwitz, Schichau-Werke in Elbing, and DWM Posen and Fabloc in Poland. Locomotives built by Jews were hauling trains to the camps. As Hitler expanded the Reich, so too did the Reichsbahn expand, taking over rolling stock and tracks from every country invaded. Without the railways, Hitler's takeover of Europe would not have happened so quickly.

It may have been that the war effort was in greater need of locomotives, but Himmler's directive still stood. Troop movements to the East and to Italy, however, were taking their toll on the ability of the Reichsbahn to cope with the demands.

Passenger carriages were attached to the train for the 289 being sent to Theresienstadt. The train stopped in Hannover and was then split up into its three remaining destinations: Bergen-Belsen, Theresienstadt and Auschwitz.

Ab Caransa, 17 years old, was travelling with his parents. Joseph, his father, was prisoner number 46, and with him was Flora, Ab's mother. They were all on their way to Theresienstadt. All survived. Ab had a particularly unpleasant experience in Dresden. There they saw some German soldiers who stood looking at the Jews. They drew their fingers across their throats indicating that they were going to be murdered. They saw trains that had writing on them – *Wir fahren nach Polen, um Juden zu versohlen*, "We are going to Poland to beat up the Jews." This must have been horrifying for everyone on the train. But it serves as another indication that it was generally known throughout Germany what was happening to the Jews. The train reached Theresienstadt on the following Friday, on the third day. Ab ultimately became a writer. Arriving with them on the train was Jacob Goudsmit, number 288. He had been a member of the cabaret group, but his exemption had run out. He was there with Izaak Veffer, number 267, and Sophie Wertheim, number 279. They were also members of the cabaret group who were no longer needed. A new programme would have to be printed, omitting their names. Out of all those sent on this transport to Theresienstadt, only 26 survived.

* * *

Gabriel Italie, the doctor of classics who was originally from Rotterdam, watched the train depart early in the morning. Gabriel was one of the observers whom we rely on for testimony regarding Westerbork. He knew there were various destinations and spoke about the train picking up 13 wagons from Belgium. This was rather sad, as Gabriel's son, Paul Marcel, had unfortunately gone to Belgium to study at a university. He had been imprisoned at Caserne Dossin (Malines-Mechelen) Camp. Do you remember how extreme the measures were against Jews in Belgium? As a stateless person, Paul was treated as all Jews in Belgium were and had been sent to Auschwitz 18 months earlier as number 924. Gabriel watched the train go as it carried a letter from the loving parents to Paul.

Auschwitz: Six wagons of Jews to Auschwitz were carrying 240 people. Among them were 29 children; the youngest was one month old. Another of the children was Fia (Sophia) Polak. She was 15 years old and sat in a wagon with 40 men. They had very little food, and there was a small barrel for water and another for bodily waste. Fia thought they were like sardines with so many people and their luggage. The only thing providing any light allowing her to look at the others came from a smoking candle. She knew that her father and three boys were keeping watch. Fia had always been protected from unpleasant things. She would decide that she would put her childhood behind her when she reached Auschwitz and accept what was real. One of the boys was sleeping, resting his head on Fia's stomach. She shared bread with her father, Isaac, who gave her some advice about never being ill. He told her to present herself as always fit and as having a good profession, perhaps a seamstress. This was sound fatherly advice from a man who loved his daughter dearly and wanted her to survive. Were any girls in Germany being given this advice by their fathers, or was it just this one Jewish father? As the doors opened in Auschwitz, Fia saw men in blue and white striped outfits jump inside the wagon.

It was Friday, 7 April 1944, the eve of Passover. Margaretha Hendrika den Arend was holding little Jaques, four months old, in her arms. She was told by one of the guards to take the child and go to the trucks. Another guard intervened and said that she was to give the baby back to its mother and to join the other women. Baby Jacques was handed to his grandmother Jansje. Together with grandfather Andries, they went on the trucks. Margaretha joined the other women entering the camp.

Out of the 240 who arrived at Auschwitz from Westerbork, 129 were admitted to the camp, 62 men and 67 women. The other 111 were murdered straightaway. A mere 20 survived the war.

The 625 Belgians arrived at the same time on the carriages attached in Hannover. Of the men, 206 were admitted, and of the women, 146. The other 273 climbed onto the motor trucks and were taken to the gas chambers.

In Brussels, a family of Dutch Jews was arrested. Moshe Flinker, his parents, Eliezer and Mindl, his younger brother and five sisters were betrayed. They would find their way to Auschwitz and arrive there the following month.

Bergen-Belsen: Herbert Kruskal and his wife, Ada Leah, were on the train. Both were medical doctors and had worked in the hospital at Westerbork. They might have felt glad to be leaving but wondered about their future. They were from Germany and were due to go

Palestine. Herbert did reach Palestine before the end of the war. He reckoned there were 100 or so going to Bergen-Belsen and another 200 travelling in coaches to Theresienstadt. He remembered some Hungarians and Romanian Jews were also headed towards Germany, but he did not know where. His recollections were correct: In his office, Rauter had papers stating that 41 Jews from Romania, women and children, were destined for Ravensbrück, and 28 Romanian men were going to Buchenwald.

In Herbert's group of 101 people were 39 children under the age of 18. The youngest had not reached three months; off she went on the transport with her parents and older sister.

At the other end of the journey, Renata Laquer, who had left Westerbork with her husband, Paul, last March, saw the transport arrive. Herbert remembered entering Westerbork where they had been met by other inmates; here they met the SS with their savage dogs. They were lined up, five abreast – roll call, selection. Old people, the sick and children went in trucks. The rest walked. They had to undress and were given other clothes to wear. Herbert was not too clear about what clothes, as according to others, those in the Sternlager wore their own clothes. Joseph (Jupp) Weiss was tasked with keeping records for the Nazis. One hundred and one were admitted to the Sternlager from Westerbork on Thursday, 6 April 1944. Precise and accurate. Not made up and not fabricated. Like all Nazi records, they were accurate down to the last number.

Mirjam Bolle had worked out from what she was told that numbers in Westerbork were dwindling. She wrote to Leo that another transport from the Netherlands had arrived but that there were not many on it whom she knew. The newly arrived were in Barracks 10 under quarantine, and it was forbidden by punishment of death to approach them and to speak to them. However, Mirjam's father, Maurits, was able to talk to them as he distributed food in the camp. They told him that there were only about 2,000 left in Westerbork at this time.

The day after the arrival of the train from Westerbork, Friday, 7 April 1944, two Jews, Rudolf Vrba and Alfred Wetzler, escaped from Auschwitz. They had managed to hide for two days in the inner perimeter of the camp in a pile of logs. Other members of the escape team or camp resistance were able to mislead tracker dogs with Soviet tobacco dipped in gasoline. The dogs were sent in a completely wrong direction. When the furore around the camp had died down, the two men escaped the camp.

How, you can ask, in a camp numbering many thousands would two be missed? It was this German obsession with accurate numbers. Count the living, count the dead and if the number reached was not the expected one, then roll call would be delayed until the discrepancy was accounted for – after which time, in the depth of winter, the number of dead would have increased. Rudolf and Alfred got to Slovakia and met the underground. With its members, they wrote a 30-page report called the *Auschwitz Protocols*. It described everything that happened in the camp and detailed the preparations for the murder of 800,000 Jews in Hungary. The report reached the West and left no one in any doubt as to what Auschwitz was – an extermination camp.

It was the second successful escape from Auschwitz within three days. That must have annoyed the Germans. Siegfreid Lederer had escaped two nights previously, aided by *SS-Rottenführer* Viktor Pestek, a devout Catholic. He was killed later, but Siegfried survived and returned to his Czech homeland.

Friday, 7 April1944 – The Nazis raided a French children's home for Jewish children.

Friday, 14 April 1944 – Greek Jews arrived at Auschwitz.

* * *

On Sunday, 16 April 1944, the Hungarian government registered Jews and started to confiscate their property. Each Jew was expected to and did record all assets, which included the value of their house, businesses, securities, bank accounts and household possessions. They were given until 20 April to register everything. They could sell their possessions, but anything sold to non-Jews after 22 March was confiscated. At the end of the month, on 27 April, all Jews were asked to register for new ration books. This was another ruse to provide a list to match up with the earlier registration. These lists would be used by Germans and Hungarians to round up Jews.

* * *

Himmler had a warped mind, fiendishly twisted. He devised a plan that Eichmann was expected to put into operation. It was simple in outline. There were about a million Jews in Hungary. If the Allies gave the Hungarian government motorised trucks for civilian use (or on the Soviet front) and other commodities, then the Germans would release the million Jews. Eichmann referred to it as "Blut gegen Waren, " "blood in exchange for goods." He recruited Joel Brand at a meeting on Tuesday, 25 April 1944.

Joel was a member of the Relief and Rescue Committee in Budapest. What must have gone through Joel's mind? He accepted the role, of course; he had little alternative. Joel travelled to Ankara in Turkey, Jerusalem and Cairo, pleading the case. He met with American officials and the Jewish Agency for Palestine. When he got to Cairo, the British were having none of that sort of nonsense, and he was arrested. First, there was suspicion of the deal, and second, if they agreed, what do you do with a million people? The rescue scheme was never implemented. Eichmann had promised the Grand Mufti of Jerusalem that none of the Jews would reach Jerusalem. It is not known whether Himmler had duped Eichmann into believing in the scheme, but he probably did because if you are in on a scheme that you know will not work, then how do you really convince others it will? Then again, they were Himmler and Eichmann. Eichmann's scheme all along was to create a rift between the Western Allies and the Soviet Union, letting it leak out that the Western Allies had provided transport for use on the Eastern Front. It could also have been a tentative approach to seek a separate peace with the Allies to join with the Germans and attack the Soviets. We can only guess how Joel felt, heart-broken perhaps, condemned to think of those Hungarian Jews, torturing himself that he might have saved them, although everyone else knew it was an impossible task, especially Himmler.

MAY 1944

ONE TRANSPORT WITH 1,635 DEPORTEES

Sunday, 14 May 1944, Erich Naumann instructed all Dutch police units to arrest all Roma and Sinti as well as anyone dwelling in caravans. Those who held Italian or South American citizenship were released along with those who just happened to live in caravans. The rest were robbed, disinfected, locked up in Barracks 65 and told not to speak to the Jews.

* * *

On Tuesday, 16 May 1944, far away in Theresienstadt, two members of the cabaret group were boarding a train to Auschwitz, Ruth Pagener, number 2171, one of the Westerbork dancing girls, and Arthur Durlacher, the singer, who was on the second part of his journey, number 2309 this time.

Himmler had time to send Mother's Day greetings to Marga.

* * *

On Thursday, 18 May, again in Theresienstadt, two more of the cabaret group boarded a train to Auschwitz. They were Izaak Veffer, number 144, a costumier, and Sophie Wertheim, number 151, another of the dancing girls.

* * *

It was Friday, 19 May 1944, and another train stood ready to leave from Westerbork. There was nothing unusual about that, but there was an excited buzz from some on the camp station. Boots seemed to gleam even more today. Rudolf Breslauer was moving among the crowds. There was nothing unusual about that either. He was often about taking photographs; after all, he was the closest Gemmeker had to a camp photographer. Gemmeker invited him into his green and white house to take photographs of himself and his guests socialising. The train was delayed too, nor was there anything unusual about that. At the front were six coaches which would carry 238 Jews to Bergen-Belsen. The Jews going there usually travelled in coaches. Behind were freight wagons, holding 453 Jews going to Auschwitz, and then at the rear were 254 Roma and Sinti people. You could say that was different, but still not unusual. At this rate, the train would not leave until 1 pm. The train would stop at Assen where it would join with a Belgian train, carrying 507 prisoners from Mechelen to Auschwitz. That had happened before. If you watched, you could see Hans Margules, walking along closing the wagon doors. His overalls distinguished him from others on the platform. Mrs. Adelaar-Furth, the head of a Montessori school, was giving a speech about how she might be old but could still work. She withdrew into the wagon, and her friends left, going back into the camp. There were not many left now anyway. Nearly all of them were on the train.

There are Gemmeker and other German officers holding sheets of thin paper and *Scharführer* Hendrik van Dam signing lists off. Van Dam was hated, despised and feared. They were chatting and smoking among themselves. A couple marched off. What was unusual? It was the fact that Rudolf had a cine camera and was filming the entire proceedings. He had filmed their coming to the train and searching their allocated space. He had filmed inside the wagons, with some hiding their faces. He caught on film one of the eight known to be sick, who was wheeled along on a hideous contraption with two large wheels, a 61-year-old Frouwke Kroon from Appingedam. Rudolf had seen the 51 children, but they are not prominent in his film record. The doors were closing, and Rudolf was standing near a truck marked for 74 people. A door closed on a young girl looking out. Rudolf captured her thin face in the narrow opening. The girl was ten-year-old Settela Steinbach from Buchten. She was a young Sinti girl, taking her last look at Westerbork camp. Settela had been arrested in Eindhoven only last Tuesday. Settela's mother called to her to pull her head in before it was caught by the door. If you watch the record carefully, you can see Settela respond to her mother's voice – just a slight movement right before the door closed. Crasa Wagner was in the same wagon and recalled the mother telling her daughter to mind her head. Crasa would survive. Settela along with nearly one-quarter of a million Romani and Sinti would die. She would travel to Auschwitz where she would die with her mother, her two brothers, two sisters, an aunt and two nephews. The families of Crasa and Settela still remember the Porajmos, which means "the Devouring" or the Pharrajimos, "The Cutting Up."

Perhaps we see her on the film, but Marianne Kloos was on this train going east, too. She survived.

Rudolf carried on filming the rest of the train as it began to leave. He even caught on film the sausages meant for the guards. Watching his film, you might think the food was for the deportees. The German guards hung on the sides of the train as it moved off. I fancied I saw Gemmeker wheeling his bicycle away. Rudolf ran with his camera and caught up to the train. He could stand outside the camp and waited to catch the moments after the handover when the train moved off into the Dutch countryside.

Bergen-Belsen: Somewhere on that train was Avraham Asher, like Settela, he was ten years old and was deported with his family. They were listed as diamond workers and also had Palestine certificates.

There were many diamond workers on the train. Slottke confirmed that. She recorded that they were going to Bergen-Belsen because Himmler was once again considering the idea of a diamond industry. They were to wait until a new camp opened where their skills could be utilised. They had been at Vught, but Himmler wanted all transferred to Bergen-Belsen. The SS Main Economic and Administrative Department noted that the diamond industry in the Netherlands ceased to operate after 19 May.

Here are a few others who were on that transport: Suse Frank, a diamond worker, Rachel Sacksoni-Levie who was a Jehovah Witness and a diamond worker, Franz Heinz, a member of the French resistance. Renata watched the train arrive at Bergen-Belsen and saw 260 diamond workers assemble at roll call. The diamond workers were not necessarily popular in the *Sternlager*, as they did not have to work and got double food rations. Hetty E. Verolme saw them "lounging" around in the sun while she was marching off with her work detail and noted that they were nicely dressed. Two new barracks were being built to house the diamond factory. The diamond workers would stay there until the following December when they were sent to Sachsenhausen.

Out of 936 sent to Bergen-Belsen, only 20 survived the war.

* * *

Auschwitz: Some 699 were on the train for Auschwitz, including Settela. On this train were also 13 who had been caught by collaborators. Gerardus Ganzevles came across two addresses where 20 Jews had been hiding and turned them in. The other seven Jews followed on a later train. Only two of the 20 Ganzevles had found would survive. Ganzevles betrayed 52 Jews in all and earned himself nearly $1,000. He had better spend it quickly.

The train arrived the following Sunday. It drew up at the new platform in Birkenau. This was one of the first trains to pass through the tower gate right into the camp. Anna Sara Fels-Kupferschmidt saw a train coming in from Hungary. This train's deportees had been travelling for seven days and were in a terrible state. The comparison with her own train did not stand. Sara had dressed in as many clothes as she could and had eaten as much as she could. Sara and the others had to get off the train from Westerbork, and young men in striped uniforms told them to leave their luggage. The luggage was put into great piles. A Dutch man walked through the crowd and told them that they should not worry and that all would be well. The older people he said were going to a separate camp. She remembered the Belgian train as well. Of the men, 250 went into the camp, and of the women, 100. Some of the women were tattooed with the wrong number, which was crossed through with another added. They had been recorded as being Belgian, and that did not suit the German need for accuracy. Would it have mattered that five women got the wrong number? Well, it did matter to the Germans. What about the Sinti? One hundred and twenty-two men and boys from the Sinti and Roma group entered the camp, as did 124 women and girls, including Settela. By the end, out of 30 Sinti or Roma survivors, 18 were children. There were 64 Dutch survivors, including seven children.

Also arriving this month were the Flinker family. The children had been born in the Netherlands, but they had fled to Belgium. They had been betrayed some days earlier and were now selected to go into the camp. Father and son together, daughters to another part of the camp, mother to the gas chamber. Just like that a family was destroyed. The mother, Mindel, was torn from them, and the beating heart of the family slowed but did not stop.

* * *

Let me backtrack a little to add a little more to the Breslauer filming. During the spring of 1944, Rudolf Breslauer got a call to go see Gemmeker. He was not unduly worried, as he was often called to see

263

the Kommandant and to be given some photographic assignment. When he arrived this time, a box sat on the desk along with round canisters marked *Agfa*. He was told to open it and took out a cine camera. His instructions were to film the life of the camp. It was Gemmeker's intention to "showcase" his model camp. In the office was also Heinz Todtman, a German Jewish journalist. Gemmeker had used Todtman to write a script for the film he wanted to make of the model camp. It would start with Gemmeker leaving the camp office and touring the camp, and it would end with Gemmeker making a nightly patrol around the camp with the moon and chimney in the background. It was Breslauer's task, together with his assistant, Karl Jordan, to turn the script into moving pictures. He was told he could go anywhere to film with Todtman. Breslauer would show how orderly the camp was run.

So this was what Rudolf and Karl did. They had little alternative. Do as Gemmeker says, or you are on the next train out. Rudolf was even allowed to leave the camp and to accompany work units working outside of the camp. He shot a lot of film here and there, but in the end, only unedited reels were found. I am sure that Breslauer made a complete film with titles and diagrams showing the productivity of the camp. This would be 3,029 workers to Bergen-Belsen, 2,470 to Theresienstadt and 91,545 to the East. Notice this diagram did not include Sobibór or Auschwitz-Birkenau. Gemmeker and Todtman's script would not highlight death camps. Is this another indication that Gemmeker knew what happened there?

From early spring until into May, Rudolf and Karl toured the camp with instructions to those "in the shot" not to look directly into the camera and to carry on as if he were not there. There are no dates for any parts of the film but one. So let's accompany Rudolf on his tour of Westerbork and surroundings, but bear in mind that these sections would be edited and spliced with shots of Gemmeker and explanatory diagrams.

The film began out in the fields with an idyllic scene of a large horse being fed, and then the horse cantered around with a foal, free as it liked. There was even time for a young boy to be put on the back of the horse. The boy looked unsure. Then there were sheep grazing in a field. There was the narrow-gauge train hauling trucks full of bricks, a scene of life on the farm. Men were filmed working the soil by hand, then the soil being farrowed by a horse towing the rake and then a man struggling as he pulled a rake over the soil by hand. A group appeared like some well-oiled machine moving up the field planting beans followed by a girl who dropped a handful of manure over the bean. Rudolf used slow motion to show the accurate aim of the girl. The work was tiring, and Rudolf caught a group resting in the spring sunshine before starting to work again. He then joined a group out into the woods, showing how trees are felled and cut up, men and women working side by side.

It must have been a Sunday. Rudolf filmed the packed church with the minster at the front behind the altar, complete with white cloth and splendid cross. They must have been the Catholic converts. The choir sang heartily, and there were close-ups of children and adults singing along to the piano. Outside a football match was underway. Gemmeker encouraged football; it gave men an interest. They liked dressing in clean kit to play in leagues. There was a large crowd watching from the touchline; the only one out of place was the referee. Obviously Gemmeker drew the line at kit for the referee, for he was dressed in long trousers and shirt. Continuing the theme of exercise, the girls performing on the field were shown; Leo Kok would draw the girls as well, later in August – Lotte Heider would be leading the girls in their routines.

Rudolf was keen to show all the many industries in Westerbork. He entered a quiet workshop where women were busy cutting and sewing pieces of cloth together. There were the finished products of elephants and other toy animals. Rudolf used stop-frame animation, and one of the elephants knocked all the others over. Then the men were making wooden toys which are painted by the women. In the *Tischlerei*, men were manufacturing all sorts of things. The foreman moved around the shop, checking and giving advice. There was sawing, planing and lathe work. Next, hand brushes and what seem to be toilet brushes were being made. From wood, the film moved on to metal and to the blacksmith's shop, and here some welding and lathe working was shown. From there, it went into the shoe manufacturing shop, where welts were stitched, heels were ground and uppers were polished. Women cut up sacking and made shopping bags and gloves; they weaved and spun and made yarn. Tailors sat cross-legged or at benches, making clothes, and from there, Rudolf went into the hot and steam-filled laundry, where Mara Rosen worked and where Etty Hillesum came looking for a lost flannel. I doubt she found it in among the mountains of clothes being washed and dried and then ironed. Huge machines were used to press sheets.

Rudolf took us back outside of the camp as men pulled trucks along on the narrow rails, with a horse at the front. Then along came a narrow-gauge engine, and Rudolf was up in the driver's cab, showing how the train was operated. The driver could have been Richard Tieg, 20 years old. He could barter coal for food from the farmers along the railway's route. Richard was a member of the resistance, and his parents were safe in Spain. The train rode across the heath, with Rudolf filming through the cab window. There were more sheep which come running to meet the train, and then on it went, through the farm, on through the trees. And in the distance was the canal with barges and men boating. It was the Stadskanaal. The train followed the bend and ran alongside a dredger where men were working. They were driving large wooden planks into the embankment to repair it. Rudolf showed that they were using pressurised water to make a hole for the plank to slip into before it was driven deeper. Then the reason for the visit of the train was shown; it was to be filled with bricks from a barge. Men and women threw the bricks, hand to hand from barge to train where the bricks were carefully stacked into the trucks. The weather was bright, and men were in shirt sleeves. Back aboard the engine, the film returned to the camp. Next there were the large flat-bedded wagons brought into camp and left on one of the sidings to be unloaded of wooden prefabricated buildings. One could think that they were for new barracks, but they were green houses. The finished buildings were shown, and the planting of seedlings, which were then watered could be seen. It might have been on Gemmeker's orders, but no armed guards were to be seen. Everyone seemed to be working unsupervised other than by foremen in everyday clothes.

Still outside the camp, Rudolf took the camera by huge piles of scrap metal from aeroplanes. Crashed planes were brought to the camp to be dismantled and sorted for reusable metal. Men clambered over the piles to find parts to break up and sort. Sledgehammers were arcing through the air and land with a crash on lumps of metal. Johnny and Jones were here somewhere. Then through the workshop, Rudolf was astride a flat wagon rolling along on rails that ran through the middle of the shop. On either side were large machines and men at benches, stretching into the distance. Rudolf paused to show how the men were working. Then electrical instruments were being taken apart; everything had to be used. There were large barrels for copper, iron and aluminium. Women stripped wires to get at the copper, so needed for the German war effort. Nothing could be wasted.

Another work-shed, shovelled stone, out of wagons and into trucks to be taken away. Batteries were shovelled up to be broken open by hand. Hundreds and thousands of old batteries for recycling. Women stripped silver foil from its paper backing, sorting it into piles. Then a long clip showed women working at heavy clothing material, cutting and stitching on machines, and buttons being attached by machine. Everyone worked to help make the uniforms for the German army. Then there was a little idyllic scene of the camp signpost receiving some attention from a "pretty girl" on a ladder. Everything looked industrious, and no one was forced to work. Rudolf had shot absolute propaganda for Gemmeker. But he was not finished yet.

Over he went to the theatre where Willy Rosen and the Bühne were rehearsing. He showed us Willy Rosen first, at his piano in the orchestra pit. Erich Ziegler could be seen at another upright piano, conducting the orchestra. The camera moved along the pit, and the film gave a good view of the musicians in the pit; some were well-known jazz musicians. We could date this to April 1944; the team performed scenes from *Bunter Abend 4 and 5.* Esther Philipse came out on stage inviting the viewer to watch a scene called *"Parkett Reihe 1,"* "The Front Row at a Theatre"; it starred Esther, of course, as the usher, with Mara Rosen (Willy's Wife), Otto Aurich, the famous Dutch dancer, with his wife, Lisl Frank, and then two famous comedians and cabaret stars, Franz Engel and Max Ehrlich. Audiences would have known Franz from his many records and his film appearances. Max was mainly theatre and cabaret but tremendously popular. The latter two were seen performing *Fröhlich und Schön.* Lisl and Otto did a dance routine, and Esther Philipse sang again. Lisl and Otto then came to life as shop window mannequins in the scene called *"Schaufenster – Reklame,"* Shop Window – Advert. Then, for some it was the highlight, Willy Rosen and Erich Ziegler *An zwei Flügeln,* on two pianos – grand pianos at that – with Esther Philipse carrying out some silly business in between. Erich was a famous pianist and a composer but nowhere near as well-known as Willy, who had well over 600 hit songs in his repertoire. It was mostly Willy's show, fronted by Max Ehrlich, assisted with the music by Erich Ziegler and rehearsed by Hans Krieg, another famous composer. Then the whole cast came forward to take a bow as the curtain finally closed, with hardly a yellow star in sight.

What a wonderfully happy and industrious camp. Everyone looked clean and healthy; they were hard-working, and no guards were to be seen. You could show it to the Red Cross, and who could criticise it, apart from the question – "Why are you imprisoning Jews?" The amount of money being generated by Westerbork transit camp must have been huge and contributed greatly to the German war effort.

Some of you are perhaps saying that I have omitted something that Rudolf filmed. Yes, I have indeed. But everything was done according to the script. Even what happened on the "Boulevard of Misery," at "The Dutch Jerusalem." That was what the camp is colloquially known as. All the Amsterdam Jews were now in Westerbork. Was ever Jerusalem so industrialised?

Rudolf filmed the trains. Families arrived at the station and descended from carriages. They were met by Jewish camp workers, notably the Flying Column in their brown overalls, with *FK* on their armbands who would whisk luggage and people into the camp and also out again if departing. There were plenty of armed Dutch police in evidence. Next some wagons drew into the station to be met by armed German guards. Again the Flying Column were on hand to help these people. No luggage. All men wore clogs. No long coats in sight. Collars were turned up as the only protection from the cold. The deportees formed into lines and marched off. They were dirty and dishevelled, and it looked as if they were standing up in everything they had. They seemed to be slave labour brought in from perhaps Vught or farther afield. The films moved then over to the theatre hall, which was the main registration hall, with long tables full of typewriters and people sitting on both sides. On one side, they volunteered information to be recorded for their *Lagerkarte*, a camp card and work card if they are staying. It was all busy and noisy. Well-dressed Jews passed over information for the Nazi records office. People handing over their money to the bank were not shown.

It was Friday, 19 May 19. These were the people going off to die, and Gemmeker was there to see them off with his officers. It was in the script. Gemmeker looked directly into the camera. In fact, he would be ringed in red later, the only time colour is used in the film. He had his importance highlighted. Was it just another day, another train, another thousand going east?

* * *

During this month, Gemmeker banned dogs. Some prisoners were able to keep pet dogs in the camp, and Gemmeker also had a dog, an Alsatian. You can see it in Rudolf Breslauer's film walking alongside the train, not far from its master. Whether the other dogs took a dislike to the Nazi dog or were just being dogs, they set upon

Gemmeker's dog. The result was that all other dogs in the camp had to go, but Gemmeker kept his dog. Anyone found in contravention of this camp order was liable to transportation, which to some was to be avoided at all costs considering the rumours about what happened when anyone went east. Now if the inmates of Westerbork knew what was happening, how was it that Gemmeker did not?

JUNE 1944

ONE TRANSPORT WITH THREE PEOPLE TO
RAVENSBRÜCK

Tuesday, 6 June 1944 – The Western Allies invaded Normandy.

* * *

Friday, 9 June 1944 – Hannah Szenes (Senesh) was arrested in Hungary. The British tried to assist the Hungarian Jews. She was parachuted into Yugoslavia with 36 other Palestinians. There she spent three months with Tito's partisans but was determined to get to Hungary. She was arrested at the border and later executed.

* * *

Tuesday, 13 June 1944 – The first V1 rockets landed on London. They were built in factories with slave workers from the Netherlands and elsewhere.

* * *

Monday, 12 June 1944 – Alfred Ernst Rosenberg, the head of the Reich Ministry for the occupied Eastern Territories, ordered the kidnapping of 40,000 Polish children, aged between ten and 14 for slave labour.

* * *

Catharina Gokkes had been running with the partisans since the previous October, since her escape from Sobibór. Her leg had healed, and she had taken part in actions against the Germans. They were forcing the Germans back out of their area. Then on Thursday 22 June 1944, the day before the Germans withdrew, Kathy was shot dead.

* * *

Friday, 16 June 1944 – Himmler sent Marga copies of two of his speeches. Marga would claim she knew nothing of what was happening to Jews in Europe.

* * *

Friday, 23 June 1944 – three women were sent from Westerbork to Ravensbrück. They were ones who held foreign citizenship, and it was "hoped" that they could be repatriated to their own countries or bartered. They could be deported but not all the way east. This was an order from Gestapo Chief Heinrich Müller, so almost coming from Himmler himself. Harster read the instructions and acted accordingly. In his office, Zöpf advised in a telegram to SS-Hauptsturmführer Fritz Suhren, Kommandant at Ravensbrück, that three prisoners were on their way to him. Suhren was a nasty piece of work. He went to Ravensbrück from Sachsenhausen, and at 36, the sadistic tendencies he had had as a child were now fully developed. His overall aim was to work the prisoners as hard as they could for as little food as he was willing to let them have. He had arrived in 1942 and was feared. Yet Suhren refused to give Dr Karl Gebhardt prisoners for experimentation. Suhren objected, as most prisoners at the camp were political prisoners and therefore were kept for a reason. Suhren then received orders from above to hand over the prisoners to Gebhardt. It is easy to see why Suhren was overruled when you know that Gebhardt spent much of his time at *Hohenlychen Sanatorium*. Himmler was a regular visitor to that particular sanatorium owing to stomach ailments and stress. The fact that Gebhardt was Himmler's personal physician therefore may have had something to do with Suhren being overruled. Gebhardt was the one who liked to infect wounds and amputate limbs as well as give large doses of radiation. I will mention here Felix Kersten, with his round jolly face with a mop of hair atop and twinkling eyes. He was Himmler's personal masseur. Felix had been German but was now Finnish since borders of countries changed rapidly after World War One. The fact that he saved Jews from deportation was later contested, but he was passing information to the Americans and was also the intermediary between Himmler and Count Bernadotte. He was playing a dangerous game, whatever he was up to.

Zöpf sent 30-year-old Jolante Arato and another Hungarian woman to Ravensbrück. Jolante had been betrayed by a Dutch woman. The strange thing was that Jolante was not Hungarian. She had met the Hungarian ambassador while a member of the resistance, and the ambassador had given her a false passport. Her real name was Yehudit (Aufrichtig) Taube. She survived Ravensbrück by creating fantastic recipes in her head. Also deported was 30-year-old Gertrud Weisz from Munich. The next day, Slottke got involved. She was responsible for suggesting these small groups travel on escorted timetabled public passenger trains. She informed Suhren that Gertrud had escaped. Slottke referred to her as the Jewess and said she had jumped from the train in Utrecht and gone into hiding. She had eluded the guard on the train in Utrecht. Only one guard had been sent with the three women. I do not know who the other Hungarian woman was or whether, like the other two, she survived.

* * *

Friday, 23 June 1944 – The Red Cross visited Theresienstadt. Rahm, the Kommandant, well and truly pulled the wool over the eyes of Maurice Rossel and the other Red Cross delegates. Flower gardens were everywhere, fake shops opened, as did a café, a bank, a kindergarten and schools. The delegation reported back favourably to the International Red Cross. The Nazis would capitalise on this beautification in the attempt to sell Theresienstadt to the world. The member of the Danish Red Cross and two members of the International Red Cross visited at the insistence of the King of Denmark. Not wanting to upset the Danes and Swedes as a whole, the charade was finally agreed to by the Germans, as long as they had time to "beautify" Theresienstadt.

* * *

Luna Cymbalist-Peres with her daughter, Rosa, and husband, Simon, were mentioned in the telex sent by Zöpf to Bergen-Belsen. They were sent east on Friday 24 June 24 1944. Within a month they were all dead.

* * *

Do you remember Catharina Frank and her son, Clarence? They were sent to Theresienstadt, and Eichmann had said she would not be sent anywhere else. She was settled in Theresienstadt by this time, where everyone made such a fuss over Clarence. Rahm had made the preparations to deceive the Red Cross visitors. He called an artist, Charlotte Buresova, to his office. He pointed to the wall behind his desk and said that he wanted her to paint a picture of Madame Butterfly or similar that he could hang there so it beautified his office. I am sure Charlotte went away wondering what to paint. As she was puzzling over what would please Rahm, she spied Catharina with Clarence. She had painted Clarence and Catharina before, when she wore a blue flamenco dress and Spanish headdress entitled "The Last Flamenco." Here was her muse. Catharina became Madame Butterfly, and the painting was placed in Rahm's office.

It was likely that soon after the Red Cross visit had occurred, Eichmann turned up. Eichmann saw the painting and identified Catharina as its subject. Catharina was sent for and was asked how she was faring. She said it was difficult bringing up her son without privacy and she could do with some extra food. Eichmann had Catharina and her son transferred to a private room where they also received the extra food from the Danish deportees she was billeted with.

JULY 1944

FOUR TRANSPORTS WITH 396 DEPORTEES

Monday, 3 July 1944 – The Red Army liberated Minsk. Hardly a handful of the pre-war population of 80,000 Jews remained.

* * *

Friday, 7 July 1944 – Admiral Miklós Horthy, Regent of Hungary, halted the deportations of the Jews. This was after Hungary had been declared *judenrein*" except for the capital Budapest. The trains had taken 437,351 Jews to the death camps.

* * *

Saturday, July 1944 – The Kovno Ghetto in Lithuania was incinerated with its 2,000 Jews. About 4,000 had been taken west, mainly to Dachau, Kaufering and Stutthof where Bruno Dey was a camp guard. He was intent upon preventing escapes, a 17-year-old boy drafted into the SS, as he was unfit for the Wehrmacht.

* * *

Thursday, 13 July 1944 – Jewish Partisans who had escaped from the massacre at Ponary helped the Red Army liberate Vilna. They freed 2,500 Jews, which were the remaining 4 percent of the Jewish population.

* * *

Saturday, 15 July 1944 – Marga Himmler complained about the prisoners from Dachau *Außenkommando* who were building an air raid bunker in the garden at Haus Lindenfycht. Himmler was afraid that he would be targeted in an air raid. By September, the work was still not finished, and Marga complained to the Kommandant in Dachau about the slow progress the prisoners, working on a starvation diet, were making. They were all replaced.

* * *

I am sorry that I cannot tell you much about someone who appeared in communications sent between Zöpf's office, Buchenwald and Gemmeker in Westerbork. Such a man was Max Kampelmacher, born on 17 June 1902 in Siret, Romania. He had not done anything other than being a Jew and a Romanian. Zöpf was hoping that Max could be repatriated, but it had not happened yet. He would be sent to Buchenwald to wait. Gemmeker was ordered to transfer him to Scheveningen ready for transport to Buchenwald. Max is not listed among the dead, so he may have survived the war. Someone else was sent to Buchenwald with Max, and that was Dr. Andries Kaas, a psychiatrist imprisoned in Arnhem. At 36 years of age, he found himself going to Buchenwald simply because he had two Jewish grandparents and was therefore a Mischling. He had been found to belong to an organisation that aided Jewish refugees and was allocating funds. It was also found that Andries had hidden a Jewish child. For some reason this greatly upset Rauter, and he had demanded that Andries be deported out of the country. Fortunately, when he was arrested, his wife, Meia, was not. She was in the last stages of pregnancy, so she was not taken by the police. Zöpf told

SS-Obersturmbannführer Hermann Pister that the train would leave The Hague at 6:00 pm on Friday, 14 July 1944 and would arrive some point in the afternoon of Saturday, 15 July. We even know the names of the escort, SS-Hauptscharführer Wies and SS-Unterscharführer Weygand. Andries lived to see his son, Willem, and he returned home a changed man after what he had seen in Buchenwald.

* * *

Thursday, 20 July 1944 – A bomb exploded at the Führer headquarters, but Hitler was not killed. There were 15,000 arrests made with one-third of those being executed, some in a most hideous fashion, hanged with piano wire.

* * *

Saturday, 22 July 22 1944 – Lvov was liberated, but 110,000 Jews were dead.

Gudrun Himmler gave thanks that her father had not been in the room on 20 July when the bomb planted by von Stauffenberg exploded.

* * *

Monday, 24 July 1944 – Soviet troops liberated Majdanek Concentration Camp where some say that at least 80,000 had been murdered. Some put it at four times that number.

That same day, Jews were deported from Rhodes and Kos to Auschwitz.

* * *

Raoul Wallenberg, the Swedish diplomat in Budapest, issued diplomatic papers throughout July and established safe houses for 33,000 Jews.

* * *

Monday, 31 July 1944, another train left Westerbork for two destinations: Theresienstadt and Bergen-Belsen.

Some 213 people were sent to Theresienstadt. On Tuesday, 8 August 1944, Karl Rahm in Theresienstadt received a telegram from Gertrud Slottke telling him what to do with Jews holding Honduran or Paraguayan passports. Her message was simple. Those two countries had issued the passports as a gesture of goodwill, and they were worthless. Zöpf informed Rahm the same day that there were five groups: 146 Jews who had helped in some way with the cleansing of the Netherlands and the country's families; 23 Jews of intermarriages in which a spouse had died or been divorced and had part-Aryan children still in contact with the parent after three months in Westerbork; 19 Jews with *Sonderanweisungen*, "special instructions"; 14 Jewish war veterans with the Iron Cross; Portuguese Jews; and finally the *Stammliste* "Veterans of Westerbork" – 11 Jews who had helped build the Westerbork camp. You remember that Eichmann had also made them a promise, and here he was delivering on it. On the third day, Wednesday, 2 August, the train reached Theresienstadt. On the train was Gabriel Italie and his family, his wife, Sara Rose, and their grown children, Paul and Ralph, and Ida, who had recently turned 23 and had survived polio. Gabriel had not had much luck. His brother Nathan had been killed the previous year at Sobibór on 26 March1943. His brother Arthur had died in The Hague on 8 August 8 1940. And Herman, Gabriel's third brother, was killed in Auschwitz on 26 December 1943. His adopted sister, Matke, had been killed 19 November 1943. Gabriel only knew of Arthur. The family's luck changed, however. Gabriel's wife and three children survived.

Luck is an odd thing. Do circumstances favour some people and not others, as if a circumstance has a life and can make choices? Is that luck? What do you say to a survivor who says that God saved them? Do you point out that God chose not to save the others? Does God have a purpose in all this that we are not aware of, as we are only human, only made in his image? Are these questions without answers?

The train consisted of a mixture of passenger carriages and freight wagons. Usually all those going to Theresienstadt or Bergen-Belsen would travel in passenger coaches. Not this time; 178 people were destined to go to Bergen-Belsen.

Friday, 4 August, four days after the train had left, Gemmeker sent the manifest to Rauter. Rauter sent five lists to SS-Hauptsturmführer Josef Kramer who was the Kommandant of the concentration camp. Kramer had arrived from Auschwitz last December. Although there were not any gas chambers at Belsen, the camp still accounted for something like 50,000 deaths. On the lists were 47 children, 23 Jews with visas for Palestine, 131 who had connections with hostile countries and could be used for bargaining, eight from the diamond industry and 17 who held foreign passports.

On this train were Lena Reindorp-van-Essen, 37, and Betzalel Siegurd-Kaufmann of Duisburg, aged 15. Lena remembered that she had been betrayed by a neighbour and then arrested by six German soldiers and a member of the Dutch Nazi Party. She had been put in the penal block at Westerbork. She knew all the others arrested at the time with her were dead. Betzalel remembered hearing gunshots on the way. They found out that someone had tried to escape and that security on the train was then tightened. When they arrived at Bergen, the person who had attempted to escape was beaten but went into the camp with the others. It was odd that they were not shot. They went to the Sternlager where there were now 4,000 people. At the start of 1944, 379 Jews had been in that part of the camp. The majority at this time were Dutch Jews.

Renate Laqueur saw that the train was from Westerbork. She found out from the newcomers that their letters had been reaching Westerbork. All those with *Austauschsperre* destined for exchange were now in Bergen-Belsen. Telegrams had come from Istanbul from the people sent to Palestine. Renate got a letter from her parents in Westerbork. They were worried, as they thought that those in Belsen did not get enough to eat. The children on the train did not fare well. Quite a few died from disease, one was murdered in Auschwitz and two went on "The Lost Train" and died at Tröbitz. Poor Jacob Elsas, who was 17, died on the day the camp was liberated, six days before he would have turned 18. After liberation, thousands in the camp continued to die, despite the care given to them by British medics, many from disease but also from eating the wrong sort of foods until a nutritionist arrived who started to give the survivors rations like those issued to people who had starved in famine in India, just shortly before.

* * *

Monday, 31 July 31 1944 – Settela died in Auschwitz. A member of the cabaret group also died that day. All I know about her is her surname, Troeder, and that she was a member of the ballet group and appeared in *Bravo da Capo*.

AUGUST 1944

NO TRANSPORTS

Thursday, 3 August 1944 – Leo Kok painted Lotte Heider and the girl gymnasts in Westerbork.

* * *

The war would come very much into the camp. Inmates often saw planes flying over, so many, in fact, that it seemed that "the birds could walk across the sky." Westerbork had wire fences and watch towers. From the air, it looked like a military camp. Harry Klafter was walking across the camp when a Lockheed Lightning swooped around and strafed the camp. Bullets bit the ground around Harry. He threw himself backwards; his friend threw himself forwards. Harry got up from the ground – his friend lay lifeless. In Barrack 85, three people were hit, one fatally.

* * *

On 4 August 1944, in Prinsengrach 263 Amsterdam, a family had been in hiding for two years since July 1942. They were hidden away from the Germans, like thousands of others. Also in the "Secret Annex" were the van Pels family and Fritz Pfeffer. They were aided by Victor Kugler, Johannes Kleiman, Miep Gies and Bep Voskuijl. *SS-Oberscharführer* Karl Silberbauer arrived with the local police, and they were all taken away. Anne Frank's diary was left behind in the hiding place. People often think Anne was Dutch, but she was German from Frankfurt and had moved to Amsterdam when she was four years old. Removal vans from the firm of Abraham Puls appeared soon after to seize belongings.

* * *

Sunday, 6 August 1944 – 60,000 Jews had been sent to Auschwitz from Łódź. The deportations continued.

* * *

Friday, 11 August 1944 – Marga Himmler noted in her diary the disgrace of officers wanting to kill Hitler and that it was a miracle he was still alive.

* * *

Wednesday, 16 August 1944 – Kurt Gerron commenced filming in Theresienstadt *The Führer has given the Jews a city*.

* * *

The Flying Column and OD often worked outside the camp. Rather bizarrely they supplemented the work of a collaborator, Willem Christiaan Heinrich Henneicke. He ran what came to be called the *Henneicke Kolonne*, the Henneicke Column. He worked for *Zentralstelle für Jüdische Auswanderung, Abteilung Hausraterfassung*. This organisation emptied confiscated Jewish houses. Henneicke also ran a group of 50 plus collaborators who tracked down Jews and handed them over to the Germans for a reward, as I mentioned. Inmates of Westerbork were used for the heavy work. Harry Klafter once worked with such a team and was driven to Zeist. He was admiring the beautiful houses from the back of the lorry. The lorry stopped, and Harry and Mr Bezem were left to clean one house. They did not do much, as no one was watching them. Two women appeared whom Harry knew to be members of the resistance known to his brother. They were there to help Harry escape. But he knew his mother would be deported by Gemmeker, so he declined. Freddy, who was Harry's brother, knew many in the resistance. One of Freddy's associates was Mijntje Leisen or "Tante Koos," who rescued children from the Jewish Creche at the Schouwburg Theatre in Amsterdam. Harry decided about half past three that he ought to show that he was willing and threw a bucket of water over the floor and began mopping. A little while later, the new resident of the previously Jewish domicile appeared. The SS man duly arrived at four o'clock and spoke to the two Jews as to how his hometown had been bombed, and he was worried about his family. If he expected sympathy from Harry, he did not get any. Harry inwardly felt joy that the Germans were being made to suffer. A few days later, Harry's mum was deported to Theresienstadt.

* * *

Wednesday, 23 August 1944 – Romania surrendered to the Soviets.

* * *

Monday, 28 August 1944 – The Slovaks started an uprising. In the fighting, 5,000 Jews were captured and killed along with 1,900 Slovaks. Around 13,000 Jews were sent to Auschwitz.

* * *

The school in Westerbork was closed owing to outbreaks of scarlet fever and polio. The children were taught in the barracks, which was not entirely suitable. First, there was an absence of teachers, and second, many of the older children who had been working were too tired to study. Again, there were complaints about the amount of room they required. Hélène Wolff wrote in one of her letters that 12 children were crowded around a table, squeezed onto two benches, which did not leave any room for anyone to get by. Yet others remembered children corners in the barracks, where children could play and not disturb anyone. All memories are different depending on the time that someone was in the camp. There was a brief return to the school, but again it was closed in November and did not reopen properly until 1945. Not everyone went to school. Some younger survivors could not even remember there being a school, unless of course it did not make any impression. Otto Kallus remembered Hebrew lessons. It taught him one word, that for "child," the rest he forgot. It really would have been "in one ear and out the other." Of course, some teachers were transported. Jacobus Valk remembered the cessation of his German lessons when Miss Schülz was "sent on," literally to who knows where. Some younger survivors told of games and organised walks between the barracks or playing out on the heath in the hot summer of 1944. Yet others recalled how there was so much organised for the youth in Westerbork. If you knew about it, it had happened. If you did not know about it, it had not. Jacobus Valk remembered the kind Mr Baruch. He gave the children rolled up newspapers and told them to swat flies, of which there were many. He promised those who swatted 100 or more would get extra "fly soup." It was fun to swat the flies, but there was no soup.

SEPTEMBER 1944

THREE TRANSPORTS WITH 3,361 DEPORTEES

Friday, 1 September1944. Gemmeker stood on a podium in the main hall. Harry Klafter was there. He heard him use words like "regret" and "sorry" as he informed everyone there that Westerbork Camp was to be evacuated. He told them that 1,000 would depart on Sunday to Auschwitz and 2,000 on Monday for Theresienstadt. The evacuation would include the baptised, the Barneveld group, the alte Kampinsassen and those on the registered lists. This meant just about everyone. Only 300 would be kept behind to run the camp. There was shock and horror on the faces as even the Flying Column realised that they would be assisting themselves to the train and preventing themselves from running away. Harry and his brother, Freddy, found their names on the list for Theresienstadt where their mother was. They made plans and escaped the camp Sunday evening.

* * *

Gabriel Italie had estimated that 800 people were being held in the punishment barracks when he left in August. Among them were Anne Frank and her family. On Sunday, 3 September 1944, a train arrived to take them away to Auschwitz. The transport was not expected, but when the bakery was ordered to bake a larger number of loaves, it was then suspected a deportation was imminent. Ronnie Goldstein van Cleef remembered a member of the camp police coming to the barracks with a German to read out the list. They thought it would be for Bergen-Belsen, not Auschwitz. Freight wagons duly arrived. A group of orphans were put onto the train. Lenie de Jong van Naarden watched Gemmeker and the other officers. Gemmeker stood there motionless and emotionless. He did not see what was happening – it was only another train. Ronnie Goldstein-van Cleef confirmed that the Kommandant was there to see the children board. The punishment barracks were empty, and the hospital was nearing empty. They were nearly all to go on the train, 70 people in each wagon. Then the doors closed. The second group were ordinary Jews. Their treatment in Westerbork was better than for those in the punishment barracks, but on the train, everyone was the same. The third group was composed of those from mixed marriages, who were no longer protected by the status of a spouse who was divorced or dead.

Sal de Liema, 30 years old, stood in another cattle cart pushed up against a woman. They started to talk, and she told Sal what he did not want to hear. The truth. She said she had been where they were headed. She had been before but was brought back to the Netherlands as a witness in a trial, and now she was returning. She told him what would happen when they arrived: 90 percent would be taken away and murdered. He told her not to tell the others. When the train arrived, Sal thought he had arrived in hell. It was dark, the Germans were shouting, and there were spotlights glaring into their faces. The Germans shouted a name, and Sal's travelling companion was taken away. She knew her fate. The Germans asked for the mothers of the children. They too were put into the lorries with the children. Sal noticed that there were no children in Auschwitz.

An escape had been made from this train. A worker from the sawmill had smuggled in a saw. Behind a wall of suitcases, they had cut a hole and escaped after the train had passed through Assen. Seven of them slipped away, and three were injured in the escape. When the escape was discovered, the wagon was emptied, and everyone else was moved to other wagons.

Otto, Anne Frank's father, was given the number B-9174. The old, the children and many women, 763 of those were on the train, went straight to the gas chambers. Anne, her mother, Edith, and her sister, Margot, were selected for labour. Edith died in Auschwitz the following January.

Frieda Brommet had not been in Westerbork long when she was transported to Auschwitz. Her family had been betrayed, having spent two years living above a bicycle shop. She watched as her father joined one line and she and her mother, Rebecca, joined another, standing near to each other. That would be the last view of her father. He was not selected to work in the camp. Frieda and her mother were taken to a large hall and renamed with a number. They undressed and were shaved all over and then showered. They were issued clothes, for Frieda a summer frock and two left shoes. Then they went to work carrying bricks day in and day out for four kilometres. There was illness after illness and spells in the hospital barracks. She lay in the bed next to Anne and Margot Frank.

* * *

Monday, 4 September 1944 was the final transport to Theresienstadt. There were 2,074 on the list, with quite a few names from those whom I have told you about. For a start, almost every member of the Bühne cabaret group was on this train, including Willy Rosen, number 576; Max Ehrlich, number 151; Mara Rosen, number 577; Esther Philipse, number 767 with her two sons; the teenager Flips Sanders, number 169; Franz Engel, number 163; Johnny and Jones, numbers 346 and 741; Leo Kok, number 364; and Hannelore Cahn, number 102. Out of the 70 or so associated in some way with the cabaret, only 19 survived the war, and two of those died within days after the liberation. Gemmeker was instructed to end the cabaret shows, and therefore the group was up for deportation. I heard a story that Willy Rosen was given a letter written by Gemmeker to

Rahm in Theresienstadt that they should receive special treatment and get good rooms. If there were a letter and the words were used were "special treatment," then it was even more cynical than writing the letter in the first place. Four of the group lingered to see the others off. Four were not being transported: Chaja Goldstein, Lotte Heider, Beatrice Lissauer and Erich Ziegler. Chaja, the performer of the dance "Ping Pong" was Polish, which may have been why she was not transported. Lotte Heider had been drawn with the other girls performing gymnastics by Leo Kok. She kept that drawing by Leo of the girls spelling out her initials. Beatrice was in a relationship with Saloman Sandor of the camp police, and this may have saved her. Erich was the accomplished pianist. Gemmeker liked music and kept him back to play a jazz version of Beethoven's Ninth to his guests.

It was also Rudolf Breslauer's family from Leipzig's turn. There were Rudolf and Bella, born Weissmann, and their three children. Ursula was about 16; then there was Stefan, aged 13, and the youngest was Marc Michael, aged eight. Rudolf had served his purpose; Gemmeker no longer need a photographer. Karl Jordan was also on the train. The assistant had to go east as well. Their film was back at Westerbork. It was a couple of hours of scenes that would never be used to showcase Gemmeker's model camp. Perhaps it would be shown to him when he was interviewed, and he would point to the fact that everyone looked well from his time spent as Kommandant of the camp. Wim Loeb, part of the photographic team, continue to work on it and to smuggle out information to the Dutch resistance.

The Drukkers were also on the train. Maurits and Erna Drukker and their two children, Elly and Alfred, were all bound for Theresienstadt.

Somewhere on this train was also one of the oldest people to die during the Shoah, Klara Borstel-Engelsman. She was 102 years old, born in 1842. As Klara was on this train, did it mean she was still fit for work? This was train XXIV/7, and Klara was number 1946. She reached Theresienstadt on 6 September three days later, where she was entered as Clara Borstel-Engelmann. She travelled no farther. Her death was recorded at Theresienstadt. Some think she died at Auschwitz, but I cannot find any record of her leaving nor arriving as Klara Borstel-Engelsman. It has been asked before: Why was there a need to murder a 102-year-old woman?

Another group on the train were Jews who had converted to Christianity. The Dutch Protestant Church had made noises about the deportations, so Seyss-Inquart promised they would be kept in the Netherlands. There was a great deal of pressure from Rauter and others for them to be deported. They had by now all been drawn to Westerbork. Seyss-Inquart eventually gave permission for them to be deported to Theresienstadt and wrote a letter of apology to the Dutch Church, saying that Jews could not be in a war zone. The Allies were advancing, and indeed some were starting to think already that the war had ended. It came as rather a shock that the certificate of baptism was now no longer their protection. Ilse Blumenthal said they had to start sorting their things and stuffing them into their rucksacks. They marched to the freight wagons, 90 people with were luggage crammed in, a barrel by the door and hardly any light inside. The lucky ones got a wall to lean against. Sasha Ben Shalom remembered the journey – how could he forget it – and that the train was left standing in a siding. The doors were flung open, and the deportees were greeted with the words "Heil Hitler" and told to hand over their watches, pens and anything else of value. Then they were shut back into the dark.

Later, they fell out of the wagons, continually shouted out. They formed up and marched off, including Eduard Meijers, an expert on the law. He had written the civil code for the Netherlands and survived to do so again.

Willy Rosen clutched a case, possibly full of music and his latest piece of prose: *"Abschied eines Alten Kampinsassen,"* "Farewell of an old camp inmate." It began with "Mein liebes Westerbork, ich muss nun von dir scheiden." He left Westerbork like a man leaving a wife. He had hoped to perform again in Theresienstadt. Some 2,074 people entered Theresienstadt on Wednesday, 6 September 1944. Oddly, Willy Rosen was not one of the original German camp inmates at Westerbork, yet he obviously came to regard himself as such, promoting himself through the camp hierarchy above many Dutch people who had arrived before him. It was rather a presumption on his part, no doubt encouraged by the favoured position in the eyes of Gemmeker. It would also be another reason for many not to like Willy Rosen and the others of the Bühne. Although Hannelore Grünberg-Klein said the poem spoke as if from their hearts, he possessed the ability to touch hearts, if not minds.

The filming in Theresienstadt, also as a model camp continued, although Kurt Gerron has been sacked, and Karel Pečený had taken over. Karel Pečený was Czech and produced "Aktualita," a newsreel company.

* * *

On Wednesday, 6 September 1944, four men were executed at Westerbork by firing squad at the back of the crematoria.

John Ancona
Johan Frederik Theodor Engers
Samuel Goldstein
Ernst Katan

Their bodies were cremated two days later. Their crimes are not known and extremely little is known about them. They may have been the four inmates Harry Klafter talked about when he said that four Jews were shot while escaping. It seems that they may have been shot after an escape attempt rather than in the attempt, something Gemmeker would be responsible for.

* * *

I must also mention a transport that left from Vught on Wednesday, 6 September 1944. Five people were transported. Records are unclear as to who they were, and it's assumed they were Jews. But they were not Jews, or at least not all of them were. These five included Corrie ten Boom and her sister, Betsie. It was the only transport from Vught to Ravensbrück in September 1944. The officials who saw to the administration of the train were Wilhelm Zöpf, Hans Albin Rauter, Wilhelm Harster and Gertrud Slottke. You may remember that Slottke was all in favour and suggested small deportations; this was one of them.

* * *

Monday, 11 September 111944 – Kurt Gerron was no longer needed to work on the film being made in Theresienstadt. In fact, he only had a very minor role anyway. He acted as an assistant, encouraging people to smile on the film. All to no avail, the film would not be seen anyway, but it stands as a testament to the perverse nature of the Nazis.

* * *

The last transport out of Westerbork left on Wednesday, 13 September 1944. A total of 268 deportees were bound for Bergen-Belsen and 11 for Auschwitz. The papers were in Rauter's office. Again, each list had the individual's number on the train, their date of birth and their occupation. The deportees were grouped. One is there at the orders of Harster. Thirty-one held Paraguayan passports, and still more diamond workers were headed for Bergen-Belsen, 24 of those. A group of 12 whose "racial origin" could not be determined as their *Abstammungsuntersuchungen* turned out somewhat vague. There were 55 whose nationality was classed as foreign, Turkish and possibly even Egyptian. Also on the train were 58 Mischlinge. Then there were 50 children who had been caught in hiding and were considered Jewish. This last little group was quite pathetic; they were children whose parents had given them over to others to hide, but they had now been discovered. I cannot recall whether I have mentioned the Kindertransport. It is possible that some of the orphans Gemmeker had been sending east were children from these transports who had come from Eastern Europe. Ten thousand children came from Berlin, Vienna, Prague, and other major cities, passing through the Netherlands, as the Germans refused the use of their ports. Not all the children were Jewish, but possibly more than 75 percent were. There were various agencies involved, mainly Jewish ones, aimed at getting Jewish children out of harm's way. Some of these were lucky and went to England and then further afield; some Kindertransport children only went as far as France or the Netherlands. In England, some children were saved by Nicholas Winton, and in the Netherlands, they were saved by Geertruida Wijsmuller-Meijer. On 14 May 1940, Geertruida saw off 74 children on the SS Bodegraven out of the port of Ijmuiden. She could have but did not go with them. The next day, all borders were closed. Many children from the Kindertransporte were trapped in the Netherlands and other countries. The Dutch took in as many of the children as they could hide, and others ended up directly in orphanages even though their parents were still alive. Many of these poor children were sent east alone. On this train were perhaps a few of these children who had lost their parents more than four years ago, children who had been moved here, there and everywhere and were lost, frightened and feeling alone. Gemmeker did not display any compassion for them. They were numbers on a list used to make up the full inventory.

Sitting in one of the wagons was 19-year-old Fredrika (Elly) Kulker. She was a seamstress but was in with the diamond workers, as she was related to one, her father, Josephus. Her mother, Grietje, was there too. She had been arrested twice and had now been waiting in Westerbork since 29 September 1943.

In another freight car was Mary Andriaansz-Groen sitting with some of the children on the straw that had been placed in the wagon. There were some rough tables and chairs too. The children had some milk and water in bottles and a wicker laundry basket filled with sandwiches. The Germans told them to throw them out, as they would get better where they were going. They did as they are told, and it was something that they would regret, as the journey was long.

They would be on that train for three days. The milk went sour. They drank all the water. Some of the young children should have still been in nappies, but there were none. They tried singing songs and telling stories, but in the darkness of the wagons, the conditions were more than depressing. It was a very hot September, and it was sweltering in the wagons. On one occasion, the train stood in the sun for hours. The doors only opened once, and the Germans came with water for the children. Water for a baby was no use, so Henriëtte Delia (Jetje) Hamburger, not yet a year old, died from dehydration on the journey. After they reached Bergen, they had to walk to the camp, but the children and Mary went by lorry.

Gideon Drach, 28, was a member of the resistance and should have gone on that transport. You remember how Rudolf Breslauer rode on the footplate of the train out into the countryside? It may have been driven that day not by Richard Tieg but by Kurt Walter. Kurt helped Gideon escape by hiding him in one of the wagons on the narrow railway. Kurt drove the train out into the countryside, and Gideon ran away. He was hidden but eventually recaptured and sent back to Westerbork, but by then the transports had ended.

Josephus Kulker died in Bergen-Belsen on the very last day of 1944. Frederika and her mother, Grietje, both survived, as did Mary.

Ribca Chichou had been sent east on the last train that left Westerbork. She went to Bergen-Belsen and was then evacuated on Sunday, 8 April 1945. She had been found with the train by American troops who gave food and medical assistance. But already suffering from disease, she died days after being liberated at Hillersleben.

* * *

On Wednesday, 20 September 1944, ten members of the Dutch resistance were executed for various robberies and arson:

Jans Diemer
Andries Diepenbrug
Wessel Jan Knot
Pieter van Laarhoven
Rendert de Poel
Geert Por
Anne Rutgers
Jan Toet
Roelof Tuin
Johannes Vis

* * *

Monday, 25 September 1944, 12 more men were executed at the execution area behind the crematoria. It was an overcast sort of day with the temperature not rising much above 14°C and hardly two hours of sunshine. These were the names of the murdered:

Pieter Teeuwes Barkema
Willem Christiaan Lodewijk Barkema
Klaas Bouma
Hendrik Date Bus
Julius Cohen
Jan Rengenier Dijksterhuis
Hendrik Otto George van der Kooi
Karsien Kriegsman
Willem Antoon Kriegsman
Claas Joseph Cornelis Rooda
Jan Smallenbroek
Pieter Berend Venema

Pieter Johan Faber and Klaas Karel Faber, both fervent Dutch Nazis responsible for murders of many Dutch, were part of the firing squad that day.

* * *

Thursday, 28 September 1944 – Churchill announced the formation of the Jewish Brigade. It would go on to fight in Italy, Yugoslavia and Austria. Young Jews were drawn to it, and when based in Belgium and the Netherlands in 1945, it would also prepare clandestinely for military organisation in British-occupied Palestine.

* * *

Friday, 29 September 1944 – much toing and froing was occurring in Theresienstadt. A train was being loaded destined for Auschwitz-Birkenau. On the train were many from Westerbork who had been at Theresienstadt thinking that they were safe. Some had been given vacuous promises by Gemmeker that they would be looked after. A number were from the Bühne who had been looking for a purpose to no avail. Some were reunited with those who had been sent ahead. Upon arrival, they were pleased to know this earlier group were still alive. Willy Rosen was trying to say his fond farewells to his wife, Mara. Both tried to comfort each other with well-meant assurances. But deep down, both knew that this would be the last time that they would be together. Mara was kept behind in Theresienstadt, and Willy was about to be deported. Gemmeker's letter, if he ever wrote one, was gone. It is doubtful that Willy would have used the reverse side for composition. It is hard to write on a sheet of paper when it is in a thousand small pieces. Willy might have bemoaned the fact that they were unlucky. Those selected had numbered 2,500, but there were not enough cattle wagons, so only 1,500 were going today. The rest would follow. Teenager Flip Sanders stayed a few more days in Theresienstadt before following the others members of the Cabaret group to Auschwitz.

* * *

Nol (Arnold Siméon) van Wesel and Max (Salomon Meyer) Kannewasser, also known as Johnny and Jones, were on the train as well. They were numbers 1106 and 932. At Westerbork they broke up aircraft; Leo Kok drew them both, and they sang once in the shows. Gemmeker did not like their Americanized Dutch accents, so they had been banned. They found themselves on this train off to Auschwitz, having been selected by Sturmbannführer Rahm. Johnny and Jones became brothers according to Nazi records at Ohrdruf camp; they could be no closer anyway. Leo Kok, number 1109, was there with them, but his need to draw was not with him that day. He sat with the others. In fact, 1,504 people on this train, from Karl Abraham from Berlin to Hertog van Zweeden from Amsterdam.

Mara Rosen may have asked Max Ehrlich to take care of Willy, and Max in his humorous way would have said it should be the other way around. It would be a kindness to think that the friends were together on the journey. But German efficiency did these things in alphabetical and numerical order. Willy was number 875 and Max was number 789, so they were probably not in the same wagon but maybe close. Five members of the cabaret group started their journey to Auschwitz. None would get to go home.

* * *

On the second day, Transport El arrived from Theresienstadt. Max Piskorz remembered they had to write a postcard to their families. When one card was short in his wagon, the guard threatened to shoot everyone in the wagon. The card was handed in. All the cards said the same thing: "I am well. Arrived safely. The work is bearable. The food is sufficient. Hope to see you soon."

Jozef Hilel Borensztajn said that one person was shot for throwing a piece of paper out of the train. They had to wait for some time with the doors closed. There were two trains running back and forth from Theresienstadt to Auschwitz-Birkenau. When the tracks were clear, they would leave one day and arrive the next. The five members of the cabaret group lined up with the men on the ramp at Birkenau. Their small amount of luggage was discarded. They were inside the camp in full view of everything going on and moved up the line to the doctor. It could have been Mengele, but few children came from Theresienstadt, so it probably was not him. With a flick of the hand, a person's fate was decided. Three went to the right, and Willy with Max Ehrlich went to the left.

There is a story that Max was recognised by a camp guard and told, at gun point, to tell a joke. Max had not been in a film for at least 12 years, and time in the camps took its toll, so he would not have looked his best and had only performed for Jews since the mid-1930s. I have tried to verify the story. I have asked around, but nothing. Maybe it happened, and maybe it did not. Perhaps Max and Willy went into the gas chamber together, undressing in public, making sure their shoes were tied together, walking naked into the shower and being pushed up against other naked bodies, waiting for whatever – water or gas? In these "showers," it was always gas. There was a noise above, a flash of light and then a rattling noise. Those nearest to the pellets of Zyklon B, the rat poison, started to feel the effects of the cyanide. The noise climbed to a crescendo.

Dr Charles Bendel from Romania had seen this procedure many times. A man on a motorcycle would arrive at the crematoria to say that a transport had arrived and that there would be such and such a number for gassing. People would be tipped out of the lorries. They were told to undress and were then forced into the gas chamber, and the doors would be shut. By a macabre twist of fate, the gas canisters would arrive in an ambulance with a red cross on the side. Mengele and the other doctors oversaw the process. The hatches in the roof were opened and the pellets dropped in. There was a great deal of noise, which subsided after three minutes. After 20 minutes, the doors were opened, and the bodies chest high across the floor were dragged out either to the crematorium or burning pits, which had been dug and filled with logs soaked in petrol. These could dispose of 1,000 corpses in an hour, whereas the furnaces could only manage that number in a day. If there was not enough room in the shower, those left over were shot and pushed into the pits. The Sonderkommandos were beaten to encourage them to drag the bodies to the pits as quickly as possible, after the collection of anything of value on or in the corpses. Dr Bendel's job was to look after the Sonderkommando, who were kept locked up away from the others in the camp to prevent what they were doing from becoming common knowledge. After a time, when they were exhausted, they would be put into the gas chambers themselves, and a new group would take over their jobs. While working, they lived. If they were of no use, they died. They could not be released, as they knew too much. How did that weigh against this Nazi ideology that it was not only their legal right but also their moral right to murder the Untermenschen, the lower orders of humanity? Why destroy Treblinka and plant it with lupins? What had they to fear? It is always the same answer; they knew what would happen to them if caught. Why run if you were doing your duty? Why hide if you were doing your duty? Why change your name if you were doing your duty? "I was doing my duty," they would all say.

OCTOBER 1944

Last month saw the end to the transports out of Westerbork. The war was not over yet. It was nearing an end, but Westerbork was reasonably safe, up in the north of the Netherlands, close to the German border. "Operation Market Garden" had started halfway through September and lasted eight days, from 17 to 25 September. It did not reach or affect Drenthe, but the government in exile with the Queen called on railway workers to stop working. About 30,000 workers went into hiding, and for a short time the railways came to a halt. The resistance spent much of their efforts hiding these people. The hope had been to curtail the German troop movements; however, the Germans just ran their own trains over the tracks. Fortunately for those in Westerbork, the capacity to transport Jews was curtailed. No doubt Slottke had trains planned, but they only travelled on paper. In retaliation the Germans restricted the movement of food supplies, which contributed greatly to the Winter Famine of 1944–45. Anywhere up to 22,000 people died, and many relied upon soup kitchens.

* * *

Sunday, 1 October 1944 – Hermann Feiner, the funny man from the cabaret group, was transported from Theresienstadt to Auschwitz as number 691 on Transport Em. He was sent straight to the gas chamber on Tuesday, 3 October when the train arrived.

* * *

Tuesday, 2 October 1944 – The Warsaw Uprising was crushed by the Germans. It had lasted two months and cost 250,000 Polish lives. The Soviet Army regrouped only a few miles from Warsaw.

* * *

Wednesday, 4 October 1944 – Olga Maria (Mara Krauskopf) Rosen, Willy Rosen's second wife, was sent as number 87 on Transport En from Theresienstadt to Auschwitz. She had most likely been told she would meet up with Willy at Auschwitz. Very soon after arriving she found everything she had been told was a lie. With her were 336 Dutch Jews. The train arrived at Auschwitz on Friday, 6 October.

* * *

On Friday, 6 October 1944, Transport Eo left for Auschwitz. On board was young Flip Sanders, number 632. With Flip were his mother, Marta, 629; his brother, Hans, 630, and his baby sister, Judith, 631. Flip helped with the revues, and while doing so, neither he nor his family were transported. His father, Henri, had left on the same train as Willy Rosen and the other men. Flip had arrived in Theresienstadt with Willy and a few of the others. Now he was leaving for Auschwitz at the same time as Esther Philipse, number 378, the singer and dancer. With Esther were her boys Leon, aged ten, and David Edward, aged eight. Her husband, Dr Salomon, had died last Sunday, but she did not know that. She too was hoping to see him again.

The following day, Saturday, 7 October 1944, the Sonderkommando at Auschwitz-Birkenau completely destroyed Crematoria IV. They had learned they were going to be killed, as Auschwitz was the last working death camp. Support from the local resistance was hoped for. They attacked the SS with hammers and axes and stones and set fire to the building. When the smoke became visible, a general revolt broke out, and several hundred prisoners escaped. Weapons hidden in Crematoria I were not used. The SS response was swift and brutal. Most of the prisoners were recaptured, and 200 who had revolted were executed. The SS discovered gunpowder had been smuggled into the camp from one of the sub-camps, leading to further torture and executions.

Monday, 9 October 1944 – Philip Mechanicus was moved from Bergen-Belsen to Auschwitz-Birkenau with 120 Jews or others who had infringed upon some Nazi directive.

Tuesday, 10 October 1944 – Fritz Bernhard from the cabaret group was sent from Auschwitz to Dachau.

Thursday, 12 October 1944 – Philip Mechanicus was shot at Auschwitz-Birkenau.

The same day, an execution of 17 men took place at Westerbork. These were their names:

Jacob Bruggema
Pieter Heertje Dijksterhuis
Johannes Jacobus Eskes
Sietse W Gjaltema

Jan Arend Grobbe
Cornelis Hoving
Allard Kwast
Christinus Wieger Lubbers
Johannes Moerman
Harm Molenkamp
Tonnis Pieter Oosterhoff
Gerard Catharinus
Oosting Pieter Sneeuw
Eduard Eugen Stolper
Anton Gerrit Swart
Pieter Tuinstra
Roelof van Weerden

* * *

Sunday, 15 October 1944 – The Nazis seized control of the Hungarian government. Olga Maria Rosen died in Auschwitz.

* * *

Tuesday, 17 October 1944 – Adolf Eichmann arrived back in Hungary. It does not take much to guess why he was there or what it would mean for the Jews in Budapest.

* * *

Thursday, 19 October 1944 – Margaretha Kahlenberg (Kok), number 365, was transported from Theresienstadt to Auschwitz where she died. She was a Westerbork girl.

The same day three more men were executed behind the crematoria at Westerbork:

Lambertus Bruulsema

Hendrik Wiegers
Lammert Zwanenberg

* * *

Saturday, 23 October 1944 – Three more members of the cabaret group from Westerbork were transported out of Theresienstadt to Auschwitz: Hannelore Kahn, number 396, and Ulla Gross, number 1059, were on Transport Et together with Jacob (Jack) Goudsmit, number 1524, a member of the orchestra. Ulla and Hannelore survived the war. Ulla ended the war at Flossenburg, married and become Ursula Wertheimer. I could not find Jack's death recorded anywhere though.

* * *

Friday 27 October 1944. Nine more men were executed at Westerbork behind the crematoria on the execution ground:

Jan Kiers
Jan Kooiker
Roelof Kooiker
Jans Medema
Johannes Pieter Moesker
Hendrik Nieuwkoop
Charles Henri Emil de Nocker
Jan Veerman
Christiaan Kuiper

* * *

On Saturday, 28 October 1944, the last train left Theresienstadt for Auschwitz. Since Tuesday, 26 October 1943, there had been 27 trains from Theresienstadt reaching Auschwitz-Birkenau. They had transported 44,124 people of whom 40,881 had been or would be murdered or die at Auschwitz. On Tuesday, 5 October, two trains left under Rahm's orders with 1,196 children and 53 carers on board. They were all been murdered upon arrival. Out of the cabaret group, the Bühne, 23 members saw Auschwitz, and all but two of those died there. The deaths continued.

* * *

Seven more members of the resistance were executed and cremated, and the ashes were buried at Westerbork on 28 October 1944:

Iman Jacob van den Bosch
Jochem Hendrik Gorter
Hendrik Ridder
Henri Rots
Adriaan Veen
Derk ter Veld
Miente Viersen

These last brought the total to 62 members of the resistance who were executed at Westerbork. All paid the price for freedom, even being executed by fellow Dutch.

On the same day, Kurt Gerron, number Ev 1284, was deported from Theresienstadt to Auschwitz together with his wife, Olga Meyer Gerson, number Ev 1285. With them was Fritz Bernhard. It was the last train to leave Theresienstadt for Auschwitz.

* * *

Monday, 30 October1944 – Kurt Gerron and Olga Gerson died in Auschwitz with another 1,865 people. Out of 2,038 people on that train, 171 survived the war.

NOVEMBER 1944

On Wednesday 8 November 1944, Eichmann saw to it that transports resumed from Budapest. The Jews were rounded up by the Germans and members of the Hungarian Arrow Cross Party. Raoul Wallenberg, the Swedish diplomat, had been saving Jews by issuing them with passports. Many of those he had issued diplomatic papers to were being transported. He pursued the convoys in his car and returned hundreds back to Budapest. He went to the railway station and rescued others. In all he, got 20,000 people to safety and kept them in what was called the "International Ghetto."

* * *

Saturday, 18 November 1944 – Catharina Frank was issued a certificate naming Clarence as her son, including his birthdate of 1 May 1943. It noted that she had arrived in Theresienstadt on Transport XXIV/4 as number 221.

* * *

You remember the van Gelder family? Irvin, his mother, father, and his sister? They were at Bergen-Belsen, but on Sunday, 19 November

1944, they were transported to Wurzach Internment Camp. Many Channel Island non-permanent residents had been deported there since autumn 1941 in retaliation for the internment of Germans in Iran.

* * *

In Auschwitz, 3,509 Jews had arrived from Sered, in Slovakia, on the first Friday of that month, 481 were gassed immediately. Then on 25 November, Himmler ordered the cessation of extermination by gassing at Auschwitz. Crematoria 1 and 2 were dismantled and the parts sent to Groß-Rosen. The Sonderkommando were made to clear out the cremation pits, to fill them with ash and to cover them with grass. Again, there is this covering up of what went on there and the keeping it secret. Yet they believed they had been right to do what they did?

* * *

One day, it might have been recently in November, Frederick Spier had been hanging around the front gate at Westerbork. What he was doing there, nobody knows, but he was not supposed to be there. He was probably just being inquisitive. Well he had the misfortune to be seen by Gemmeker. He and his mistress, Frau Hassel, were strolling through the camp. Gemmeker had been shooting out on the moors, perhaps as he carried a shotgun with him. He spotted Frederick and shouted at him to get away. Frederick did not move quickly enough, almost as if he did not hear Gemmeker or was ignoring him. Gemmeker's bile rose, as did his shotgun. The report was loud as the shot hit Frederick. Frederick was taken to the hospital and had numerous shotgun pellets removed. Now you might think that Hassel would have been pleased that Gemmeker had exerted his authority. Not in the least. He was berated by her for not warning her so that she could cover her ears. Hassel was quite evil. When Gemmeker was away, consorting with Eichmann and the others, or sulking around the house in Düsseldorf visiting his wife, Hassel played at being his deputy. She knew how to use his name to get what she wanted. Jews would change direction if they saw her coming their way.

Jacob Boas told a few stories that demonstrate Gemmeker's temper and Hassel's influence. There was a gardener who did not take off his hat quickly enough – deported. A boy who broke a window – his mother was deported. There was also the young woman whom Gemmeker heard impugn Germany – deported. And, of course, the 50 who were deported because a small boy had hidden himself and delayed a transport. Jacob was only a baby at this time but related these stories as heard from others. Barry Spanjaard told a story about how Gemmeker just looked and said nothing. Barry and some other teenage friends had been really bored one night and risked punishment by sneaking out of the barracks with suitcases. If they were caught, they risked being accused of trying to escape. What were they up to if not escaping? They took the suitcases to the communal washrooms. There they played cards, a harmless activity, but against the rules nonetheless. Unfortunately for them, Gemmeker was out walking. Perhaps he could not sleep, or he had been up to some personal mischief of his own. He must have heard the noise of the card players and walked in to see what was happening. The noise ceased. There was stunned silence. To say they were scared witless at being caught by the Kommandant is rather an understatement. But Gemmeker did not do a thing. Barry thought he had got away with it, until they got a severe beating the next morning from their barrack leader. One could not have predicted the odds of bumping into Gemmeker.

DECEMBER 1944 TO APRIL 1945

On Friday, 15 December 1944, Wolf Drukker died at Sachsenhausen. It was coincidental that he died near Berlin, where Willy Rosen and the others had performed, yet they died far away in Auschwitz. Wolf had played in the cabaret orchestra at Westerbork and ended up in Sachsenhausen, a place notorious for beatings and murder. There would have been a reason for his having been sent to Sachsenhausen rather than the other camps where the majority went.

The next day, Saturday, 16 December 1944, the Germans launched their last offensive of the war in the Ardennes. About 100,000 German soldiers died, and the same number were taken as prisoners of war.

* * *

As the Soviets advanced, Himmler ordered the evacuation of death and concentration camps. He also ordered the destruction of "evidence."

I will keep asking – why? They believed they were doing the right thing and that history would thank them for ending the Jewish reign in Europe. Yet they were anxious that the Soviets should not find evidence that they had been systematically murdering not only Jews but also Soviet POWs, Slavs, Poles and anyone who did not fit in with their scheme of things. The Germans had made great play of the discovery of the mass graves of Polish officers, murdered by the Soviets, by releasing evidence to the world. They had also duped the International Red Cross at various places, especially Theresienstadt.

A film was made at a late stage in the war to convince the world that the Jews were treated fairly. And even before the outbreak of war, they had tried to trick the world into denying Jews any sanctuary. This was the story of the MS St. Louis, which had sailed from Hamburg to Cuba with 937 Jewish refugees. The Nazis had manipulated things so that the Jews were refused entry into Cuba. They were refused entry into American and Canadian waters, too, and to English, Dutch and French ports. This all played into the hands of the Nazis, who could then turn around and say to the world that everyone had turned their backs on these Jews. Their end was as much the responsibility of the world as that of Germany. The captain of the ship refused to return to Germany until he had found sanctuary for all the passengers. The ship sailed into Antwerp Harbour about five weeks after it had left Hamburg. Then Neville Chamberlain, the British Prime Minister relented, and accepted 32 percent of the passengers. They did not know it, but they were the very lucky ones. The others were accepted by France, Belgium and the Netherlands. Captain Gustav Schröder then took his empty ship back to Hamburg and his own anonymity. Of the 620 passengers who returned to the European mainland, about 254 did not see the end of the war. Of course France, Belgium and the Netherlands were not expecting Germany to invade and thought they were offering a safe haven to those Jews. The Nazi's plan did not work; the world did respond, if not all that enthusiastically.

* * *

On Friday, 22 December 1944, Himmler wrote to his wife bemoaning the fact that they would not be together for Christmas. He told his family about the presents he had sent. He celebrated that he was now in command of "his" army group, which he had joined 17 years earlier as a cadet. He added he would send on a fur coat. These presents were in short supply, but Himmler had his choice of confiscated property. But he might possibly have paid for them rather than straightforward looting. Other women had given up their fur coats to send to the Wehrmacht soldiers serving in Russia that first winter back in 1941–42.

* * *

Stalin wanted to impress at the Yalta Conference and ordered the complete liberation of Budapest. By Tuesday, 16 January 1945, the Soviets had liberated Pest, the eastern part of Budapest.

* * *

Wednesday, 17 January 1945 – The Soviets liberated Warsaw.

* * *

On Thursday, 18 January 1945, the Soviets were approaching Auschwitz. Nearly 66,000 prisoners were evacuated through "death marches" to move them west to other camps, or to their deaths if they faltered. Many Dutch prisoners were among these. Louis de Wijze was one. In Auschwitz, Louis de Wijze had made friends with an influential Jew who provided things the SS wanted. He had managed to get a job tending rabbits and enough food to keep him alive. But he was one sent on one of the evacuation marches. He moved from camp to camp and, on the third occasion, made a successful escape to the American lines. The camp continued to run; the crematoria were dismantled and then blown up as the Soviets approached.

Here also was Leon Greenman. He was to march the 90 km to Gleiwitz, and from there he would go on to Buchenwald. His suffering was to continue.

On Thursday, 18 January 1945, Fritz Bernhard from the Westerbork cabaret group died in Dachau. He had been born in Berlin on 21 April 1899, and he died at Dachau, near Munich, the first Nazi concentration camp, at age 44.

* * *

Back in Auschwitz with guards no longer in the camp, a surreal atmosphere had descended. Used to following orders and stringent routines, those left wandered around looking for food. They wondered what they should do. Those too ill or those who had lost their will to live gave up and died where they were before the Soviets arrived.

On Saturday, 27 January 1945, the Soviets liberated Auschwitz and all its sub-camps. They found 7,650 inmates still alive and the bodies of a further 600 inmates, who had died after the Germans had left. They did not know what to say when they entered, but they knew they had to save these people. Lorries laden with bread arrived the next day. Let me just tell you what they found in the warehouses that had not been destroyed: 350,000 men's suits, 837,000 women's garments, thousands of pairs of shoes, piles of glasses, prosthetic limbs, toothbrushes, suitcases, baby clothes and so forth, along with eight tons of hair, packed ready for shipment. Perhaps there are still pieces of furniture in Germany filled with human hair from Auschwitz.

The Flinker girls, Esther, Malka and Leah, were still in Auschwitz. They had survived. Their brother, Moshe, and their father were sent to Echterdingen Labour Camp. Like many others, they contracted typhus and were sent to Bergen-Belsen. The girls knew none of this; they just knew that their mother was not with them and had joined the Heavenly Kommando on arrival. They had not seen her since they arrived, so this was their only certainty. They would discover that their brother, Moshe, the diarist, and their father, the provider and carer, had only just died in Bergen-Belsen. But they would meet up again with their younger siblings and survive in a way, without their mother, their father and their older brother. They would treasure his diary and share it, so he would not be forgotten in their new life in Israel.

Those saved by the Soviets would follow a circuitous route farther east before being allowed to return to their homes in the west. For some from the Netherlands, the Soviets did not arrive soon enough, as they had been sent on to other camps, either in open cattle carts of by foot. Dead bodies littered the countryside, most with a single death shot to the head administered in cold blood.

* * *

There were literally hundreds of camps that were still operative at this point in the war. Murders and beatings were still occurring in Dora-Mittelbau, Flossenburg, Buchenwald, Mauthausen, Dachau, Bergen-Belsen and Sachsenhausen. Dutch people were flung far and wide, existing in absolute misery across the whole of Europe. The Jews had experienced a further Diaspora.

In Westerbork, sometime in February 1945, Maurits van Dam was assaulted by the German guard Heinz Lemke. Lemke accused Maurits of stealing some potatoes. Somebody had stolen some potatoes. Some potatoes were missing, and perhaps a German had taken them, and to cover the theft, Maurits had been accused. Lemke pulled Maurits to see Gemmeker. On the way, he hit Maurits so hard in the right eye that he collapsed. Maurits was told to tell the truth – in other words, to confess to the theft. They met with Gemmeker, who believed Lemke, and Maurits was sent to the "S" Barracks. He remained there until Liberation Day.

* * *

Tuesday, 13 February 1945 - Dresden was devastated with huge numbers of civilians killed. Firestorms paid witness to Goebbels' declaration of "Total War" and the reaping of the storms he had promised, but his rhetoric did not envisage it being his own people but their enemy. It is possible that 100,000 people died. The true figure will never be known, as Nazi sources manipulated the numbers to make the Allies appear inhumane. Recriminations will be made against many, reasons will be sought, but for many it was a form of justice for what had been done to them. The Himmlers noted in their diaries that Goebbels had doctored the numbers.

* * *

Rudolf Breslauer, the photographer, was also somewhere in the middle of Europe. He could have been in any one of a hundred camps, or on a death march, or sitting in a train, but on Wednesday, 28 March 1945, he died "somewhere in Europe." Another life touched by Gemmeker and extinguished. Ursula Breslauer said in an interview that her father had known their fate after talking with Kommandant Gemmeker. Her father never told her what Gemmeker actually had said, but it had left him in no doubt as to the fate of those going east. How do we accept Gemmeker's plea that he knew "nothing" of what happened when the trains had left?

The deaths of those from Westerbork continued across Europe.

* * *

On Wednesday, 28 March 1945, the film that Kurt Gerron was supposed to have made in Theresienstadt was completed. Kurt had been dead for many months by now. The film would never be shown. But it would serve as a reminder that the Nazis and their like are not to be trusted, that they will lie and kill and lie about the lies and the killing. "The Führer gives the Jews a City" fooled no one but the Swedish Red Cross staff who were there in that city. The coffee shops closed as soon as the Red Cross had left, the facades were taken down, and the trains recommenced.

* * *

Saturday, 31 March 1945 – Arthur Durlacher, the opera singer from the revue group, died at Bergen-Belsen.

* * *

Wednesday, 4 April 1945 – Ohrdruf Kamp was liberated.

* * *

Jules Schelvis, his family already dead, survived a death march and found himself in Vaihingen near Stuttgart, on Sunday, 8 April 1945, surrounded by French soldiers.

* * *

Simon (Dixon) Dekker, also from the revue group, was not so fortunate. The next day on Monday, 9 April 1945, he died in Bergen-Belsen. His wife, Mina Felicitas de Silva, survived to see the liberation before she died at Bergen-Belsen. Their daughter, Renee, also died.

* * *

I told you about Mischa Gelber and his family. They had been sent to Bergen-Belsen, and they knew the British were coming, but it would not be for them. On Tuesday, 10 April 1945, they were all deported east. They were on a train and did not know where it was headed. They were taken from the Sternlager. Mischa would say later that only six out of 1,250 families in that part of Bergen-Belsen were untouched. Although that was not right. Everyone who went through that camp was touched in some way. What Mischa meant was that only six families survived intact, and that would be immediate families, not extended ones. Nearly every Jewish family across Europe lost someone, every Soviet family, every Polish family, every Romani and Sinti family. So many families without a number. One family that did survive together from Bergen-Belsen was that of Eddy Boas.

* * *

On Wednesday, 11 April 1945 at Buchenwald, 21,000 are liberated. In among those was Leon Greenman, but he would remain there a few more weeks before being allowed to leave on 24 April. He met a British journalist who wrote up his story, describing him as "The Barber of Buchenwald" who came from Forest Gate. His British family found out that he was alive, but when he searched for Else and Barney, there was no sign of them. Nor would he find any sign of his Dutch family or his Dutch friends.

* * *

You are probably wondering, and want to ask about, what was happening at Westerbork. The deportations ceased, and camp life continued. Dutch patriots were brought to the camp to be imprisoned or shot. The gates remained closed, and the guard towers remained manned. Gemmeker continued to run the model camp. He knew the war would soon be over, and he was making plans.

On 11 April 1945, the day that Buchenwald was liberated, Gemmeker fled the camp at Westerbork with some of the other officers. He had received a telephone call from Willem van der Veer. What was said? Willem told him to speak English because in a very short time he would have plenty of opportunity to speak it. That may have been enough to frighten off Gemmeker and the others. It may have been that Willem knew what might happen, that at the last moment there might be mass killings. By ringing Gemmeker and saying they were already in the village, there would not be enough time to organise such a thing. But before he left, Gemmeker had a conversation with Schlesinger, the Jewish administrator, and handed him a pistol. He told Schlesinger he was leaving and that he might need of the pistol to protect himself. Now if Gemmeker had acted properly and had employed Schlesinger in an administrative capacity to oversee the actual workings of the deportations, why would he have given Schlesinger a revolver to protect himself? Protect himself from whom? Also, why was Gemmeker running away? Why not just surrender to the Allies? He was after all doing his job, following the *kriegsnotwendig*, "needed during the war." Why did he need to hide? Who was Schlesinger to be threatened by?

The answer was simple. Gemmeker knew that his involvement in the camp would be seen by the Allies as part of what was to be called a "war crime" and that Jews might wish to take revenge on Schlesinger. So Gemmeker was getting out of it. He also left a poster saying the camp was handed over to the Red Cross. Helena Fuchs had watched them leave. She said they could only find one car that would work because the rest had been disabled by Van Buren. Gemmeker's driver, Van Laer, had taken a car and gone off to find the Canadians. He came back with a motorcycle and told Gemmeker the Canadians were close. Helena and Selfried Fuchs watched Gemmeker made his departure. They were approached by Gemmeker, who asked Selfried to give them a hand, but he kept his hands firmly behind his back. Gemmeker said that if they were to meet again, then perhaps Selfried could tell him how the liberation went. Werner Löwenhardt was there too, watching. He remembered seeing Frau Hassel sitting on the running board of Gemmeker's Mercedes. You would have thought she had had her head in her hands, but no. She was cradling a bust of Hitler on her lap. Gemmeker returned to the car, and they both got in and drove off, out of the camp for the last time, with Hitler. Did the bust get back home to Düsseldorf with Hassel and Gemmeker?

Gemmeker left Drenthe by the flood defences and went to Amsterdam. There he occupied himself as an administrative leader, as an office boy, whose sole responsibility during the war had been to push pieces of paper around.

* * *

Abraham Mol remembered Wednesday, 11 April 1945. Gemmeker had left, but there were Germans all around, outside of the camp. The camp was on the frontline. We all know that elsewhere other camps were being demolished and the prisoners either forced marched away or shot. There was a distinct danger that a group of German soldiers might take it upon itself to take reprisals against the inmates. If Gemmeker had stayed, he would perhaps have had enough authority to prevent this from happening. There was talk about leaving and going out into the world outside the camp, but they chose to stay and take their chances here in the camp. With SS and Wehrmacht units about, someone on their own wearing a yellow star was an easy target. Their fears were soon allayed.

When there is a vacuum in the control mechanism, a feeling typically exists that it is necessary to have it filled to ensure stability. Other posters had been distributed around the camp from the new administration under Aad van As, joined by five others who oddly enough included Schlesinger, who handed control to Aad as soon as Gemmeker had left. Aad was the only Dutch member of the Dienstleiter. It was expected that the work in the camp would continue as usual with reduced hours but that there would be punishments for those who upset the smooth and orderly running of the camp. I find this strangely odd, as most of the work was for the German war effort.

Aad van As was talking to as many as could get into the large hall when he was interrupted and told he was wanted on the telephone. He wondered who it could be. "The Tommies are here!" came the reply. Not Tommies, but Canadians. Who cared? Many ran out and towards the farm to meet the Canadians and to guide them to the camp.

On Thursday, 12 April 1945, a Canadian tank flattened the camp wire and drove into the Westerbork. Shortly before, the Canadians had been planning to shell the camp. It had been strafed by aircraft in the belief it was a military camp. Samuel Schrijver, a member of the Dutch resistance, had escaped from the camp on Wednesday evening and then swam across the Oranjekanaal. He met with Canadian Brigadier Jean Allard, and after some effort, persuaded him not to shell the camp, as the SS had gone and with them, their collaborators. Still being cautious, the Canadians sent in a tank first. The act of the tank crushing the barbed wire walls was a symbolic action the detainees much appreciated.

They were shouting with joy and crying with tear-streamed faces. Kisses and hugs for anyone, any of the 876 prisoners left in the camp and for the Canadian soldiers of the Second Infantry. Cigarettes were handed out, as was chocolate. Aad van As was asked if he wanted to raise the Dutch flag. As it was being hoisted, the Dutch National Anthem was sung, and before he knew it, Aad was hoisted shoulder height and tossed up and down, light as a feather. Captain Morris of the Second Infantry explained the situation outside to the now residents. As free as they would have liked to feel, they could not leave. They could not go out into the chaos of the war's end, at a time when death was futile but more common than it had ever been in the preceding days, months and years. The 500 or so Jews would have to stay where they were until July, when they could return to their home or strive to make a new life somewhere else in the world, a further Diaspora. There would be some returning from elsewhere in Europe hoping to restart a life in the Netherlands, the land of their birth, only to find that there was little joy for their return, an emptiness that would lead them to move on. First, however, came the realisation that they were standing at a door and could look in and out at the same time. These were confusing times, during which they had to wait for the war's end before stepping over that threshold and forging a new life.

* * *

Sunday, 15 April 1945 was a day that many at Bergen-Belsen would remember, as it is the day they were saved. The British found 60,000 inmates still alive, with piles of corpses lying around to which those alive from the camp were immune, but not so the British troops. It was documented on film, all of it, including the earth movers used to speed the dead to their graves. The emaciated survivors continued to die from disease and food that was too rich, literally, killed by kindness. The Nazis had attempted to dispose of many prisoners. Some 25,000 had been killed, but the process had been curtailed by the Jewish resistance in the camps. In the camp were 54 Dutch children of all ages who had been shielded by Luba Tryszynska, a Polish mother who had lost her own child. One day she had heard children whimpering and gone in search of them. She had found a large group of Dutch children that had been cast out by the Nazis to die.

Luba took them back to her hut and with the help of the other prisoners, hid them, telling them to be quiet. Luba secured extra food for them and aid from Nazi overseers and even the Kommandant. Upon liberation, Luba escorted the children back to the Netherlands to look for remaining family members and others who would take them in. Little wonder she became known as the "Angel of Belsen." These were the children of the diamond workers and became known as the "Diamantkinder."

Jacob (Jaap) Hillesum should have been in Bergen-Belsen but was on a train in the middle of nowhere, a train that seemed to have been forgotten, The Lost Train. He was not alone; others from Westerbork on this train as well.

* * *

This Train. The Lost Train. How do you lose a train? In the confusion at the end of the war, many things were lost. Lives were lost. In those last few months, German soldiers died at a rate higher than in any other part of the war. Thousands of innocents on death marches were shot. Thousands of innocents were dying from innumerable diseases. So many people were just looking out for themselves, without a care for those around them. Desperation makes monsters of us all. And there were many monsters, previously confirmed in that family by their deeds when they themselves were not in a desperate situation. Skulking around were those who knew they would be sought for the deeds they had done. They killed witnesses to their crimes, covered up their identities, went to ground or sought assistance to find new lives far away from Eastern Europe. If you were responsible for a train of 2,500 people and your life was in danger, you run! You would leave them. They became lost.

We need to start this event at Bergen-Belsen. This camp held the Sternlager, the part of the camp where Jewish prisoners were kept ready for exchange in situations that would prove beneficial to the Nazi elite. Himmler was behind this. Who else? He was already negotiating for his life, though the Sternlager inmates would no longer be exchanged for Germans elsewhere in the world at this point. What Germans living away from the war would have wanted to return to a Germany they knew had been levelled? At this stage of the war, Himmler was only interested in saving one life in exchange for released Jews. They were also a bargaining "chip" in local situations. Yet oddly enough, camp guards would flee before approaching Allied troops. Why was that? They fled from the Soviets and had cause to after the atrocities committed by the Germans in the Soviet Union, but they also fled from the Americans and British and other Allies. They knew an SS uniform now made them stand out. It had done before, but they had been the elite then. Now they would be prized prisoners themselves. But they could not hide the tattoo under their arm of their blood group. But what do you know? Himmler was canny enough not to have been tattooed.

But what about the train? Bergen-Belsen was about to fall into Allied hands. Thousands of prisoners needed to be moved. On Tuesday, 10 April 1945, three trains left Bergen-Belsen. It was some feat to have put together three trains at this stage of the war. But then to move them to Theresienstadt was beyond Eichmann and the Reichsbahn. One train made it to Theresienstadt, and the other shunted east and west through Germany until it was liberated near Magdeburg, Willy Rosen's hometown. There were a number from Westerbork on the third train, including Marion Blumenthal with her family, Dr Jacob Hillesum (Etty's brother), Steven and Marion Hess, both aged seven, with their mother, Ilse, and their father, Charles. The Hess family had also managed to stay together. But there were many on the list of "Tröbitz Jews" who remain in Tröbitz to this day. The Lost Train left Bergen-Belsen for Theresienstadt where they would remain held hostage. The track and route for this train was just a meandering sojourn through Germany. Allied aircraft targeted anything that moved on the railways. Fighter aircraft were equipped with weapons that could easily destroy a train. Although the Germans had placed white flags on the train, the pilots had little idea what was inside, and by this time of the war, no one had any trust left in the Nazis, and what had been discovered by many was now common knowledge. If a man did not really have any idea what the war was being fought for, he did now. The train was strafed and bombed but miraculously survived, even though it stopped, and the Nazi guards all jumped clear. The train left Bergen-Belsen and headed north to Soltau, then east to Uelzen, north to Büchen, east to Hagenow Land, south to Wittenberge, south-west to Spandau and Berlin, and south to Senftenberg and then east to Tröbitz. Of the 2,500 who started the journey, 704 died, either on the train or at Tröbitz. There were numerous trackside graves. One of those belonged to Jacob Hillesum. He died and was buried in Berlin, one week into the journey on Tuesday, 17 April 1945. Each day the Germans would walk down the train ordering the dead to be brought out. The prisoners were given picks and shovels to bury the dead. This went on for 14 days, stopping, bombing, hiding, suffering, dying and burying. Misery was not a strong enough word. There was no food, only what they could forage when the train stopped. Had anyone thought of escape, what was there to run to in Germany?

Steven Hess told the story of how they ate leaves off the trees or drank grass soup for nourishment or ate rotten vegetables they could scrounge along the way. His mother cooked them on a little Sterno stove. His father was late one day returning to the train, and it had left without him. His thoughts were for his family. He ripped off his yellow star and followed the train as best he could. He secreted himself on another train and hid in a station. There he recognised his old train and was reunited with his family.

Marion Blumenthal remembered the first day on the train on Monday, 9 April 1945. They walked to the train from the camp and got into the trucks, 50 per truck, so they had some room to stretch out. A water bucket in one corner, and the slop bucket was in the farthest corner. They sat and waited for the train to move. They were fearful. After all, trains meant death. The Sternlager was being emptied. The train did not move; it still did not move. Marion watched as some got out of the wagons. There was no shouting from the guards. They ventured a little farther down to the stream and washed in the clear cold water. All afternoon the train stood. Fires were lit, and a little food cooked – half rotten root vegetables found near the track in a pile. It was night, and they were herded back into the wagons, by the guards. The train stood all night. It was now Tuesday. The train stood in the spring sunshine. More prisoners arrived. The wagons became fuller. Sometimes there were as many as 80 in each. Each of them was given a large chunk of bread and was told it was for eight days. The Nazis thought the journey would last eight days and that a large piece of bread would be enough. Late that night the train moved, but only 15 miles. The doors were opened to allow for the dead to be buried. The train was incubating typhus; one was dead within a few days of infection.

One of the Kapos from the camp was on the train as well, Jacques Albala, a Greek. Marion had little sympathy for the man. He was brutal towards the Dutch Jews, especially when German guards were in view. He had to struggle for his own position in the camp against his second in command, Walter Hanke, a Berlin criminal. Yet there he was, one morning burying his own son. He was perhaps a little

323

more fortunate than other Kapos who had remained behind. Many of those were lynched by the inmates. Let me dissuade you if you think the wagons were not too bad – if there was only typhus. There was dysentery. Many were too weak to use the overflowing slop buckets and voided their bowels where they lay. Others had pleurisy or tuberculosis and wounds that would not heal. Marion had such a wound. If not treated, it could lead to death or at the least amputation. She was too young to realise it, but her parents knew. Can you imagine the difficulty in trying to keep such a wound clean in those conditions? It was a source of nourishment for the lice, which Marion had to pick off one by one and crack between her nails. Marion was about ten years old. What sort of life is this for a child? Marion had a task from her family. Her parents knew that drinking bad water could lead to all sorts of illness, so they needed boiled water to drink. Where would they get boiled water? The answer was the locomotive at the front of the train. It was Marion's task to go to the engineer, to smile and to ask for water from the engine. It was hot and rusty, but it was safe to drink. Marion remembered the journey through Berlin where the train stopped. She could see the bombed buildings against the skyline as the train stood in a yard. She would have watched the others bury the dead; perhaps Jaap Hillesum was among them. Moving south into farming regions, an SS guard would accompany them as they tried their luck at begging at the farmhouses. Sometimes they were lucky. Sometimes they were extremely fortunate in that the house was empty, the occupants fleeing the Soviet "hordes." Goebbels had told the populace about the rapes, and many committed suicide rather than face the Soviets.

Then one day, the doors of the wagons opened, and soldiers jumped in demanding their watches. Not the SS this time, but the Soviets. They were free. Little Eddy Boas told the story about his brother jumping down from the train and coming face to face with the Soviet soldiers. But it was not the end of their suffering. They were near Tröbitz. It might be a haven for them. The Soviets told them they did not have any food but that others were coming, which indeed they did. It was Monday, 23 April 1945, the day their comrades reached Berlin.

* * *

On Wednesday, 19 April 1945, Gudrun Himmler arrived home to find her mother in discussion with friends about going to Vallepp in the Alps with Frau Heydrich on false papers. It was to be a secret, but they were taking many possessions with them.

* * *

Tuesday, 20 April 1945 was Hitler's 56th birthday, not worth celebrating, but that same day, Himmler was found to be playing a deadly game. Felix Kersten, his masseur, has been working with Count Bernadotte who had arranged to save Nordic citizens, but this did not include Jews. Himmler had agreed that 8,000 Scandinavian citizens would be spared. Bernadotte had 36 buses and 12 trucks painted white and traversed Germany to collect prisoners from Neuengamme. By early April, they had saved 4,700 but not one Jew. Hillel Storch, a Jewish refugee from Latvia living in Sweden, pleaded for Jews to be saved. He was replaced in negotiations by Norbert Masur, a Swedish Jew, and a member of the Jewish World Congress. On this Tuesday, the 20th and the next day, Norbert met with Walter Schellenberg and Heinrich Himmler. Himmler had intimated that his hands were tied while Hitler was alive. That very day he had been to the bunker in Berlin to wish Hitler a happy birthday. Then he had travelled 70 kilometres north with Schellenberg to meet Norbert and to discuss the release of Jews. He had even told Norbert that it had not been his intention to persecute Jews who supported Germany. Norbert could not believe the situation, that he was face to face with the man who personified what would later be called the "Holocaust." It was agreed at that meeting that 1,000 Jewish women from Ravensbrück could be saved. Bernadotte's buses were detoured to include the women's camp. Also included were 423 Danish Jews from Theresienstadt.

Unfortunately, one bus was strafed by an allied fighter, and the driver and 12 survivors were killed.

* * *

Wednesday, 25 April 1945 – The Americans and Soviets met on the river Elbe near Torgau.

* * *

Saturday, 28 April1945 – Mussolini was shot by partisans as he tried to escape, dressed in a pith helmet and a German uniform. Colonel Valerio read out the death sentence. The body was then displayed in Milan.

Hitler found out about Himmler's duplicity. He stripped him of all authority and ordered his arrest.

* * *

On Sunday, 29 April 29 1945, Dachau was liberated. Hidden among the typhoid patients and cared for by Dr Jan Cornelius Boswijk was Jozef Wins. Jozef had to be admired for his tenacity and endurance. He survived the salt mines and was on a forced death march to Dachau. Nearly 2,000 set out, but only 792 arrived, Jozef among them. The rest lay beside the road or in ditches, dead from a shot to the back of the neck. But eventually it all proved too much even for Jozef, and he confided in Dr Boswijk that he could not go on. Jan took him and hid him among those suffering from typhoid. Not many guards would visit those sick with this. Each day Jan brought Jozef food and cared for him. Then on that Sunday, Jozef was free. Jan, too, was free after nearly two years of imprisonment, where his help for others indicated how high he stood in the ranks of men.

* * *

The Soviets guided those who could walk from The Lost Train to a small village called Tröbitz. There were houses and very few Germans but some food. Marion found a house and discovered ham hanging from the rafters. In dire circumstances, a Jew can eat non-kosher food, and that day was one such circumstance. They knew to eat slowly and not overfill their stomachs. Some ate too quickly and died. The houses were well stocked. The occupants had not taken everything with them. Perhaps they had heard the Soviets approaching and fled in what they were standing. There was room enough for all the Blumenthals, but they slept together for security, as it was something they had not been able to do.

More Soviets arrived, also seeking food and offering assistance to the Jews. Marion was transported every day to have her leg treated with an early antibiotic. But the typhus lice were in Tröbitz. Everyone, including Marion, shaved their heads. A large communal grave was dug, and each time a new body was added, soil was scattered over it. It is probably here that Max Friedman, who was the manager at the Turkish restaurant in The Hague, was lying. He succumbed to typhus. He had survived since his deportation from Westerbork and through his time at Bergen-Belsen to die here at Tröbitz.

The Hess family were in another house. There was Ilse and Charles with their twin children, Steven and Marion. They had found an abandoned farmhouse and were living in it. Marion remembered that the first Soviet soldiers were crazy, and it was dangerous to go out when they were about. The Soviet soldiers were not to know that these families were victims of the Nazis, just like their own families back in Russia. Then after nearly two months, the gum-chewing Americans arrived in the village. Steven saw his first-ever black person. He thought it might be "Black Pete," the helper of the Dutch Santa Claus. They learned their first English words – "gum" and "Hershey." These were children who could not remember sweets, flowers, toilet paper or clean white sheets, which frightened Marion, for they were too white. The Americans took them to Leipzig. There they found themselves in a prison camp with other Germans, but these were Nazis. Charles got a lawyer who argued their case, and after ten days they were freed.

The Blumenthals were not so fortunate. Although they were together, even in Tröbitz, Walter was in poor health. The radio had told them of Germany's surrender and that the war was over; if they felt safe it was with trepidation because they were not home with the doors locked and well-stocked cupboards. They were hundreds of miles from whatever had been home in an unknown village. In the spring, Marion and her family found a little more food, as planted vegetables were becoming ripe to eat. The number of deaths from typhus fell in May but rose again in June 1945. This time, Marion's father, Walter succumbed. He had contracted typhus. The Nazis had tried to kill them in the last moments of the war, and they had survived. They were free again, but deprivation took her father. Walter Blumenthal died in Tröbitz on 7 June 1945. Albert dug his own father's grave. The body was laid to rest and the grave marked with old bricks, just like children burying a loved pet in the garden. But this was their father. There was no rabbi to lead the ceremony, no handcrafted coffin, no headstone to mark a brave man's life. He was 48. He had his family to say Kaddish and mourn for him.

Somewhere in Tröbitz were Mischa Gelber and his family too. They had survived. Mischa would grow up to see his own family around him.

* * *

Monday, 30 April 1945 – Hitler committed suicide.

That same day, the Soviets reached Ravensbrück and found less than 3,500 prisoners left at the camp. Towards the end of March, nearly 25,000 inmates had gone on a forced death march, including Rozette Lezer. They were liberated by Soviet troops at about the same time as those in the camp. They told of a Soviet officer riding into the camp on a beautiful white horse. Some women prisoners were reported to have been raped by the Soviet soldiers.

Towards the end of April 1945, the Jews and others at Camp Westerbork became aware that prisoners were being brought to the camp. These were not Jews or even Dutch Jews but Dutch men and women. They had been arrested by the new Dutch authorities on a charge of collaboration with the enemy. Although those remaining in the camp were possibly pleased that these people were being caught and quite quickly, it may have seemed odd that they should be on the same site with them. There was some satisfaction in seeing these people incarcerated and that the world had finally caught up with them and their deeds. But this time it was the Royal Hamilton Infantry that ensured that local authorised people were in the watchtowers. Some were Jews who were until a short time ago prisoners of the people they were now guarding.

Gemmeker had fled to Amsterdam and busied himself, hoping to hide away and merge into the background. But he was identified and arrested. Upon interrogation, his past came to light, as did the fact that he might be of interest to those in the army tasked with finding Germans who had committed atrocities. Someone in the Allied forces saw how ignominious it would be for this proud German officer were he to be sent not to a camp with other officers but back to Westerbork. Word would soon have sped round the camp that Gemmeker was back. The surprise would have turned to some hilarity when the circumstances became apparent. I wonder whether Selfried Fuchs told Gemmeker what liberation day had been like. Gemmeker was joined by other Nazis.

Wednesday, 2 May 1945, Theresienstadt was taken over by the Red Cross, and the organisation learned of the truth regarding what had really happened. The other train from Bergen-Belsen did indeed reach Theresienstadt. The Drukker family were still there and had been since September 1944. Alfred had managed to stay with his parents and had worked at the crematoria, not realising that the ash he was handling was all that remained of other Jews. Erna did not think it a suitable task for her son and managed to have it changed.

He then worked in the garden. Maurits was engaged in strenuous work outside of the ghetto in a group made up mostly of Dutch Jews. Theresienstadt was still sending food further east to German troops. Among other survivors was the wife of Leo Kok, Kitty, the sister of Louis de Wijze.

The Dutch started to sing their national anthem. The German Jews from Westerbork started to join in but ceased after objections from the Dutch. Petty? Now it seems so. But we were not there. We had not been through what they had. We have no idea how they felt, how any of them felt – Dutch or German.

* * *

Saturday, 5 May 1945 – Mauthausen was liberated. The camp was handed over to the Austrian police as the SS left the camp on the following Thursday. All those, bar one, who worked in the crematorium had been murdered to prevent their telling what had happened there. When the Americans arrived, they found that some of the guards at the sub-camps had been murdered by the prisoners. They had also repelled an assault by German troops. The American troops disarmed the old police and Volkswehr and then moved on. Among the survivors were Simon Wiesenthal and Leo Kok, the Dutch artist.

* * *

Sunday, 6 May 1945 was a day that Max Garcia would not forget, meeting with American soldiers near Ebensee in Austria. Max Garcia's full name was Meyer Rodriguez Garcia, and he had been at Auschwitz since the last week of August 1943. He had been arrested with his family in Amsterdam in June 1943; they had fled to Belgium and then back to the Netherlands. They had spent a short time in Westerbork before being sent to Auschwitz. His father had been a diamond polisher, but that did not save him. Max's father and mother were gassed that last week of August 1943 together with other members of the family. By Friday, 31 August 1943, Max was the only survivor. He was admitted to Camp 1 and stayed there, even surviving a burst appendix. He was only saved by a doctor for the sake of curiosity. Max was just number 139829 to the Nazis. With the approach of the Soviets, he was put on a forced march and ended up in Ebensee Labour Camp. He then worked for the Americans, seeking out members of the SS. To honour the memory of his lost family, Max would go talk to anyone about his experiences and his views on life.

* * *

The Germans surrendered on Tuesday, 8 May 1945. Gerhard Durlacher was released by the Soviets, far to the east. He returned to the Netherlands and ultimately became a famous sociologist and writer.

* * *

On Wednesday, 9 May 1945, Heinrich Himmler committed suicide in British custody. He was detained while trying to escape disguised as an ordinary soldier. The architect of the Holocaust, convinced that it was right and that he would be thanked, did not stay around to find out. The Germans signed a second surrender document with the Soviets, and the "Great Patriotic War" came to an end.

* * *

Saturday, 12 May 1945 – Leo Kok, who had been imprisoned at Mauthausen, was moved to Sankt Wolfgang in Ebensee but succumbed to poor health and died. He did not get to be reunited with his wife, Kitty, who survived.

* * *

Monday, 6 August 1945 was the day Katharina Frank and Clarence were repatriated to the Netherlands. But they do not stay; they felt they were not welcomed back with open arms.

* * *

Tuesday, 20 November 20 1945 – The War Crime Trials Commence in Nuremberg.

AFTERMATH

Westerbork Camp was demolished in the early 1970s with only the Kommandant's green and white house surviving. Today the site is a museum and a memorial to what happened there.

After the war, some 16,000 Jews came out of hiding in the Netherlands and were joined by 4,500 deportees making attempts to pick up their lives. David Cesarani in his book *Final Solution* details all of this. Yad Vashem has recognised 5,778 Righteous Among the Nations from the Netherlands, second highest only to Poland.

The days after the war were a difficult time for the Dutch. There were very mixed emotions, and reasons were sought as to why some Dutch behaved as collaborators. Nearly 25,000 Dutch men had joined the Waffen-SS to fight against the Soviets on the Eastern front, believing that Bolshevism was a real threat. Collaborators were shot in those early days following the liberation.

Those who had shielded the Jews mainly kept quiet, and their heroism was not celebrated in those years. Eddy Boas could not understand why his family and others, who were Dutch, were treated so terribly. He only recently on his 80th birthday received news that Dutch Prime Minister Mark Rutte has apologised for the behaviour of Dutch bureaucrats towards the Jewish Dutch population 75 years later. Eddy said that even though it is 75 years late, it is better than no apology, and he had lived to see it.

The King of the Netherlands, Willem-Alexander, similarly apologised that his great-grandmother, Queen Wilhelmina, seemed indifferent to the plight of the Jews. Reception of his statement has been initially one of surprise, as he was the first member of the Dutch royal family to speak in this way. The Dutch Railways agreed to pay out 50 million euros in 2019. The French government agreed a similar amount of 47 million euros in 2015. It was paid to survivors, surviving partners and first-generation children. Germany had agreed reparations in 1951. Since then, it has paid out 71 billion euros in the form of pensions and welfare payments. Everyone recognises that money itself is inadequate, as it does not bring back the dead.

When 104,100 people are treated to such degradation, how is that measured? Families lost more than 103,000 members; how is that loss calculated? When 16,000 hid for fear of their lives, how is that recompensed? When thousands fled to other countries, how is that justified? Every single person who went through Westerbork either lost their life or most of it through what they suffered. How do you make it up to them and their families? And who can forgive on such a scale?

Even today arguments continue to take place; one of the most recent being about Jewish children, being brought up as Christian by their adoptive Dutch parents.

From a laughable fringe group in the 1920s to an organised machine in 1939, the Nazi Party demonstrated how an extreme group can take control of the masses and engineer them to exercise the group's will through the promulgation of appealing ideals. Westerbork and all other Nazi concentration camps stand as testament to what could happen again when a population is swayed by speeches of hate and blame or stand by and do not speak out.

Denial of the past does not build a better future.

SHORT BIOGRAPHIES

Aad van As worked quietly at the camp ensuring that the food he was supplied with was properly distributed. He was able to ensure that six members of his service team were not deported. But he could not always do this. Many were sent east, with only five of his team surviving. Aad wanted to know what was happening in the camp, so he hid notes in the wagons hoping for a reply. He never got any.

Adolf Löwenhardt was from Hemer in Germany. He was born on 9 October 1889. He perished at Auschwitz on Wednesday, 11 1944. He died together with his wife, Julia (Julchen). They kept a butcher's shop. Adolf had brothers: Salomon, Isidor, Max, Hugo, Emil, Julius, Siegmund and Hermann. All nine siblings had served in the German Reichswehr in the First World War. All of them died in the Holocaust. His sister Julie died in hospital in 1941. Her two daughters, Paula and Emma, died in the Holocaust. Adolf's other sister, Johanna, survived and went to America.

Arthur Pisk was the head of the Jewish Administration Police Force. Jacques Schol had recruited some of the longer-term Germans to assist with the internal running of the camp. Pisk and the Ordnungsdienst became hated by many members of the camp. It was they who ensured people got on the trains. There were many younger members made to be runners for Pisk and Schlesinger, both boys and girls. When the war ended, Pisk disappeared. He certainly left the Netherlands and was reported by Aad van As to have made a new life in Australia, probably trying to forget the 104,100 men, women, children and babies he had ensured boarded the trains while his own deportation was deferred.

Captain Jacques Schol was a retired army captain who was selected by the Dutch authorities to take over command of the newly constructed camp in Drenthe to house the large influx of refugees, mainly German Jews. He was to take over from Syswarda on 16 July 1940, following the German invasion in May. Schol himself had a certain antipathy towards Germans but seemingly some sympathy for these German Jews who came to be regarded as the camp aristocracy. He recruited some to assist with the internal running of the camp. Kurt Schlesinger was appointed *Oberdienstleiter*, Dr Fritz Spanier was appointed chief medical officer and Arthur Pisk acting as chief of the Ordnungsdienst was charged with keeping order. New regulations were posted. All mail was censored, anyone leaving the camp needed a permit and there was to be no cycling in the camp. He served under the first two SS Kommandants, Deppner and Dischner. Schol felt that by running a strict regime, the Germans could be kept at bay. Some saw it as doing the Nazis' job for them. But reports made to Seyss-Inquart alluded to Schol's easy behaviour towards the Jews. His replacement was recommended. On 1 July 1942, the SS officially took over. Schol was kept in office until January 1943 when Gemmeker sacked him.

Cornelis Johannes (Kees) Kaptein was the police officer from The Hague. He had sent perhaps 2,000 Jews to Poland and appropriated much of their property worth millions of guilders. He was tried in April 1948 and found guilty of persecution of Jews. Shortly before his execution, he converted to Catholicism. He was executed on 21 July 1945.

Corrie Ten Boom, or Cornelia Arnolda Johanna ten Boom, resisted the Nazi invasion by hiding Jews. From May 1942 until 28 February

1944, the family harboured Jews. Eventually, she was caught after being sold to the Nazis by an informant called Jan Vogel. The whole family were arrested and sent to Scheveningen, but six Jews in the house were not discovered. As many as 30 people were arrested that day in the ten Boom house. Corrie and her sister, Betsie, were sent to Vught. Casper, the father, died in hospital after spending ten days in Scheveningen Prison. Then on what I believe was Wednesday, 6 September 1944, they were both sent to Ravensbrück. Betsie was not in the best of health and succumbed on Saturday, 16 December 1944. Only 15 days later, Corrie was released. She was told later that her release was a clerical error, as all the women her age had been sent to the gas chamber. Corrie had not been home long before she threw the doors open to disabled people seeking safety. Arnolda Johanna (Nollie) and Willem ten Boom survived the war, a sister and brother of Corrie.

Edith Stein, also known as St Edith Stein or St Teresa Benedicta of the Cross, died at Auschwitz on Sunday, 9 August 1942. She had been born into an Orthodox Jewish family, but like many teenagers, found atheism. She completed a doctoral thesis at the University of Göttingen and obtained an assistantship at Freiburg University. She was drawn to the Catholic faith and was baptised on the first day of 1922. She did not possess an Aryan certificate and had to give up her teaching post in the School of Education at Speyer in 1933. She then went to Köln and entered into the Carmelite Order. She took the new name of Teresa of the Cross. In 1938, she and her sister, Rosa, also a nun, were sent to Echt in the Netherlands. Both left Westerbork on Friday, 7 August 1942. Both went to the gas chamber two days later. Edith was made a saint in October 1988 by Pope John Paul II. Critics say she died as a Jew not as a Catholic martyr. At no point did Edith seek to be spared death. It is possible that some Catholic Nazi may have interceded at some point, but she chose to die with the Jews, following the teachings of the Catholic Church, and could therefore be regarded as a martyr.

Friederich Weinreb was a Hassidic Jew. He was an economist but was famous for duping many of his fellow Jews, by selling them exemptions, along the lines of Calmeyer. In this case they were fictitious. He claimed after the war that he was giving people "hope" and that as the war was going badly for the Germans, his clients would escape deportation. It is thought that perhaps 70 of his clients died with many being deported. In 1976, his claims were investigated, and it was found they were a tissue of lies. He was later convicted as posing as a medical doctor and on charges relating to sexual offences. He fled to Switzerland and died in 1988. He was a swindler and a collaborator.

Hans Margules was in Westerbork a long time. He had escaped Germany shortly after Kristallnacht with his brother, Pieter. He landed in Westerbork on 10 January 1940. He turned his hand to many projects. He helped build the new barracks needed for the Dutch Jews who were to come to the camp. Hans should have been on the first transport east on 15 July 1942, but his mother had managed to get a sworn statement that he was only half Jewish, which meant he could stay in Westerbork. He liked to draw and would draw people if they asked. He started to draw greeting cards and a few other things which he was given cigarettes or other things for. When the theatre started, he helped design the sets and built the seats. He also had a hand in the book given to Gemmeker. He became a member of the 20-strong fire Bbrigade as well. In the summer of 1942, the brigade was given the new duty of the Ordedienst. They were like the camp police force and responsible for ensuring order to and from the trains. Hans found it hard ensuring people got on the train. Among them were friends and families of the other men who were members of the OD. He found it painful that many felt that the Ordedienst were the ones sending inmates away to the East, most likely to die. It was a strange situation. Gemmeker continued to make use of the Germans who had been at the camp a longer time. It therefore seemed to many that they were collaborators. Some indeed may have been that by helping more willingly and with a certain voracity. Hans knew that he might be there the weeks following a transport. He spoke German and wore a uniform of sorts, a brown overall. The rift between Dutch and

Germans grew wider, and resentment brewed. This was likely one of the reasons the Dutch acted vehemently when the Germans joined in the singing of their Dutch national song at Theresienstadt when it was liberated. The Dutch generally had been made to feel very much on the bottom rung of the ladder in Westerbork. They often wondered why they had been treated differently. It was not their choice to be there. This was one small way of expressing their indignation and knowing that there would not be any further repercussions. No longer would those Jews with four German grandparents get preferential treatment. Yet some of those Germans had adopted the Netherlands as their home and felt strong kinship for the Dutch taking them in after they had fled the Nazi regime in Germany.

Kurt Schlesinger and his wife, Thea, were arrested by the Dutch police at the border of Germany and the Netherlands and interned at Westerbork in February 1940. Simon Hornman described him as a big man with the head of a bull. He wore a black jacket together with riding breeches and shiny black boots. He looked every inch like a German officer, but for the yellow star on his chest. Schlesinger had been a mechanic but rose through the ranks of the German Jews interned in the camp. When the Germans took over the camp, they encouraged the Jewish administration to continue, but to their duties was added that of organising the lists for transport. The chief administrative officer was Captain Jacques Schol, but he was dismissed by Gemmeker and replaced by Schlesinger. He came to be regarded by some as the "Lord Mayor" or even "King of the Jews." Schol had shown himself to be anti-German. Most of the internees were German. Gemmeker appointed someone he felt would be more amenable. It can be of little doubt that Schlesinger knew what was happening. He had eyes and ears everywhere. He saw himself as a "buffer" between the SS and the Jews. In this, he was able to protect some groups or even alleviate some of the suffering. He learned of all the news and information coming back from the camps – that Jews were being murdered. He oversaw the transportation of thousands of people. His reward was the delay of his own transportation and omission on that very last transport in September 1944. It seems he did not need to use the revolver he had been given to protect himself. He stayed in the Netherlands to testify on behalf of Gemmeker at the latter's trial. When news reached Schlesinger that questions were being asked about his collaboration, he left for the United States. He died there in 1963. While Schlesinger was enjoying his privileged position and deferred deportation, he oversaw the deportation of 104,100 people to the camps in Eastern Europe. Of those, 76,297 were murdered upon arrival to those camps, 26,711 died from disease or were murdered before the end of the war and only 2,197 survived to say what had happened. No action was taken against any of the German Jews who had been members of the camp administration. Questions were asked, but none were arrested and tried in any Dutch courts. There is little doubt that many German Jews abused their positions. Philip Mechanicus noted how they behaved; they commanded, shouted, barked, snarled, shrieked and intimidated just like any Prussian soldier, something Etty Hillesum and Gabriel Italie would agree with.

Lippmann, Rosenthal & Co. or Liro was a Dutch Jewish Bank. It was appropriated by the Nazis, and its employees effectively worked for the German state. They confiscated Jewish accounts, oversaw the sale of Jewish possessions and received art works and so forth to be sold. High Nazi officials had their pick, and the best pieces were sent to museums in Germany. The bank took money from those being deported or arriving at the camp. After the war, no one really wanted to have anything to do with the bank and its reputation. Not terribly surprising. The bank was taken over by Hollandse Koopmansbank.

Martin Uffenheimer – You might remember he escaped the camp by changing into another person actually inside the wagon and then walking out the front gates. This method of escape was used a number of times, and it meant that someone had disappeared from the train rather than escaping from Camp Westerbork. Martin thought that 21 probably escaped from Westerbork, although others put the number higher. Jan Smit thought the number was 30.

Salo Muller – Salo went into hiding as a child, escaping from the Schouburg Nursery, and then to escape the Nazis, he was shielded at eight addresses. He lost both his parents in the Shoah. The last words his mother spoke to him were: "See you tonight and promise to be a good boy," the title of one of his books. Only recently, after years of perseverance by Salo, has the Dutch Railways agreed to pay reparations for its part in transporting Jews during the Holocaust.

Viznitzher Rebbe is the title afforded to the leader of a Hasidic dynasty founded by Rabbi Menachem Mendel Hager in the small town of Vizhnitz. At this time, it was Moshe Yehoshua Hager, who lived to be 95 and died in 2012.

Willem van der Veer was a hero in more senses of the word than can be imagined. Before his involvement in the Westerbork episode, he was a hero many times over. He had fled to the Netherlands in May 1940. He was a member of the Marechaussee and left on his bicycle to support Queen Wilhelmina. Her ship did not turn up, so he made other plans. He rode that bicycle all the way to Brest and got a boat to Plymouth. He joined the commandos and fought with Mountbatten in Burma, but after contracting malaria, he was forced to return to England. In October 1944, he was dropped into Arnhem. Although in pain from the bad parachute landing, he escaped capture by hiding in the headquarters of the German general in charge of policing operations. He slipped away and began training partisans in Drenthe and surrounds. As part of Operation Amherst, French paratroopers were dropped in Drenthe, where they would secure key points. Westerbork was on the route for Amherst. He knew the French were close to Westerbork village, so he rode his bicycle to meet them. He was stopped by German troops on the way, but an Allied fighter plane appeared, and they ran for cover, leaving Willem to escape. In the village of Westerbork, he seized the mayor and made him fly the Dutch flag to welcome the French troops. In fact, the mayor and the councillors had met to be ready to surrender, and the mayor's wife made had made everyone coffee. It was then he made the phone call and frightened off Gemmeker.

Adolf Haas was SS-Obersturmbannführer and Kommandant at Niederhagen-Wewelsburg and Bergen-Belsen concentration camp from December 1943 to December 1944. He was labelled as incompetent and corrupt and was assigned to duties at the front. He took part in an execution of an SS officer in April 1945 and then simply disappeared. He was declared dead in 1950. If anyone knew whether he was still alive, nothing was ever said.

Adolph Eichmann's story is well known. This was the man who declared he would die happy even though he had five million deaths on his conscience. He had been responsible for the deportation of that number of Jews. The eventual total was more than that, as Eichmann did not accept any responsibility for those killed by the Einsatzgruppen. He escaped Berlin but was captured by the Americans. Somehow, not realising whom they had, he was not watched closely enough and escaped. Moving around Germany, he avoided capture and settled in Lower Saxony. Few knew what he looked like, as he was a behind-the-scenes worker and did not parade around for everyone to see. He visited without the film cameras. Then in 1950, he went to Argentina on false papers. In 1960, the Mossad discovered his whereabouts. He was captured, drugged and secreted out of Argentina to Israel. He faced a trial, which was televised and recorded. Transcripts are available to read in which he does not deny the Holocaust or the numbers were presented to him. He simply claimed he had been merely following orders. He was found guilty and sentenced to death by hanging. The sentence was executed on 1 June 1962.

Albert Ganzenmüller was the undersecretary of the Reich Ministry of Transport. He was responsible for the transportation of Jews. He was one of the old Nazis. Even though he held a doctorate in engineering, he had taken part in the Beer Hall Putsch in 1923 with the other original members of the Nazi Party. He had been in the Brown Shirts (SA) and reached the rank equal to colonel. He worked for the Reichsbahn. In 1942, Albert Speer recommended him, and

Ganzenmüller was appointed deputy general director of the German State Railways and undersecretary of State at the Reich Ministry of Transport. One of his first tasks was to deal with a complaint about the slowness of trains to Sobibór. Ganzenmüller replied to the effect that they would do their best to ensure that trains ran smoothly to Sobibór as they were doing to Auschwitz. Karl Wolff, adjutant to Himmler, thanked him for this. After the war, Ganzenmüller escaped via the ratline to Argentina. There was an amnesty in 1950 which benefited him. But then the correspondence between Himmler and Wolff came to light in 1957, and investigations were reopened. Nothing much happened, and it was not until 1973 that formal charges were made against him that he had aided and abetted the murder of millions of people in the war. But his mind was wandering at age 68, following a heart attack, and the case halted in 1977. Ganzenmüller, however, lived a vigorous life until 1996 when he was 91.

Albert Konrad Gemmeker came from Düsseldorf. Many have recorded what they felt about him. When Wilhelm Willing asked what the Kommandant was like, he found out that he made inmates shiver and tremble. Lotte Ruth Kan was pleased to have met him and thought him very honest. She hoped that because she was of a mixed marriage that he might leave her alone. That was first impression. She found that once Gemmeker had decided something, that was it. Philip Mechanicus believed Gemmeker never really showed his true heart. He thought he had iron hands in velvet gloves and an unpredictable nature. Gemmeker was fond of saying that he had had a good upbringing, a good *Kinderstube*. Philip cited many actions that would not be taken by such a person. Again, Etty Hillesum saw a cruel, cold and insecure man behind the smiling façade. She thought he looked like a cross between a well-groomed hairdresser and a man who frequented a pub for the "bon viveur." Everyone saw his fiendish schemes. If you have a kindly man, on who cares for "his" Jews, why are you afraid when a small thing happens, like a ball from a football match hitting his bicycle and knocking it over with a clatter? Jacobus Valk was surprised when nothing happened.

Surely, if you accidentally knock over the bicycle of a gentleman, one should not expect any repercussions. After Gemmeker's arrest and detainment at Westerbork, he was moved to the prison at Assen. He was questioned there and confirmed he had taken up his post on 13 October 1942, the same day as Hassel had. He described Lemke's actions at Barrack 51, where he was in charge. He mentions other SS men and Dutch Marechaussee, Lubbecke, Reiser, Sleik, Van Dam, Van Laer and Van Eck. He was very careful in his statement not to incriminate himself. Gemmeker supported Lemke's statement about how Lemke had looked after the prisoners in the punishment barracks and that he would have seen to all their needs. Gemmeker had to wait until January 1949 for his trial to start. Before his trial, he was imprisoned for nearly 45 months while he was interviewed and interrogated. Throughout this time, he vehemently denied knowing what happened at the death camps in the East. This was his defence at his trial. He had acted with sympathy in those very difficult times and thought that the 79,800 people he had sent to the East to work, which included babies, orphaned children and the elderly way past working ages, were to work for the Fatherland. Of those he sent east, only 2,084 survived, 62,628 were murdered on arrival and 15,088 died before the war's end. Information now available would have to ensure that Gemmeker received a longer sentence than the ten years that he was given. The prosecution had asked for 12 years. When Queen Juliana came to the throne, various offenders were granted "grace," including Gemmeker. He was released on 20 April 1951. He returned to Düsseldorf, and his doctor, from before the war and at Westerbork Camp, was again Dr Fritz Spanier. Two years later, Gemmeker remarried and lived a life more akin to that of a recluse. He continually maintained that he had known nothing of the killing camps and that he was not an anti-Semite. Yet his distaste for Jews could be seen for everyone at the Jewish Psychiatric Hospital at Apeldoorn when he was present at the evacuation. It showed the total of his humanity towards Jews. The patients had been beaten and piled on top of one another in the lorries. They were packed so tightly, they had a job to shut the tailgate. Children were thrown in with the other patients. Then when the train was going, the nurses were asked to volunteer to accompany the patients to work in the new hospital or to come home if they wished. In interviews for television, Gemmeker again repeated his mantra that he knew nothing. Gabriel Italie wrote how he could never trust the statements that the Germans made about working in the East. How was this? Gabriel could not trust Gemmeker's promises. Gabriel was no different from many others who all distrusted Gemmeker. Now why was this? Was this because they knew more about what was happening than Gemmeker did? I find this hard to believe. Gemmeker tried to have people believe that he did not know what even the Jews knew. Is this why they did not trust him? Gemmeker was not that naïve. Was Gemmeker not asked about his conversations with Eichmann or Alfred Käsewieter, who had accompanied the trains? Was he not asked about his briefings or told of the rumours that circulated the camp? This man must have lived in a bubble or blamelessness., Then in 1967, the German judiciary filed charges against Gemmeker. Yet no evidence could be found to prove his willing involvement in the Holocaust. No one asked him about his meeting with the SS Architect Winne, who visited and stayed at the camp and was instrumental in its construction as well as being well versed in the other camps such as Auschwitz. Nor was Gemmeker's reaction noted when he was told what happened in the East to all the Jews he sent there. What was his reaction when he supposedly heard for the first time about the death camps? Did he express any regrets or profound sadness or just continue to state his innocence, his duty and lack of knowledge? Gemmeker died 30 August 1982 at age 75. He took to the grave whatever it was he had said to Rudolf Breslauer and that Rudolf was too afraid to tell those he loved.

Anton Burger, known as Toni to his confidants, became Kommandant at Theresienstadt from July 1943 to February 1944. It was he who ordered the whole camp to parade in freezing weather. Out of 40,000 people, 300 died from hypothermia. He then went to Greece and was another arrested at Alt Ausee. He was tried in a Czech court and sentenced to death. In 1947, he escaped. He returned to his hometown under a false name but was again arrested in March 1951; he managed to escape again in April. He then disappeared. He worked in the Essen region under the name Wilhelm Bauer, who had been involved in the Theresienstadt film. Burger disliked Bauer but chose his name despite that Burger had personally murdered Bauer. In 1994, the deception was discovered, nearly two years after Burger's death.

Arthur Seyss-Inquart was the civil overseer for the occupied Netherlands from May 1940 to April 1945 when Hitler appointed him as part of the Nazi government that was to follow him. He was an anti-Semite and intransigent in his Nazi beliefs. He tried to ensure that all Jews were deported from the Netherlands. His main belief was that in Germany. He had been strongly opposed to the Allied air drop of food and supplies for the beleaguered Dutch in the Hunger Winter of 1944–1945. He was arrested on a bridge over the Elbe and later sent to Nuremburg for trial. He was found guilty and hanged on 16 October 1946. Shortly before death, he sought solace in the Catholic Church.

Bernhard Henschel, born 7 July 1893 in Breslau, was a senior police officer in the Dienstelle of Organisation Schmelt at Sosnowitz. He was tasked with the sorting of prisoners from the train station when trains stopped on the way to Auschwitz. Annelies and Herman Rens believed that this man and Henschield were one and the same. Henschel was responsible for the deportation of forced labour to camps and factories. He was captured in Sudetenland in May 1945 and executed by shooting on 4 September 1946.

Elisabeth Helena Hassel-Mullender was the wife of Untersturmführer Hassel, also from Düsseldorf. Inmates described her as the epitome of femininity, which made her doubly dangerous. She had divorced Hassel and had started a relationship with Gemmeker, for all intents and purposes, as his wife. It had started when she was Gemmeker's secretary. They lived together in the green and white Kommandant's house. She was always in the background and accompanied Gemmeker as he walked through the camp. She was there when he hosted parties for Nazi bigwigs or for the Jewish entertainers Gemmeker would host after the revues. An interview with Hassel was not one to be savoured, and she was not one to grant favours. She was hard and unmoving. Hermann Schliesser noted that when Gemmeker was away and she was deputised, even the SS hid from her because of her angry spirit. After the war, she was arrested and kept in custody to give evidence against Gemmeker at his trial. She was not found guilty of her involvement at Westerbork as Gemmeker's evil genius or his angry partner. She assimilated herself back into German life in Düsseldorf. Her local doctor was also Dr Fritz Spanier. Her relationship with Gemmeker ceased. When interviewed by the Assen police, Hassel confirmed she had started as secretary at the camp on 13 October 1942. In her capacity as secretary, she said she spoke with Gemmeker and other camp officers. She claimed she was present during discussions when Gemmeker decided what was to be done when the "low-ranking" residents of the camp had committed "reprehensible" acts. She could not recall any conversations between Gemmeker and Max de Jong. She did not know him, but she did know Heinz Lemke quite well. He was in charge of the punishment block, Barrack 51, she said.

Erich Deppner left Westerbork under a sort of cloud for mismanagement but with a congratulatory telegram from Himmler. Deppner's role in killing was repeated when 1,500 prisoners were sent from Scheveningen to Vught when the Allies broke through to Paris and Brussels. They were mostly members of the resistance and were housed in a bunker-like building from which there was little chance of escape. In late July, early August 1944, Deppner was sent to Vught to carry out Hitler's *Niedermachungsbefehl* of 30 July 1944, the order to kill terrorists and saboteurs as quickly as possible. The 1,500 had been tried before, and this order was enacted. Deppner was familiar with the Dutch resistance and put together a list of 450 names. They were executed on his orders. In early 1945, Deppner was recalled to Berlin where he was captured by the Soviets in May. He was released in 1950. The Soviets obviously did not know who he was. Deppner was then recruited by Operation Gehlen, an American-controlled security service and the *Bundesnachrichtendienst*. Both organisations knew his past. The Netherlands sought his extradition from Germany, but this was always refused. Eventually, he was tried in Germany for his role in the execution of the Soviet POWs but was acquitted. He died in 2005 when he was 95 years old. Deppner oversaw the deportation of 14,237 Jews to the East. Of those, 43 survived to see the end of the war. 5,468 were murdered upon arrival and 8,726 died before the liberation of the camps.

Erich Naumann was recalled from the killing fields of German-occupied Poland in the East to take over as commander of the Security Police in the Netherlands in September 1943. He was in post until June 1944 when he was succeeded by Karl Schöngarth. He was a highly prized prisoner of the Americans when he was caught and was questioned at the Nuremberg Trials. He was executed at Landsberg on 8 June 1951.

Ernst Kaltenbrunner was head of the Reichssicherheitshauptamt, RSHA, the Main Office of the Security of the Reich in Berlin. He had made a name for himself in Austria and was duly promoted by Himmler. Kaltenbrunner toured various camps and was given a demonstration at Mauthausen of the three killing methods: shooting, hanging and gassing. Five people for each method were used. He was instrumental in rounding up Italian Jews. At the end of the war, he was the head of all German forces in the south. He returned to Berlin. You might have seen the film in which Hitler left the bunker to decorate some soldiers with the Iron Cross; among them was Alfred Czech. He was 12 years old. Kaltenbrunner was also there at 1.94 metres tall. Czech was the boy whom Hitler pinched on the cheek. Kaltenbrunner later ran and fled to the Totes Gebirge near Alt Aussee, where he threw his seal in the lake. He further tried to hide his identity by claiming he was a doctor. On 12 May 1945, the Americans were told by the assistant local mayor, Johann Brandauer, that some men were hiding in a mountain cabin. A patrol was organised, including four paroled Wehrmacht soldiers. Special Agent

Robert Matteson called on the men to surrender. He was unarmed. Kaltenbrunner, his aide Arthur Scheidler, and two SS men came out. Kaltenbrunner still maintained he was a doctor. But since when do doctors need to run away? When the group returned to the town, Kaltenbrunner was unmasked by none other than his mistress, Countess Gisela von Westarp, who saw him across the town square, shouted out his name and ran over to hug him. Kaltenbrunner was the highest SS officer at the Nuremburg Trials. He missed part of the trial due to minor strokes but recovered. He claimed he was not responsible for contributing to the Holocaust, that it was all Himmler and that he, Kaltenbrunner, had brought it to an end. He was found guilty on three counts and hanged on 16 October 1946.

Ferdinand Hugo aus der Fünten had met Gemmeker on several occasions and had visited the camp. He served the head of the Central Office for Jewish Emigration in Amsterdam and was responsible for many arrests and the seizure of physically and mentally ill patients. He threatened mixed-marriage Jews with deportation so that they agreed to sterilisation. He was captured and had to wait until 1950 for his trial. He was found guilty of war crimes and sentenced to death by a Dutch court. It was commuted to life imprisonment. There was a public outcry when he was released in 1989. He was deported to Germany and settled in Duisburg where he died just under three months later.

Franz Fischer was another I mentioned. He was responsible for the transportation of 13,000 Jews from The Hague. He also treated Jews very badly, even those married to Dutch people. He was known as the "Jew Fischer." The Canadians captured him, and the Netherlands requested his extradition. In March 1949, he was sentenced to life imprisonment, but then a special court sentenced him to death in July 1950. Queen Juliana was averse to the death penalty, so it was commuted to life imprisonment later in 1951. He suffered perpetual dreams of being chased by Jews who would beat him. At the age of 88 in January 1989, he was released. He died the next September.

Franz Novak was the Austrian SS-Hauptsturmführer who was Eichmann's timetable expert. He set the times of departures and the length of journeys. Without his expertise, the trains would not have run on time. In March 1933, he joined the Nazi Party, and in April 1933, he joined the SA. He joined the coup against Austrian Chancellor Engelbert Dollfuss in July 1934 but had to flee to Yugoslavia when it failed. He then went to Germany and joined the Austrian Legion. In 1938 following the Anschluss, he returned to Vienna as Eichmann's deputy at the Central Agency for Jewish Emigration. In 1939, he was at the opening of the office in Prague. Novak told centres for Jewish deportations how many Jews were to be put on the trains and when. In March 1944, he went to Budapest with Eichmann to organise the deportation of Hungarian Jews. He was responsible for having organised at least 707 deportation trains, 87 of them from the Netherlands. Novak disappeared at the end of the war. Following the repeal of the War Crimes Act in 1957 in Germany, he resumed his real name and surfaced again. In 1961 when the Eichmann investigations were underway, warrants were issued for the arrest of Eichmann's staff. Novak was arrested in Vienna at his print shop in January 1961. He faced many trials where he was acquitted or had the sentence overturned. He spent a number of years in custody and was found guilty of not providing adequate food, water and conveniences for the Jews he sent on the trains and eventually sentenced to seven years. Because of the time he had spent in custody, he was released immediately. Austrian President Rudolf Kirchschläger granted him a pardon in 1974. He was responsible for sending well over half a million to their deaths. He died in 1983 in Langenzersdorf, in Lower Austria.

Fritz Suhren was the Kommandant of Ravensbrück concentration camp for women from August 1942. He had a simple policy, which was to work the prisoners to death. He provided inmates for Dr Gebhardt to experiment on. When he was asked to release the prisoners Himmler had agreed to, he refused. He kept a few prisoners for insurance purposes. As the Soviets approached, he took Odette Sansom, a British agent, to the British lines, as he thought she was

Winston Churchill's niece. Sansom testified against him at his trial, where he was found guilty and hanged in 1950.

Gertrud Slottke was Harster's thin-faced secretary. She was a bit more than a minute taker or letter writer, as she was actively involved with the deportations. She proposed lists and actions and was complicit in the deportations and murder of those from Westerbork Camp. She went to Westerbork to engage with the transportation of Jews and to Bergen-Belsen to the Sternlager. She interviewed Philip Mechanicus a number of times, and he recorded the exchanges. Barry Spanjaard described her as one of the ugliest women he had ever met and as a living nightmare. She was childless and hated children and took delight in destroying happiness. Philip said she was like a bat. Ab Carnasa also saw her as sexless and as a fanatical anti-Semite. Inmates joked that the red and black Putsch ribbon she wore on her chest helped her remember where her breast was. Part of her responsibilities included finding Jews who would make good hostages or who were of significant "interest and value". She also worked in Ravensbrück Camp. Upon one visit to Westerbork, it was commented that her skirt needed to be ironed. It became lost, and the whole camp was turned upside down looking for an Aryan skirt among the Jews. The words almost "giggle" off the page as Philip wrote them. Slottke was caught by the Canadians and interned at Hilversum. She was later released in May 1945 and was classed as a follower. For the next 14 years, she became buried in everyday life, joining various women's groups and leading some. Then in 1959 an investigation was undertaken into the deportations from the Netherlands. She found herself under scrutiny and was brought before a court on charges implicating her part in murder. Slottke denied knowledge of the exterminations, even though she had been to Bergen-Belsen and Ravensbrück. She expressed no shame or regret for what she had done. She was found to be complicit and in 1967 sentenced to five years' imprisonment. Owing to illness, she was released in May 1971 and died the following December.

Gudrun Himmler was Heinrich Himmler's daughter. I use her circumstances in the book as a stark comparison with those of Dutch and German children in Westerbork. She had a pampered life as one would expect for the Reichführer's daughter. She was the ideal Nazi child. She grew up to have complete faith in her father and in what he was doing. She never had any doubt that the right way to handle European Jewry was through genocide. After the war, she raised funds for struggling members of what had been the SS and its many factions through the *Stille Hilfe*, "Silent Help." She was the "flamboyant Nazi princess" until her death in 2018.

I suppose one could not expect any more of Gudrun than the person she grew up to be. She was indoctrinated at an early age with Nazi ideology by both parents and was told of her father's importance time and time again. She was told how indispensable he was to Hitler and that her father was always right. Would we not all like to believe that of our fathers? But many children of the Nazi hierarchy came to terms with the sins of their fathers, some even joining the church and others speaking out against Nazi ideology, yet holding on to the loving side that their parent showed them. Gudrun, however, never made that step on her journey. She blamed her treatment by the Allies after the war for the way in which she saw things. My view is that if both she and her mother had shown some contrition and acknowledgement of the fact that murder of any one person is a crime, they might have been treated differently. But they took this high-handed approach towards Germans as well. When mother and daughter left various detention centres, other detainees were glad to see the back of them. She encouraged the generations that followed to hold Himmler and others in esteem and celebrate their memory. In some respects, she was no better than her father.

Hans Albin Rauter was the highest-ranking SS Officer in the occupied Netherlands. There he instigated many punitive actions and oversaw the various camps and prisons throughout. It he who ordered that ten Dutch men be executed for every single German killed by the resistance. If one Dutch collaborator was killed, this meant death for three patriotic Dutch men. Rauter was given command of the Maas front as a Waffen-SS general after he had proved himself at Arnhem. He was severely wounded during an attack by Dutch resistance fighters on the evening of 6 March 1945. Reprisals resulted in the deaths of 262 hostages. The attack had not been aimed at Rauter; it was unfortunate for him that he was travelling on the route the partisans were on. The resistance were dressed in German uniforms and looked as if they were a normal patrol stopping vehicles. They were unaware that Rauter had ordered that military vehicles were not to be stopped by patrols, and a firefight broke out. He feigned death and was taken to hospital when he was found by a German patrol. The British arrested him in hospital. At the end of the war, he was handed to the Dutch authorities. He was tried by a special tribunal and condemned to death. The sentence was confirmed by a higher court in January 1949, and he was shot on 24 March 1949.

Hans Georg Calmeyer was a lawyer and worked for the Germans in The Hague from 1941 to 1945. It was his job to decide the racial standing of some Jews. He had to decide whether they were legally partly or wholly Jewish. Calmeyer knew he was being lied to and given false evidence, but he quite simply saw it as a means to thwart Nazi legislation. He handled 6,000 cases and was able to classify 3,700 people as "fully Aryan" or "half Aryan." Compare this with the same office in Berlin where only ten percent of pleas were granted, and you can see that Hans was quite liberal in his decision making. Gertrud Slottke complained about his actions in 1943. Hans vehemently denied he was being over generous or even sabotaging Nazi intent, although he admitted it after the war. Then in early 1945, it was decided to seize his papers to examination them, but the Allied advance meant this did not happen. But Calmeyer did class 2,300 as Jews; they were deported, and many of them died. Hence he was complicit in this regard. Whatever one thinks, he was honoured posthumously by Yad Vashem 1992 as "Righteous Among the Nations" and that is good enough for me to accept he did what he could and that it was more than some did. The Schindler from Osnabrück died in 1972.

Hans Paul Oster was, I suppose a "good" Nazi. He had been kept in the German Army of the Weimar Republic but had to resign in 1932 following his discovery at a German *Karnival* in the French-occupied *Rhineland*. German officers were not allowed in this French-occupied zone. However, he found new employment with Hermann Göring in the secret police unit he was setting up. Oster later transferred to the *Abwehr*, the German intelligence department, rising to become the deputy to Admiral Canaris. Both men were not ardent Nazis and in small ways demonstrated resistance to Hitler and his intentions. They were involved in saving the lives of Jews. Oster told his friend Bert Sas, the military attaché from the Dutch embassy in Berlin, about the impending invasion of the Netherlands. He told him not once but 20 times. Sas was not believed, and Hitler punched through the Low Countries, repeating the *Blitzkrieg*. Oster began to build a network of resistance with the knowledge of Canaris. Canaris had been sending agents to Britain who were very easily captured. Hitler was horrified at the numbers and flippantly told Canaris to use Jews, so Jews were parachuted into Britain and promptly gave themselves up. The Oster Network grew and recruited high-ranking officers. The Oster group was able to supply British-made bombs for use in insurgent activities. Then in 1943, Oster was uncovered and placed under house arrest. Oster had provided Abwehr identities to 14 Jews, who had escaped with the help of the theologian Dietrich Bonhoeffer. Admiral Canaris rather foolishly kept diaries. The Gestapo were given blank authority following the July bomb plot. Canaris had instigated the Netherlands War Scare. Through intelligence activities, he made the British aware that Germany might invade the Lowlands and use the Dutch airfields to strike against Britain. Canaris knew of the appeasement group in Britain, which he considered dangerous. This manufactured scare shook the British and made them more cautious in their dealings with Nazi Germany, which was Canaris's intent. During the war, Canaris established links with his British counterpart through Zurich and Spain, perhaps even the Vatican. He had even helped Rabbi Yosef Yitzchok Schneersohn escape from Warsaw. Himmler was suspicious of the Abwehr, and in February 1944, he had it disbanded and Canaris placed under house arrest. With the July bomb plot, two Abwehr officers committed suicide. It was then the Gestapo and SS looked for evidence to implicate Canaris, which is when they found his diaries that exposed him, Bonhoeffer and Oster. Canaris was arrested three days after the bomb plot. Oster had not taken part in this, but Stauffenberg had taken over Oster's lead. Many, including Canaris, were tried at "The People's Court" by Judge Roland Freisler. Canaris, Oster and Bonhoeffer were all sent to Flossenburg Concentration Camp and were viciously hanged on Monday 9 April 1945.

Heinrich Lindner the SS-Sturmbannführer, Nazi Party Nr 673414 and SS Nr 18274, was involved in the Organisation Schmelt at Sosnowitz. It appears he survived the war but just before extradition from a British prison camp to Poland for trial, he committed suicide on 11 January 1947 at Fallingbostel.

Herbert Johannes Wölk, party number 278643, was one of those men who disappeared from view – not from those who knew him, but from those who wanted to know of him. He was head of security in Rotterdam and spent much of his time in a splendid house on the city's outskirts called "The Garden of the Forest." It had once been owned by a Jewish man called Bos who had fled to America. There Wölk kept rabbits. Louis Berkelouw, a prisoner, had to care for the rabbits. His wife was trying to get Louis freed, as he was only half-Jewish, and his parents were not married. When it came to Christmas, Louis was expected to kill the rabbits, but Wölk made other arrangements because Louis had cared for these animals all year and had become attached. Then in March 1944, Louis was sent to Westerbork. His wife, Cornelia, rushed to the Security Service offices with her son and pleaded with Wölk. She had written letters and had probably seen Calmeyer, but to no avail. So what did this SS-Sturmbannführer Wölk, number 15429, do? He made calls, and Louis was returned the same day. Not only that – he was released. So Lages and aus der Fünten claimed at their trials that they were following the orders of this monster. It was the same SS-Sturmbannführer Wölk who was responsible for the deaths of 72 Dutch citizens as well as numerous Jews who were rounded up in

Razzias and deported. In 1950, he was sentenced to 20 years' imprisonment for war crimes, specifically for the murder of civilians and resistance fighters. He had ordered seven sets of executions involving 66 victims and two shootings known as "The Silver Fir Campaign." He was released after 13 years and deported back to Germany in 1963 where he submerged from view.

Johann Kotälla, although not featured in the recounts about Westerbork, was known as *The Beul of Amersfoort*, the "Executioner of Amersfort." Even though he was being treated for psychiatric problems, he was regarded as fit for duty. When it was *Appell*, roll call, he would beat and kick prisoners as well as stamp on them and kick the men between the legs. He was also in the execution squads. When caught, he had changed into a Luftwaffe uniform and ditched his SS uniform. It was a display of common sense for anyone seeking to hide their true identities. He obviously knew that SS uniforms were not the best sort of clothes to be found in at the end of the war. In December 1948, he was sentenced to death, but after many psychiatric examinations, his sentence was commuted to life imprisonment in December 1951. He was imprisoned at Breda. In October 1973, he suffered a stroke which debilitated his right side. Treatment allowed him some use. He went on hunger strike for a month in 1974 and received the "Last Rites" in May 1975. He died in 1979. His ashes were sent to Germany but rejected, as the country knew him as Kotälla. They were re-sent with the spelling as Kotälla. If you are morbidly interested, you can see the club he used to beat prisoners with on display in a museum.

Josef Hugo Dischner, the alcoholic, was replaced by Polizeiinspektor Bohrmann and sent back to Lemberg in Ukraine where he had come from. In 1944, he then went to fight in the Waffen-SS. Borhmann was replaced three days later by Gemmeker. Dischner died in 1989 aged 87. He deported 11,168 people to the camps in the East. Of those, only 76 survived; 8,201 were murdered on arrival, and 2,897 died before the war's end.

Karl Rahm followed Burger as Kommandant at Theresienstadt from February 1944 until the end of the war. He oversaw the making of the film *The Führer Gives the Jews a City*. As soon as that film was finished, the ghetto was stripped of all the beautification, and within one month, 18,000 people had been sent to Auschwitz. He beat prisoners and was present when they were tortured. Yet he could almost be friendly towards some prisoners, especially those from a working-class background from Vienna. He would exempt some Jews from deportation, especially for a bribe. On 5 May 1945, Rahm evacuated the ghetto of SS personnel and fled. He was captured soon after by Americans in Austria. In 1947, he was extradited to Czechoslovakia and put on trial. Having been found guilty of crimes against humanity, he was hanged four hours after being awarded the guilty verdict on 30 April 1947.

Marga Himmler married Himmler in 1928. They had three children. At the end of the war, they fled south but were captured by Americans and moved around to various internment camps. She was interrogated many times and proved to be a difficult woman, not only for the Americans but also for other Germans in the camps. From the end of the war until 15 January 1953, she faced many denazification tribunals, which she appealed against, but at each one, starting at the lowest level, she found herself a step higher and was ultimately classified as Category II. This meant she was regarded as an "Activist, Militant, and Profiteer" and was therefore an incriminated person, *Belastete,* and was sentenced to 30 days of special work. She also lost her pension rights and the right to vote.

"Merchant Henschield" – see Bernhard Henschel.

Oskar Gröning was a clerk from Lower Saxony. His mother died when he was four. He trained as a bank clerk but was immediately conscripted into the army when war was declared. Gröning wandered into a hotel and joined the SS who were recruiting there. He got his wish of joining an elite force. He was given training to serve in camps and was stationed at Auschwitz where he dealt with foreign currency. It was his job to sort the notes and put them away for safekeeping. Like the others, he profited. He made a request for transfer, but it was turned down. He witnessed the gassings and knew what had happened first-hand. He was captured and worked for some time in the United Kingdom on a farm. He returned to Germany perhaps in 1948 and settled down to a normal life. It was not until the middle of the 1990s that he had a conversation with a Holocaust denier. He wrote about his experiences to the writers of a denial pamphlet. He then received calls and letters from deniers, who denied his evidence. He started to speak publicly about the Holocaust and wrote his memoirs for private use. He was interviewed for a television series, *Auschwitz: The Nazis the Final Solution*. He did not believe that he had done anything wrong and openly stated that children were killed because they could grow up seeking revenge, exactly Himmler's point. Gröning almost became two people: the one who was part of the system and its beliefs, although he was not actively involved in the killing, and the other who spoke out against Nazi ideals and asked for forgiveness from the Jews for what had happened. He was prosecuted for his part, in 2014, as an accessory. A total of 60 witnesses came forward and spoke about Auschwitz. It was three months later that he was found guilty of being an accessory to the murder of 300,000 Jews. At the age of 93, he was sentenced to four years imprisonment. One of the witnesses, Eva Mozes Kor, said it was too late for such a sentence. She would have preferred that he was sentenced to continue to talk publicly against the neo-Nazis and felt the custodial sentence did no good at all. In March 2018, Gröning died in hospital while waiting to start his sentence. He was trying to challenge Holocaust deniers but by doing so implicated himself. There were thousands of others who did not face any sort of justice. Perhaps Eva was right; he was achieving more speaking out than he would have in prison.

Otto Bene, although he was in Seyys-Inquart's office in The Hague, was really no more than Joachim Ribbentrop's "eyes and ears." Deportations were reported to him but not organised by him. He passed the information back to Berlin. He could of course influence others through his position. He suggested that 4,000 Jews could be deported each week, and he decided that Jews baptised into Christianity were still Jews and could therefore be deported. He was imprisoned after the war but released in 1948 and disappeared into a normal life, working for the brewery Asbach Urhalt in the *Rhineland*, which many of us will have drunk if visiting. He died in 1973.

* * *

I have mentioned quite a few doctors who conducted experiments at the camps and will quickly detail what happened to them. You will see that some escaped any retribution and that the sentences awarded differ in length. Many only served partial sentences.

August Hirt was an SS-Hauptsturmführer and head of the department of anatomy at the Reich University in Strasbourg. He requested permission from Himmler to form a collection of Jewish skeletons. Himmler told him he could have as many as he wished. SS-Hauptsturmführer Bruno Beger went to Auschwitz and selected 115 prisoners who were then murdered. Eighty-six skeletons were taken to form the collection. Hirt committed suicide on 2 June 1945, but his death was not confirmed until the mid-1960s during which time he had been tried in absentia.

Carl Clauberg was a German gynaecologist who carried out sterilisation experiments on women at Dachau, then Auschwitz and finally at Ravensbrück where the Soviets captured him. They him and sentenced to 25 years. He was released early, in 1955.

Eduard Wirths was the chief medical officer at Auschwitz. He had been described as an ardent Nazi. This seems self-evident given that worked at Auschwitz; even his younger brother could not stand it. However, he did his best to protect medical practitioners among the prisoners. One prisoner, Langbein, claimed Wirths had saved 93,000 lives in 1943, in controlling a Typhus outbreak. He was interested in sterilisation but never personally conducted the experiments. It was Wirths who organised the prisoner selections on the ramps. He ended the war with the rank of SS-Sturmbannführer at Mittelbau-Dora concentration camp in Thuringia. He was captured by the British but committed suicide in September 1944.

Emil Kaschub was tasked with identifying the methods malingering German soldiers used to escape the war. Part of his research was to infect healthy people at Auschwitz with toxins and infections. The infected skin was not only photographed but also excised. Witnesses stated he injected prisoners with liquid petroleum. After the war, he secured a post as head of surgery at the Bethanien Hospital in Frankfurt. He died in 1977, never facing any charges. Evidence does not even seem to be have been collated for any trial.

Horst Schuman conducted sterilisation and castration experiments at Auschwitz. He was interested in the use of X-rays for mass sterilisations. He also infected people with typhus in an attempt to find a cure. He ended the war at a military hospital in Saxony, was captured in January 1945 and was released the following October. He worked as a sport doctor in Gladbeck but was identified in 1951. A warrant for his arrest was ordered. He served as a ship's doctor for three years and applied for a German passport in Japan in 1954. He then sought refuge in Sudan and worked at the hospital in Khartoum. He was recognised by an Auschwitz survivor and fled to Ghana where he received the protection of Kwame Nkrumah. He was extradited in 1966 but released from prison during his trial in 1972 owing to poor health. He lived another 11 years and died in 1983.

Johann Kremer was professor of anatomy and human genetics at Münster University prior to the war. He joined the army and served in the SS for nearly three months at Auschwitz. He carried out post-mortems while the individuals were alive to extract fresh living material for his research into the effects of starvation. He was present at some executions and punishments. He was sentenced to death, which was commuted to life imprisonment by the Polish president. He was released in 1958, when his sentence was adjusted to 10 years, having only served a fraction of a life sentence. He died in 1965.

Josef Mengele of course is a name many people know. He was associated with work on twins, so the fact that he specifically targeted children seems to make his crimes worse. His work was flawed from the start, as many of the twins were not mono-zygotic, identical. He volunteered for medical service with the Waffen-SS in 1940. He saw active combat and was awarded the Iron Cross for rescuing two soldiers from a burning tank. He was wounded in mid-1942 and declared unfit for military service. In 1943, Verschuer encouraged him to seek transfer to Auschwitz. Here he took part in the selection on the ramp of those who were to die immediately. He was able to select subjects for his perverse experiments and was known to whistle as he did so. He also oversaw the use of Zyklon B. His twin research was supposedly to increase the hereditary superiority of the German race. He had a kind side for the purpose of make the children pliable and malleable but thought nothing of having them killed to examine results of his experiments. He went to Groß-Rosen camp in January 1945 and fled from there a month later. He was captured by the Americans, but at that point, his name was not on the list of those being sought as major criminals. He was released at the end of July calling himself Fritz Ullman. He even went back to Soviet-occupied areas to recover his notes that he had hidden. Then, using the name Helmut Gregor, he made use of the ratline to escape Europe, going to Argentina in 1949. There are numerous stories about his life in South America, with sightings and feigned death, being chased by the Mossad. In 1979 he suffered a stroke while swimming and drowned. He was buried under the name of Wolfgang Erhard. Still there were sightings, and still he was hunted. It was not until 1992 with the use of DNA that the body was officially recognised as being that of Mengele. Repatriation to Germany was refused, and the skeleton was used as a teaching aid at the University of São Paulo where many Jewish exiles lived.

Karl Gebhardt was the superintendent at Hohenlychen Sanatorium and was Himmler's personal doctor. He specialised in traumatic wounds which he induced and then infected at Ravensbrück and

Auschwitz. He was tried, convicted and then hanged at Landsberg Prison on 2 June 1947.

Otmar Freiherr von Verschuer used Mengele's research to advance his own career. Towards the end of the war, he took his papers west towards the Americans. Although authorities in Frankfurt labelled him one of the most dangerous Nazi activists, he was never brought to trial and was awarded the professorship of human genetics at the University of Münster. He was examined by de-Nazification tribunals, but nothing incriminating had been left because Verschuer had most likely destroyed it all. He was fined 600 German marks. He died in a car crash in 1969.

* * *

Wilhelm (Willi) Zöpf worked for the Sicherheitspolizei and SD in The Hague. He contributed to the deportation of 55,000 Jews to concentration and death camps. He was, among others, responsible for the deportation of Anne Frank and most of the cabaret group on the very last train out of Westerbork. He managed to disappear after the war but was tracked down in 1959 when the Netherlands requested his prosecution. This did indeed take place, and he was sentenced to nine years imprisonment. He died in 1980.

Wilhelm Harster was commander of the Security Police and SD in the occupied Netherlands. He was responsible through his office for sending all Jews in the Netherlands to the East. He celebrated in a telegram to Reichskommisar Seyss-Inquart when 100,000 had been deported. Harster was arrested by the British in Bolzano, Italy. He was sent to the Netherlands and tried at The Hague. Found guilty of war crimes, he was sentenced to 12 years imprisonment. In 1955, he was deported back to Germany. Using false statements, he managed to get himself classified as a "victim of Nazism." He was then working as a government official. Investigations took place in Vienna and other cities, and it was found Harster was meeting with other people who had belonged to the SD and had connections to South Tyrol separatists. He was again tried. Harster was given 15 years in 1967 but by 1969 was free again, upon receiving a pardon. He died in 1991.

Willy Paul Franz Lages as head of the Central Bureau for Jewish Emigration was responsible for the deportation of all Dutch Jews and other Jews in the Netherlands. He was arrested at the end of the war and put on trial. He was found guilty of war crimes and sentenced to life imprisonment. In 1966 he was released on humanitarian grounds against the background of vociferous objections from the Dutch public. Humanitarianism was something he had not extended to anyone in the Netherlands during the war. He lived another five years and died in Braunlage in Harz, Germany.

APPENDIX

Collaborators executed by the Dutch:

J.E. Feenstra, commander of the Marechaussee in Gelderland

J.H. Ganzefles, "Jew Hunter"

G. Rollema, commander of the Landwacht in Noord-Brabant

M.A. Ridderhof, betrayed many resistance groups

H.P.M. Bartelsman, member of the Henneicke Column

F.H. Meyer, member of the Henneicke Column

G.H. Sanner, leader of the "blood-squad"

J. Berendsen, chief constable of the police

A. Harrenomee, inspector of the police in Velsen

P. Wichers, betrayed Jews and other people in hiding

Tj. van der Weiden, mayor of Velsen

J.H.A.M. Driehuis, guard at Ommen concentration camp

Ans van Dijk, the only woman and the only Jew to be executed

D. Eykelboom, leader of the Landwacht in Zwolle

P. J. Faber, member of execution squad

Maarten Kuiper, detective in the Dutch police present at the arrest of Anne Frank

W.C. Mollis, detective in the Dutch police

M. Jansen, murder and mistreatment

O. Bouman, murder and mistreatment

J. Suykerbuyk, complicit in murder

A. Kaper, sergeant in the Dutch police

P. Schaap, member of an execution squad

C.J. Kaptein, arrested more than 600 Jews

E.C. Drost, murder and torture

J. Lamberts, murdered seven boys

S. van Droffelaar, murdered seven boys

F.W. Koot, member of the Henneicke Column

A. van der Waals, betrayed and blackmailed countless resistance members

J. Herdtmann, supplied NSB members with German uniforms during the invasion

A.J. Pieters (a.k.a "Steinbach"), leader of the SS-Jagdkommando Steinbach

All were buried in unmarked graves, and their locations are still kept secret.

* * *

Germans executed by the Dutch:

L. Heineman, shooting of resistance members and suspects, member of execution squad

J. Bogaard, SS

H.M. Verwayen, SS, member of execution squad

K.P. Berg, commander at Amersfoort concentration camp

R.W. Lehnhoff, commander at Amersfoort concentration camp

W.A. Albrecht, commander of the Sicherheitsdienst in the province of Friesland

* * *

Himmler was instrumental in awarding titles and grades. Here are those mentioned:

SS Title	Wehrmacht Equivalent	Mentioned in Book
Reichsführer	None	Heinrich Himmler
Oberführer	None	Walter Schellenberg
Obergruppenführer Senior group leader	General	
Gruppenführer SS Group leader	Generalleutnant	Wilhelm Harster
Brigadeführer SS-Brigadier leader	Generalmajor	Hans Fischböck
Obersturmbannführer SS-Senior assault unit leader	Oberstleutnant	Adolf Eichmann Rudolf Höss Heinrich Lidner Adolf Haas Hermann Pister
SS-Sturmbannführer (SS-Assault unit leader)	Major	Joseph Hugo Dischner Wilhelm Zöpf Karl Rahm Herbert Aust Herbert Johannes Wölk Eduard Wirths
Hauptsturmführer SS-Head assault leader	Hauptmann/Rittmeister	Fritz Suhren Josef Kramer Franz Novak Ferdinand Hugo aus der Fünten Franz Reichleitner Joseph Mengele Ernst Mös/Moes
Obersturmführer SS-Senior assault leader	Oberleutnant	Albert Konrad Gemmeker Max Horn Anton Burger
Untersturmführer SS-Second/Junior assault leader	Leutnant	Hassel
Sturmscharführer SS-Assault platoon leader	Stabsfeldwebel	
Hauptscharführer SS-Chief platoon leader	Oberfeldwebel	Wies
Scharführer SS-Section leader	Unterfeldwebel	
Unterscharführer SS-Junior section leader	Unteroffizier	Weygand Oskar Gröning
SS-Rottenführer (SS-Squad leader)	Obergefreiter	Viktor Pestek

ABOUT THE AUTHOR

Jonathan Gardiner was born in England in 1953, to parents who had both taken part in World War II but had not witnessed the full horrors. He was educated at his local Grammar School in "middle England" and then went to College in London to train as a teacher.

He taught in primary schools for nearly 40 years and ended his career as a well-known headteacher. He is married with two children. In the past 10 years Jonathan has become interested in Jewish Performers in Weimar Germany. He has helped to research the life of Willy Rosen, a famous Jewish composer and song lyricist, imprisoned at Westerbork.

This book is a culmination of a life-time's reading and interest in the Holocaust. A story that he felt needed to be told.

NOTES

The Gentleman Kommandant

1. After the war, 20 percent of the Royal Netherlands Marechaussee were punished for their war service; de Jong was sentenced to 12 years for his violence and zealous collaboration.
2. Theresienstadt is the German name for Terezin. I will use Theresienstadt instead of Terezin, as the ghetto and camp were of Nazi design and not Czech.

September 1943

1. Werner became known later to Simon Wiesenthal in his search for Nazi perpetrators.

SUGGESTED FURTHER READING
AND SOURCES

Agassi, Judith Buber, *"Jewish Women Prisoners of Ravensbrück"*, Texas Tech University Press, 2014, Lubbock, Texas

Balfour, Michael Ed., *"Theatre and War 1933-1945, Performance in Extremis"*, Berghahn books, 2001, Oxford

Boas Eddy, "I'm not a Victim – I am a Survivor", Eddy Boas Publishing, 2017, Sydney, Australia

Boas, Jacob, *"We are witnesses"*, MacMillan, Square Fish, 2009, New York

Bolle, Kees W., *"Religion and Global Culture: New Terrain in the Study of Religion and the Work of Charles H. Long"*, Rowman & Littlefield, Lexington Books, 2003, Lanham

Cesarani, David, *"Final Solution"*, MacMillan, 2016, London

Closel, Amaury du, *"Musique et camps de concentration,"* Conseil de l'Europe, *2013*

De 102.000 Namen Lezen Kamp Westerbork, https://102000namenlezen.nl

Drobniewski, Francis, *"Why did Nazi doctors break their 'hippocratic' oaths?"*, Journal of the Royal Society of Medicine ,Vol 86, September 1993, London

Dussel, Ines, *"Truth in propagandistic images. Reflections on an enigmatic corpus"* (Westerbork 1944) Historia y Memoria de la Educación 8 (2018): 59–95 Sociedad Española de Historia de la Educación, Spain

Felder, M., Minca, C., & Ong, C. E. (2014), *"Governing Refugee Space: The Quasi-Carceral Regime of Amsterdam's Lloyd Hotel, a German-Jewish Refugee Camp in the Prelude to World War II"*, Geographica Helvetica, 69, 365-375, https://doi.org/10.5194/gh-69-365-2014

Flinker, Moses, *"Young Moshe's Diary: The Spiritual Torment of a Jewish Boy in Nazi Europe"*, Yad Vashem, 1965, Jerusalem

Fransecky, Tanja von, *"Escapees"*, Berghahn Books, 2019, Oxford

Friedlander, Henry, *"The Origins of Nazi Genocide"*, University North Carolina, 1997

Garcia, Max R., *"Speech to be delivered on Saturday, May 12th, 2012 at KZ Ebensee"*,

https://memorial-ebensee.at/website/content/stories/Aktuelles/en_reden_2012.pdf

Gardner, Paul, *"The Unsung Family Hero: The Death and Life of an Anti-Nazi Resistance Fighter"*, Hybrid Publisher, 2020, Melbourne, Victoria

Gerstenfeld, Manfred, *"Wartime and postwar Dutch attitudes toward the Jews; Myth and Truth"*, Jerusalem Center for Public Affairs, JCPA.Org, VP:412, 3 Elul 5759 / 15 August 1999, Jerusalem

Goni, Uki, *"The Real Odessa: How Peron Brought The Nazi War Criminals To Argentina"*, Granta Books, 2003, London

Greenman, Leon, *"An Englishman in Auschwitz"*, Vallentine Mitchell & Co Ltd, 2001, Elstree

Hafer, Edward, *"Cabaret and the Art of Survival at the Transit Camp Westerbork"*, Colloque Musique et camps de concentration Conseil de l'Europe, 7 and 8 November 2013, https://rm.coe.int/090000168047d194

Helm, Sarah, *"If this is a woman?"*, Abacus, 2016, London

Herinneringscentrum Kamp Westerbork, https://kampwesterbork.nl

Herzog, Rudolph, *"Dead Funny"*, Melville House Publishing, 2011, New York

Hillesum, Etty, *"Interrupted Life - The Diaries of Etty Hillesum"* (Eva Hoffman), Persephone Books Ltd, 1999, London

Himmler, Katrin and Wildt, Michael, *"The Private Heinrich Himmler"*, St Martin's Press, 2014, New York

Himmler, Margarete (Marga/Magda), *"Tagebuch"*, Jürgen Matthäus: "Es war sehr nett", Auszüge aus dem Tagebuch der Margarete Himmler, 1937–1945, https://werkstattgeschichte.de

Holocaust CZ, https://www.holocaust.cz

Holocaust Matters, https://www.holocaustmatters.org

Wally M. de Lang, *"Het Oorlogsdagboek van Dr G. Italie"*, Atlas Contact, 2011, Amsterdam

Joods Monument, https://www.joodsmonument.nl

Kirsch, Jonathan, *"A Scandalous Theory of Defense and Herschel Grynszpan"*

https://www.myjewishlearning.com/members-of-the-scribe/a-scandalous-theory-of-defense-and-herschel-grynszpan/

Koker, David, *"At the Edge of the Abyss: A Concentration Camp Diary, 1943-1944"*, Northwestern University Press, 2012, Illinois

Krausz, Don, *"Under the Shadow of Transports"*, Holocaust Information Center, Yad Vashem The Central School for Holocaust Studies, Document 3914, Jerusalem

Lazan, Marion Blumenthal and Lila Perl, *"Four Perfect Pebbles"*, Greenwillow Books, 1996, New York

Lemkin, Raphael, *"Axis Rule in Occupied Europe"*, The Lawbook Exchange, Ltd, 2008, Clark New Jersey

Levi, Primo, *"If This Is a Man"*, Abacus, 1991, London

Mechanicus, Philip, *"In Dépôt. Dagboek uit Westerbork"*, Atheneum, 1985, New York

Mirjam Bolle, *"Letters Never Sent"*, Yad Vashem Publications, December 2014

Moraal, E. M., *"Als ik morgen niet op transport ga, ga ik 's avonds naar de revue"*, *Kamp Westerbork in brieven, dagboeken en memoires* (1942–2010), PhD Thesis Amsterdam University, September 2013, UvA-DARE, Amsterdam

Muller, Salo, *"See You Tonight and Promise to Be a Good Boy. War Memories"*, Amsterdam Publishers, 2017, Oegstgeest

Nijstad, Leo Kok Jaap, *"Getekend in Westerbork. Leven en werk van Leo Kok 1923–1945"*, Balans, 1990, Amsterdam

Nizkor Project (The), *"The Trial of Adolf Eichmann"* , http://www.nizkor.com/hweb/people/e/eichmann-adolf/transcripts/

Polak, Joseph A., *"The Lost Transport"*, Commentary Magazine, September 1995, https://www.commentarymagazine.com

Ridderbos, Jan, *"Kroniek van de Jodenvervolging te Assen"*, Assen, 2016. Also: USHMM DS135.N5 A8754 2016

Sands, Philippe, *"East West Street"*, Weidenfeld & Nicholson, 2016, London

Schütz, Raymund, *"Translation of the Sakrau Report"* – Dutch Red Cross, Academia Edu, March 2013, https://www.academia.edu/22180300/ZALfJ_Sackenhoym

Sefer, Ellen Ben, *"The Courage to care: Nurses facing the moral extreme"*, The Australian journal of advanced nursing: a quarterly publication of the Royal Australian Nursing Federation, 2004, Melbourne

"Slave Labour in the Nazi Camp System", https://www.zweitausendeins.de http://www.dpcamps.org/ZA_Eng.pdf

"Sobibór Interviews", https://www.Sobibórinterviews.nl

Tate, Tim, *"Hitler's British traitors"*, Icon Books Ltd, 2019, London

Terezin, http://www.terezin.org

"The Ghetto Fighter's House", https://www.gfh.org.il/eng אוס 000241

"Todesurteile sowjetischer Militärtribunale gegen Deutsche (1944–1947): Eine historisch-biographische Studie", Editors: Andreas Weigelt, Klaus-Dieter Maller, Thomas Schaarschmidt, Mike Schmeitzner, Vandenhoeck & Ruprecht GmbH & Co KG, April 2015, Göttingen

United States Holocaust Memorial Museum, https://www.ushmm.org

Van Rens, Annelies and Hermann, *"Tussenstation Cosel"* https://verloren.nl, 2020, Hilversum

"Wannsee Protocols", https://prorevnews.wordpress.com/2014/06/30/minutes-of-the-wannsee-conference/ June 2014, The Progressive Review, Washington

Westerbork, Kamp Archieven Nederlands, Hooghalen

Wyman Institute, http://enc.wymaninstitute.org/?p=113

Yad Vashem, https://www.yadvashem.org Yad Vashem Har Hazikaron, Jerusalem

Zande, Petra van, *"An Open Door"* , Tsur Tsina Publications, 2017

Made in the USA
Coppell, TX
16 August 2023